A VISIT TO EUROPE.

A

VISIT TO EUROPE.

BY

T. N. MUKHARJI

WITH A PREFACE BY N. N. GHOSE, ESQ., BARRISTER-AT-LAW.

———

CALCUTTA:
W. Newman & Co., 4, DALHOUSIE SQUARE.
LONDON: EDWARD STANFORD, 55, CHARING CROSS.
1889.

All rights reserved.

PRINTED BY J. LARKINS,
OXFORD MISSION PRESS, 132, LOWER CIRCULAR ROAD,
CALCUTTA.

Dedication.

TO

THE PEOPLE OF GREAT BRITAIN AND IRELAND,

IN GRATITUDE

FOR THEIR KINDNESS TO THE AUTHOR

DURING

HIS SOJOURN IN THEIR COUNTRY.

PREFACE.

Mr. T. N. Mukharji and two other Indian gentlemen were deputed by the Government of India to the Colonial and Indian Exhibition held in London in 1886. He stayed in Europe for about nine months, from April to December 1886, and travelled largely in England and on the Continent. He had no intention of writing an account of his travels and had therefore kept no notes of his journey and collected no materials for a systematic work. On his return to India, he was requested by some friends, and in particular by the Manager of the *Indian Nation*, to contribute to that journal, from week to week, a narrative of his experiences. Mr. Mukharji consented, and, relying upon his memory, and a few cards of invitation, catalogues and guide-books which he had preserved, he wrote his account which was published for about a year and a half in the *Indian Nation* in weekly instalments. The present work is mainly a reprint of the weekly contributions. Such alterations as have been introduced relate more to form than to substance. The work has been, though the articles were not, divided into chapters; and such adaptations as were necessary to secure greater continuity and coherence than existed in the articles, have been made. I had the privilege of looking over the proof-sheets of the work, as well in the earlier as in the later stage. This is my only apology for accepting the honour which Mr. Mukharji conferred on me when he requested me to write the preface. And readers who remember the circumstances under which the work was written and originally published, will understand how observations which are in the nature of comments on current topics (*e.g.* pp. 253-257) have found a place here.

Mr. Mukharji is an unambitious writer. If I may presume to make any comments on his style at all, I may say that it is terse and idiomatic, and, above all, free and easy. He is blessed with a poetic vein and often indulges in metaphor, but is hardly ever obscure. The exuberant energy of his nature finds expression in his style, and to purists he may appear to have taken some liberties with the English language, for, in all seriousness and fully conscious of the risk of the adventure, he has actually coined a word here and a word there. His first endeavour has been to express himself; and in carrying it out with perfect freedom, he may have occasionally trodden under foot some conventional rule. Several of his comments on social life and manners have a touch of irony; but Mr. Mukharji is never bitter. Topics are discussed, about which opinions may differ as to standards of reasonableness; but the element of suavity will never be missed even in the most uncompromising of Mr. Mukharji's criticisms.

The book is not a mere narrative but a compound of narrative and reflection. Mr. Mukharji's journey was more analogous to that of Arthur Young than to that of Sterne; and his account is at once a register of observations and a repository of ideas. Mr. Mukharji is at his best in the observation and description of details. The descriptions of the "banker at home" (p. 41), of the "poor couple" (p. 45), and of the Houses of Parliament (pp. 311-312), may be cited as instances. It is not ordinarily that the writer of travels sheds so much of dry light on the details of the life of a foreign people. The record of details is probably the most valuable part of the book. Nearly as valuable are the reflections which sometimes accompany the descriptive portions. The reflections on the "city" of London (p. 40) will probably be found to be striking, alike in point of accuracy, condensation, and sweep of the imagination. The description of "sights" seems to be sometimes a little too overweighted with historical details; but superfluity will naturally be regarded as more excusable than deficiency of detail. And an historical account of grand edifices, or of institutions associated with them, is sometimes the only way of conveying a vivid idea of them. Mr. Mukharji's observations on matters social, religious, and political, especially where they touch questions of principle, will probably excite controversy in some quarters; but it will scarcely be possible not to acknowledge their relevancy or the independent spirit in which they have been made. His estimates of the Hindu character and the English, are sure to be closely scrutinised. In so far as they tend to make this a stimulating piece of work, they may be regarded as a desirable feature. Having regard to the origin of the work, it would be strange if it did not contain useful information on such a subject as Indian products,—raw or manufactured,—or the uses to which they might be turned, or the mode in which they might be developed. No reader is likely to be disappointed on this head. The chapter on the "Exhibition and its Visitors" contains as much practical information as could be introduced without breaking the continuity of narrative or impairing its interest. The concluding chapter will be especially interesting to Indian readers, for, though they have had placed before them descriptions of England and English life by their own countrymen, this is probably the first time that they get from the pen of a native of India a published account of his experiences on the European continent.

Taking a general view of the whole work, I may observe that it has a great moral significance. Here is an account of the experiences and ideas of a native of India who knows his own country and has seen a great deal of Europe and European life. Mr. Mukharji has travelled very largely in India and has had exceptional opportunities of studying the realites of Indian life. In Europe too, in consequence of his official position, he found easy introductions to the highest classes of society and learnt more in nine months than could be learnt in a much longer period by one not so favourably situated. He saw a good deal of humbler life also. He went to England not as a young student but as a grown-up, practical man of the world, brought up in the heart of Hindu society and steeped in Hindu traditions. The observations and reflections of such a traveller ought to be of interest alike to the Hindu and the European. The Hindu cannot fail to regard the account as something like a revelation; and the European will learn to see himself as others see him. Above all, all parties will realise the far-reaching effects, moral, social and political, of a visit to Europe. Mr. Mukharji is still an esteemed member of Hindu society. He has not incurred those social pains and penalties which he dreaded (p. 27). This is evidence that Hindu society, or rather Hinduism, is acquiring plasticity. And it would be well if plasticity were fully developed, for change is the condition of life, and incapacity of change can only mean death. What Mr. Mukharji especially regrets is the hidebound condition of

Hindu society. And while his book inculcates the principle of change in the direction of progress, he and others like him are among the main solvent influences acting upon a hardened social régime. No nation, left to itself, has improved to any great extent, and whatever tends to bring Indian life and ideas into contact with English, is desirable even more in the interests of India than of England. The travelled Hindu, if he is quiet, condescending and social, becomes a source of instruction to his countrymen and a centre of influence among them; while his familiarity, acquired at first hand and not through the reading of novels and newspapers, with Western habits of thought and life, puts him in complete sympathy with the dominant race and qualifies him to be an interpreter of the Government to the people.

N. N. GHOSE.

CALCUTTA:
March 22nd, 1889.

CONTENTS.

DEDICATION	. . . .	v
PREFACE	. . . .	vii
CHAPTER I.—On the Way	. . . .	1
,, II.—First Impressions	. . .	27
,, III.—The Exhibition and its Visitors		64
,, IV.—Notes and Observations	. .	139
,, V.—The Excursions	. . . .	196
,, VI.—Last Days in England	. .	310
,, VII.—In the Continent	. . .	331
INDEX	. . . .	399

A VISIT TO EUROPE.

CHAPTER I.

ON THE WAY.

ON 12th March 1886, the steamer "Nepaul" left Bombay for England. No mail-boat ever felt the throbbing of so many Hindu hearts as did the "Nepaul" on that spring evening when she proudly cut her way across the Indian Ocean towards Aden. Well might she be proud; for, it is only through ships that England has been able to achieve the great destiny which she has been called upon to fulfil in the history of the world. Prouder was she now at the result of the moral influence of England in her vast empire of India, which enabled so many of her sons to break through the trammels of caste, to rise above old prejudices and superstitions, and to seek education and enlightenment at the very fountain-head of modern civilisation. There were the stalwart Panjabi from Lahore with his wife, sister and child, two Hindu merchants from Delhi, a Lala from the North-west Provinces, a Musalman from Aligarh, a Marhatta from Bombay, two Brahmans from Bengal, a Kayeth from Orissa and four Christians from Goa, all going on different errands to the great country which governs the destiny of India. Thus, the representatives of many nationalities of India on that day stood on the deck of "Nepaul" and watched the change which the waters of the Indian ocean gradually underwent from a greenish colour to an azure hue as the shores of their native land faded from their sight, and the noise of the surf that dashed on the Mahálakshmi rocks grew fainter and fainter. The sun had finished his day's work and prepared to retire for the night. Gradually he ceased to send forth his dazzling rays to the world below, his orb grew larger and milder, and at length putting on a red garb, which shed on the western firmament a glory of deep crimson, he suddenly dived into the blue waves of the distant horizon. The shades of evening now enveloped the world, and the reflection of the stars played backwards and forwards on the broad bosom of the ocean as the ship rolled up and down. On the shore, now scarcely visible, the light of the Colaba light-house began to flash in its revolving course round the tower-head, shewing to distant mariners the approaches to the Apollo-Bunder. We all stood on deck, our mind struck with awe at the novelty of the scene that presented itself to our sight. Gradually, as the darkness grew deeper, and nothing could be seen but the white foam of the phosphoric waves that continually beat on the sides of the vessel and as often fell back broken and baffled, we began to speak with hushed voices, and exchanged notes on the length of the voyage, the dangers of the sea, the sufferings from sea-sickness and subjects of a like nature that presented themselves to our inexperienced minds. The Indian ladies, bashful and child-like as they are, crouched in a corner, terrified at the vast expanse of water that surrounded us on all sides, and already complained of a swimming sensation in their heads.

It does not take long for natives of India to know one another. Our habits of life are such that we cannot do without mutual help. We share our joys and sorrows with our friends, neighbours and relations. We do not consider it rude for a stranger to ask our names, our place of residence, our caste, our profession, our destination, and the object of our mission. "Where are you for, brother?" would be the first question of one Indian to another, if both are going the same way. That was how the *Thugs* could carry on their nefarious trade with such ease, and that is how robbers now put their unsuspecting victims to sleep by means of stupefying drugs. So in half an hour we all knew each other on board the steamer, and were as friendly as a small number of Indians could be in a strange place among strange faces.

Most of my countrymen have no idea what a passenger ship is. It may be compared to a large house with all the comforts and conveniences of high life. First there is the deck, paved with wooden planks nicely fitted in, which before being cleaned and washed by a strong stream of water flushed through long India-rubber pipes, is every morning scrubbed with sand and rubbed with a rude brush made of cocoanut, with shells on, cut into two. Here passengers take exercise by walking up and down the two long passages left free on either side of the vessel. Or, one can sit under the awning and converse, or read, or play chess or other games, the materials of which are kept on board. In some vessels there is a smoking room on deck, nicely furnished, where the men assemble and smoke away the long tedious hours, when the ship, the sea, the waves, the flying fish and all other things no longer wear a novel aspect and have ceased to throw the mind of a new voyager into constant raptures. Occasionally, if the weather is fair and warm, the piano is brought up on deck and a lady favours the passengers with music. Down below, there are two long rows of cabins on either side of the vessel, each containing two, three or more berths for the accommodation of the passengers. Most of the passengers, however, pass the whole day on deck, and many sleep there in the night, if it is not too cold. In many vessels the dining saloon is in the middle, between the two rows of cabins, but in some it comprises the entire breadth of the ship for a certain distance. Here the meals are taken, and after the meals, it is used as a sitting and a writing room; specially when the deck above is uncomfortable owing to heat or unfavourable weather. The different meals supplied by the ship are regular feasts that contribute not a little to biliousness and sea-sickness from which most passengers suffer. Cases of heat-apoplexy in the Red Sea have sometimes been attributed to over-feeding. Early tea between 6 and 7; breakfast between 8 and 9; lunch between 1 and 2; afternoon tea between 3 and 4, and dinner between 6 and 7, form the daily routine of meals. Except the two "Teas," each meal is substantial, consisting of many courses, in which meat forms the chief component of most dishes. But there is ample allowance of bread, rice, potatoes and vegetables on which a vegetarian can subsist with comfort. Even a Hindu, if he so minds, can preserve his caste by putting up his pot on a fire which the officers can doubtless find for him in some nook or corner of the vessel. A small library is maintained in such passenger vessels from which books can be borrowed on payment of a trifling subscription. In some vessels there is a Lady's Room too where non-smokers sit, and where the piano is kept. Thus a first class passenger ship is practically a well-decorated, well furnished palace with all the comforts and luxuries of civilised life.

On board a vessel each day is so like another that there is scarcely anything worthy of record. We were always in the midst of a vast circular expanse of deep blue water, at the circumference of which the azure sky bends and touches the whole heavens, looking like a huge convex basin inverted upon the sea. No living creature meets your eye, except occasionally a white seagull, which sits easily on the water and slides up and down as the waves rise and fall. When the ship nears her, she rises in the air and flies now on this side of the vessel, now on the other side. Her movements excite the killing propensity of the sportsman passenger who hurries down from the deck to his cabin for his gun, but before he can unstrap the case, the seagull has finished her survey of the vessel and has taken a different course. When he returns to the deck with his gun, the sportsman only sees her a little white speck which is soon lost among the foam of the distant waves. Now and then we also saw the flying-fish rise in a shoal of a few feet above the surface of the water and run a race among themselves ; the greater number of them soon fall into the water with a splash, but the race is continued between two or three until the winner lastly drops into the sea, dry and weary. Occasionally, when we were entering the events of the day in a diary, which all of us rigorously kept for the first few days of the voyage but which everyone abandoned as it gradually fell into arrears, we were called up to deck by the sound of the gong, signifying that a ship had been sighted. Numerous naked eyes were at once strained to look towards the horizon, and eye-glasses directed towards the spot where a tiny black object broke the monotony of the wilderness of water. The small black object soon developed itself into a large vessel as the two ships neared each other, when they exchanged signals and her name and destination were soon known to us.

We passed our days in this way until, six days after we left Bombay, we saw before us the bleak hills of Aden. Accustomed as we are to luxuriant vegetation surrounding us on all sides, these naked precipitous hills looked extremely dreary to our eye. They are of volcanic origin ; the mass of lava reflected various colours, brown, grey, dark green, as the midday sun shone upon it. The crater formed by these lofty hills is occupied by the town of Aden which forms a portion of the little peninsula of Aden on the southern coast of Yemen in Arabia Felix. Our ship gradually came to shallow water, bringing up mud and sand as it neared the harbour. Little boats and canoes started from the shore to meet us, and they surrounded our vessel as soon as we dropped anchor. Some of these were occupied by little dark boys who threw themselves into the sea and swam near the ship crying incessantly, "I dive, I dive," which means that they will dive for two-anna silver bits if any one will be so kind as to throw them into the sea. In this they are very expert. As soon as a silver piece is thrown into the water from the deck, a height of about ten feet, they would dive after it. The transparent water, stirred by the waves, shews them the spot where the bright silver piece is sinking, which enables them to catch it before it can go many feet under the surface of the water. Most of these boys are of African descent, being children of men who come from the Somali Coast in search of employment. They generally take a temporary wife at Aden, and after a short time go back to their homes, leaving their wives and children to take care of themselves. The mothers are taken up by new immigrants from the same coast, and the children, as soon as they are able, take to begging, stealing or "diving." The Somalis have a curious custom of treating their women as other Muhammadans treat their men, and it is said that the practice is followed by some Arab Tribes. Many Jews and Arabs came to our ship with ostrich feathers and eggs. Passengers passing through Aden purchase considerable quantities of these feathers which are used for the decoration of lady's hats. They are chiefly brought from the Somali Coast. For retail sale ostrich feathers are made into small bunches containing four feathers each, a bunch of the best quality being sold at Rs. 20 to Rs. 30. Black feathers are not liked, a bunch of which sells for Re. 1 to Rs. 8. In Africa, they hunt the ostrich by the aid of a female bird. The hunter conceals himself under her wing and makes her advance towards a wild ostrich. When sufficiently near he shoots at the wild bird with a poisoned arrow.

We went ashore at Aden, and then the place looked still more desolate. A joke is current among seamen to the effect that it is a capital offence to pluck the leaves of or otherwise injure a tree in Aden. Why? Because there are *no trees* in Aden. We saw some small shrubs, however, on many of which the aridity of the climate has reduced the cellular tissue and favoured the production of spines. In the native town which lies about two miles inland within the hills, there is a little public garden, which does not possess a single big tree. Plants which assume the dimensions of big trees in India, are reduced to mere shrubs in Aden. We saw our *Bak* tree in this garden (Sesbania grandiflora, *Pers.*) with flowers upon it, but the plant itself is reduced to a mere shrub scarcely five feet high. The most interesting sight to be seen at Aden is its reservoirs. Since the foundation of Aden the question of water-supply has always been a difficult problem, to solve which various attempts have been made from time immemorial. The rainfall is next to nothing, being only three to four inches in the year. From the earliest times great care has been taken to store this little rain-water in reservoirs not only in Aden but in all parts of Arabia. The dam of Mareb was constructed for this purpose 2500 years ago. More than fifty such reservoirs exist in Aden, but all of them are out of repair except thirteen which have been reconstructed by the British Government with the co-operation of the Sultan of Lahej. Water from these reservoirs is sold in limited quantities to the public at one rupee for 100 gallons. But this water is not fit for drinking. Of late condensers have been established both by Government and private companies, by the aid of which pure drinking water is obtained by distillation from the salt water of the sea. The bazar of Aden scarcely differs from that of an Indian town, the same filthiness and the same irregularity everywhere. But wherever the Englishman has gone, he has brought in his train commerce, peace and prosperity. Aden has recovered her ancient commerce which she lost owing to the tyrannous conduct of her former rulers, and the constant struggles for supremacy that she witnessed in the last century. We found numerous coffee-houses where the Arabs and Somalis sip night and day a decoction of the coffee husk. The prohibition of wine and spirits has, since the time of Muhammad, made the Arabs look for other stimulating substances. Coffee is one of their discoveries. Another is the *káth*, the produce of a plant of the name of Catha which grows on the mountains of Yemen. The Arabs chew this drug as a pleasurable excitant. At one time there was doubt in orthodox Arab mind whether the use of coffee and káth was in accordance with the principle laid down in the sacred Koran, "Thou shalt not drink wine or anything intoxicating." Learned men of renown were ranged on both sides and considerable discussion went on for some time. But the question was at length settled by Fakhrud-in Makki and other learned Musalmans, and coffee and káth are now in universal use among the Arabs of Yemen.

Those of our countrymen who delight to stretch their imagination in order to discover the wonderful performances of the ancient Hindus, will be glad to learn on the testimony of Ibn El Mojawir, a Muhammadan historian, that Aden was the "Andaman Islands" of Das Sir, the ten headed giant (Rávan), where he used to send convicts sentenced to transportation for life. It is said that there is a well somewhere among the hills of Aden, through which a tunnel exists communicating with India. About this tunnel the historian says:—"It is stated to me by Mubarik Il Sharoni Maula, father of Mahammad Bin Masud, that the monster (Das Sir) stole the couch of Ram Hyder's wife from the Province of Oudh, and flew with her until he rested on the summit of Jebel Seera. He then said to her, 'I desire to change your form from that of a human being to that of a Jinn,' and they began to wrangle, and Hunweet, who was an Efreet in the form of an ape, hearing them quarrel, dug this passage from the city of Oojein Bikrami under the sea until it terminated in the centre of Jebel Seera, and he completed it all in one night. Issuing from the passage he found her (Ram's wife) sleeping under a thorn tree on the top of the hill, so he took her on his back and descended with her into the passage, and ceased not to proceed with her until he arrived at Oojein Bikrami about daybreak, when he delivered her to her husband, Ram Hyder, who became blessed with two male children by her, one of them was named Luth and the other Kus, and hers was a long story and requires a lengthy narration, but the passage exists to this day." That there was considerable commercial intercourse between the Indians and the Arabs in ancient times there is no doubt. In the above account the story of the abduction of Sitá by the ten-headed giant of Ceylon has been curiously mixed up with Vikramáditya who came in a much later age, and an entirely different version has been given of the rescue of Sitá.

On our return we found the vessel getting ready to weigh anchor. Goods booked for Aden were delivered, and a cargo consisting chiefly of coffee was being taken in. A steam launch towed unto the side of our vessel barges containing coal and water which were duly transferred to the "Nepaul." At the proper time each man was at his place near the anchor. The Captain standing on the bridge gave the order to "heave up." There was no bustle, no hurry, no noise. It was all work, done with the utmost precision and regularity. Not a moment was lost. The discipline maintained on board a ship was a wonder to us. Every body knew his duty, and he performed it with alacrity. Thus not the slightest confusion happens even when winds roar and waves rise mountain high.

We left Aden on the afternoon of 18th March. The same evening after it was dark we passed the Straits of Babel Mandeb, the Báb-Darwaza of the Arabs. In a short time we saw the Light-House of Perim, a small island in the Red-Sea. Its position, commanding the outlet of the Red-Sea to the Indian Ocean, was considered of some importance from a long time, but it was never permanently inhabited nor occupied by any nation, until the British erected a light-house in 1857, and placed in it a small body of troops. Albuquerque, the Portuguese navigator, visited it in 1513 and erected a large cross on the top of one of the hills. In 1799 the East India Company temporarily occupied it, when Napoleon was preparing to invade India by way of Egypt. A story is related in the "Lays of Ind" about an attempt made by the French to take possession of this island, which led to its final occupation by the British. It is said that a French Man-of-War arrived at Aden with secret instructions to hoist the flag of France on this island. As a matter of courtesy the British Resident at Aden invited the officers of the French Man-of-War to dinner. After dinner when the glass went freely round, the French Captain secretly confided to the British Resident the object of his mission, on which the latter immediately sent a gunboat from Aden to take possession of Perim. Next day when the French commandant arrived before the island he saw that he had been outwitted by the British officer: the English flag was proudly floating over the highest hill in Perim.

It took us four days to cross the Red Sea. We were told that owing to excessive heat this part of the voyage was always trying to passengers, but fortunately a cool breeze blew from the north, and we had an agreeable time of it. We passed many island rocks which rear their heads high above the water. At one place there are seven, known to mariners as the Seven Apostles. We saw herds of porpoises in the Red Sea whose frolicsome habits gave us great amusement. These porpoises would come near us as soon as they saw us from a distance, and would for some time swim, jump high in the air and gambol in all sorts of ways. In going through the Red Sea land is often visible, sometimes the African side, and at other the Arabian coast. The African coast is fringed with sunken coral reefs which render its navigation extremely difficult. More inland, a range of high mountains runs from north to south parallel to the sea, the mountains of Massowah and Soudan, the abode of gums and gum-resins. The same wildness characterises the feature of the east coast. High hills break the country as far as it can be seen, which look dry and parched from a distance. As we drew north towards the Gulf of Suez the shore on each side came nearer and nearer. This was probably the spot where according to the Bible the Red Sea became dry to allow a safe passage to the Israelities when pursued by the Egyptian horde under the Pharaoh who persecuted Moses. We sailed close by the African shore as we approached Suez, where we arrived at ten in the morning on the 23rd of March. Here the "Nepaul" delivered the Indian mails to the Egyptian railway which carried them across the Delta to Alexandria. There another steamer of the P. and O. line waited to take them on to

Brindisi, a port in Italy. From Brindisi the mails again go by rail to Calais, and thence across the Channel to London. We did not go ashore at Suez, for there was no time. As soon as the mails were delivered we started and entered the Suez Canal.

This Canal is one of the greatest feats of modern engineering. The narrow neck of land called the Isthmus of Suez joined Asia with Africa, but separated the Red Sea from the Mediterranean, hence steam vessels going from Eastern Asia to Europe had to go round the Cape of Good Hope. The distance from Calcutta to London by way of Suez Canal is 7950 miles, and by way of Cape of Good Hope it is 11,450 miles, hence by the opening of the former route a voyage of 3500 miles has been saved. The advantage of cutting a canal across the Isthmus was obvious from ancient times and various attempts were made in this direction from time immemorial. About 2500 years ago a canal was constructed from the Nile to the Red Sea: it has silted up, but various traces of it exist to this day. Napoleon, when he was master of Egypt, had the ground between the two seas carefully surveyed, with the object of cutting a canal navigable for large ships, but the expulsion of the French from the country put an end to his scheme. M. De Lesseps, a French Engineer, however, successfully accomplished the great work which has conferred immense benefit to the whole human race, by the impetus it has given to the commerce of the world. The difficulties always experienced were owing to the treacherous sandy soil, which made the whole country a perfect desert, to the want of drinking water and to the difference of level between the Red Sea and the Mediterranean. M. De Lesseps took advantage of the natural lakes of bitter water in the Isthmus through which he carried his canal, he invented new machines for excavation and dredging purposes, he brought sweet water by pipes from the Nile; in short, by great perseverance and ingenuity he overcame all the difficulties, and succeeded in making a canal deep enough to allow a passage to the largest Man-of-War existing in the world. But it is not broad enough to allow two vessels to go abreast of or pass each other. Stations with a broader margin of water have therefore been established, and the Canal is worked on the same principle as a single line railway is worked on land. The construction of a second canal or the broadening of the existing one, *i.e.*, to make it a double line canal, is now under contemplation. Many crores of rupees were spent in the construction of the Suez Canal. M. De Lesseps is a poor French Engineer. He could not, and he did not pay all this money out of his own pocket, but obtained it by sale of shares on the joint stock system. Intelligence, education, power of organisation, enterprise and perseverance can do anything. Individuals possessing such qualities, and performing results like the Suez Canal bring credit to the nation they belong to. A nation's best recommendation is its own works; we should bear this well in our mind. Considerable difficulty is experienced to keep the Canal in good order, for loose sand is constantly coming in from above to fill it up. In some places its sides are protected by masonry walls, at others reeds and sedges have been planted to bind down the soil by their roots. But still the dredger is constantly at work. No traffic is allowed during the night. It took us therefore two days to pass through the Isthmus, and arrive at Port Said on the other end of the passage. Of late ships with electric light have been allowed to pass through the Canal during the night.

We went ashore at Port Said, but as it was in the evening after it was dark, we could not see much of the place. We however saw various coffee houses, small theatres, and gambling shops. The dregs of all European countries gather here; Port Said is therefore noted for its immorality. On 25th March during night time we left Port Said and entered the Mediterranean. We received fresh passengers in Egypt, among whom was an American Missionary of a certain persuasion. He was delighted to see a magnificent crop of heathens on board the vessel, and he at once set to commence his harvesting operations. He began from the beginning, and told us first all about the Creation. He told us about the rebellion in heaven, about the creation of Adam and Eve, about their fall, and all the subsequent results that came out of it. We on our part told him our version of the story. We said that we Bráhmans came out of the Creator's mouth, our warrior caste came out of His hand, our trading caste came out of His thigh and our cultivating caste came out of His feet. He laughed at what is related in our books, and said that our account of the Creation is simply absurd and entirely false. He wondered how our people could put faith on such a childish story. This gentleman then especially warned us of the Satan, whose constant delight is to take human souls to the place where he lives, not a very comfortable place we were told. He firmly believed that the world would come to an end within five years, and therefore earnestly urged upon us to prepare for that final catastrophe. Interesting discussions of this kind were however soon interrupted. The wind rose, the weather became unpleasant, high waves dashed against the vessel, making it roll heavily, the whole deck was inundated with spray, and both the Missionary and his audience felt that they were going to be turned inside out. Most of the passengers were now sea-sick, but I was not one of the number, and cannot therefore describe the queer sensation which people indisposed in this way are said to feel.

On Sunday the 28th of March we entered the Port of Valletta, the chief town of the Maltese Islands. Malta is a British possession in the Mediterranean. It is 58 miles from Sicily and 179 miles from the African shore. It was a clear morning, and we could see the summit of Mount Ætna, although the distance is 128 miles. We went to see the Government House at Valletta and other interesting places. The former is a large edifice with a broad staircase paved with white marble. In one of the rooms we saw many specimens of tapestry, two hundred years old, representing the four quarters of the globe. There is a large armoury attached to the Government House in which the armour, used by the Knights of St. John in their constant fight with the Musalmans, has been carefully kept. Two documents have also been carefully preserved here; one is the bull creating the Order of the Knights of St. John of Jerusalem seven hundred years ago. The other is a charter, dated the 4th March 1530, by which the Emperor, Charles V, granted the Maltese Islands to these brave Knights after their expulsion from Rhodes by the Turks. We also saw the Cathedral of St. John, which contains a rich collection of inlaid marble and Brussels tapestry. Thence we went to the Hospital of the Knights, a large building, in which there is a room more than five hundred feet in length without a central support. In one of the churches we saw dried bodies of monks kept in niches on the walls of a subterranean vault. Altogether Malta is a very interesting place both for its past history and its present position as an important outpost on the highway between India and England. Its fortresses constructed by the Knights and kept up by the British Government are simply impregnable. Caffarelli said to Napoleon, when the latter obtained possession of Valletta through the treachery of some of the Knights, "It is well, General, (Napoleon was then a General) that some one was within to open the gates for us. We should have had some difficulty in entering had the place been entirely empty." The Maltese are a sturdy, brave but impulsive people, somewhat addicted to stabbing, and are bigoted Roman Catholics. The women have good features and dark eyes. Their language has 75 per cent. Arab words in it which fact leads to the supposition that they are of Arab origin, but on the other hand not a single man can be found with the oval face characteristic of that nation. Malta is such a rocky little island that the soil on which cultivation is carried on is said to have been imported from Sicily. At any rate every bit of earth found in the crevices of the rocks has been carefully utilised and made to yield crops or bear fruit trees. Maltese oranges are celebrated all over Europe.

The same evening we left Malta and the head of our vessel was now pointed towards Gibraltar, the next halting station. The weather was calm and the sea was like a sheet of glass. The sea-sick passengers had now recovered, and the Missionary resumed his proselytising efforts.

In answer to his arguments in favour of Christianity one of our friends remarked that he was quite mistaken in supposing that a man could not be good without being a Christian. All Christians were not good, nor all Hindus bad. Nay more: the Hindus as a nation were more peaceful, more merciful, more God-fearing than any other nation upon earth. It was more necessary for a bad Christian to be good than for a good Hindu to be a Christian. The Christian religion teaches men to love their neighbours, the Hindu religion teaches men to love every living thing as their ownselves. "To do good is virtue, to do harm is vice" is the short definition of virtue and vice given in the Hindu religion. But taking all round neither do Christians obey entirely the precepts of Christianity, nor do Hindus follow those of their own religion. In this matter the fault lies more on the side of the Hindus. So many corruptions have crept into the Hindu religion that no wonder an outsider would be shocked at the absurd practices found in India. The burning of widows and infanticide will be an everlasting shame to the Indian people, and it must be gratefully admitted that the abolition of these cruel customs is due to Christianity or rather to the liberal principles of a people who recognise Christianity as their religion. A Bráhman is now considered a demi-god, not for his sanctity and purity, but because he is born a Bráhman. Religious observances in India now mainly consist in not eating certain kinds of food. To eat forbidden food is a more heinous crime than to commit murder, to steal or to lie. A man does not lose his caste by committing such offences, but he does if he eats what is prohibited. It is a greater sin to kill a cow than to slay a low-caste man. Even the virtues of the Indian people have often been reduced to such a twisted form that they have become vice. They have been taught to be kind to things having life. So they hire men to have their blood sucked by vermins. If these practices were Hindu religion then the Hindus ought to be made Christians or Muhammadans as fast as possible. But it is hardly credible that the sages of ancient India whose knowledge and wisdom were so profound could have meant to teach their descendants rules of life as followed at the present day. "You will ask, Sir," continued our friend, "if those of my countrymen, whose mind has been opened by western education have given up such baneful practices. Alas, no. The formation of our society is such that it is not easy to do so. It requires a large amount of self-sacrifice and moral courage as is not given to average men. Failing to do what in their inmost heart they felt they should do, they gradually bring their mind round to suppose that it is patriotism to uphold all such national malpractices and finally seek for them subtle explanations and mysterious meanings, until they are made to assume such a spiritual aspect as to bewilder and deceive both themselves and their less advanced brethren."

We were now sailing close by the African shore. There was an old gunner in the ship who had passed and repassed these seas since his childhood. He explained to us the various landmarks on the Tripoli, Tunis, Algiers and Morocco coast. In the name of religion, how many cruel things have been done in all parts of the world! Perhaps no part of the world witnessed so many acts of sanctified rapine, murder and violence as that including the seas and countries from mount Arrarat to the Pillars of Hercules. After the Crusades, the Knights of Malta continued for some centuries to exterminate, wherever they could, the followers of Muhammad on the east side of the Mediterranean, while to the west the Moors of Tunis, Tripoli, Algiers and Morocco, for three hundred years proved their religious earnestness by robbing and enslaving thousands of Christians with the aid of their invincible piratical ships. Poor Shaikh Sadi relates in his Gulistan—how he was taken prisoner by the Christians while in a retired place among the hills of Palestine he was saying his prayers, and how he was taken to the Tripoli market and sold as a slave. In the same manner thousands of Christians, taken prisoners from vessels captured by the Moorish pirates, were every year bought and sold in the bazars of Northern Africa.

On the morning of Wednesday, the 31st March, we sighted the snow-covered mountains of Spain. Shortly after, we rounded the little promontory of Gata, and during the whole day sailed along the Spanish coast. In the evening we anchored before the famous fortress of Gibraltar. When we arrived here the sky was overcast, and it was raining. We could not therefore go ashore, but next morning we could see from the deck the commanding position which Gibraltar occupies as the key to the Mediterranean. It rightly bears for its arms a castle with a key hanging on to the gate. The fortress is constructed in a mass of precipitous rock. This rock and Mount Abyla opposite to it on the African coast were called by the ancients the Pillars of Hercules. Gibraltar is almost an island, being connected with the mainland by a narrow isthmus of sand, which sometime or other must have been covered with water. Strong as it is by nature, it has been rendered impregnable by modern improvements. In 1704 it was taken from the Spaniards by a combined attack of the English and Dutch fleets, since which time it has remained in possession of the British, although various attempts were made from time to time to recover it either by force or stratagem. In one of the many sieges which the English sustained in it, a queen of Spain rashly vowed that she would neither take food nor drink as long as the British flag floated over Gibraltar. But she undertook an impossible task. In vain did thousands of Spaniards recklessly sacrifice their lives in repeated assaults on the fortress; the English flag still waved defiantly over the summit of the unconquered rock. At length, the British Governor, taking pity on the unfortunate queen, chivalrously took down the flag for a few moments to fulfil her vow in its literal sense. During the five years' siege from 1779 to 1783 in which the French and the Spaniards combined against it, they bombarded the fortress from ships the sides of which were thickly padded with straw, to prevent shots penetrating them. Four hundred pieces of the heaviest artillery played upon the fort from these battering ships. The garrison was very much harassed, and the Governor knew not how to destroy or drive away those padded vessels. It is said that a drunken soldier suggested to him the idea to "give them red hot." He followed this idea, and caused cannon to be loaded with red hot iron balls and immediately fired into the straw pads on the sides of the enemy's vessels. This had the desired effect; in a very short time many of the enemy's ships were on fire, but they were not totally destroyed or dispersed until more than four thousand red hot balls had been poured into them. The strength of the fort can be best understood from the fact that while the enemy lost upwards of 2000 men, the British had only 16 killed and 68 wounded. Such small loss on the side of the garrison was largely due to the guns having been placed within tunnels excavated on the side of the rock, the muzzles of which we could dimly see peeping through small apertures. The Straits of

Gibraltar which separate Africa from Europe are 12 leagues long, and 8 leagues in width at their western and 5 leagues at their eastern extremity.

On the 1st of April we passed the Straits of Gibraltar and entered the Atlantic Ocean. The sky was clear and the sun shone bright, which enabled us to have a good view of that great expanse of water which only four hundred years ago was considered as the limit of the earth, and which the boldest navigator never attempted to explore. What changes have been wrought upon earth since that time! Civilised man has now established his supremacy over every quarter of the globe. Races of one-legged men, and men with long ears, one of which they spread as a carpet while with the other they covered their body as a blanket, have disappeared from the face of the earth. But no part of the world has since then seen such wonderful changes as the unknown continent on the other side of this vast ocean. Mighty cities now uplift their tall steeples and chimneys where four hundred years ago the density of the forest scarcely permitted the evening breeze to pursue its rustling course through the luxuriant foliage of pines and larches. Powerful locomotives now drag palatial salons over plains and hills where formerly the bison and the deer dozed and ruminated after their midday meal. The earth and the sea have been made to yield food, clothing, and the comforts of life to millions where only a handful of savages could hardly eke out a precarious livelihood by hunting and fishing. The bounties of nature are for him who can best use them. Those that cannot must make room for those that can. So it has been in America and Australia, and so it will be in Burma and all over the globe.

Although the weather was calm, big waves came from the west and struck on the side of our vessel. This caused her to roll heavily. At each roll she seemed to stand on her side and the bulwarks were about to touch the surface of the water. It was impossible to walk, nor could we feel ourselves at ease when sitting on deck, for fear of slipping down into the water as the ship stood upright on her side. Lying down we were afraid of being rolled out from the bed. Plates and dishes were kept on the table within a sort of wooden framework, as otherwise they would fall down and break to pieces. One of our friends asked what would the ship do in a tempest if she rolled from side to side on such a calm day? Some one answered that on such occasions she usually revolved round her axis. Notwithstanding this swell near the coast, the navigation of the Atlantic in this part of the ocean, specially in going from Europe to America, was always easy and free from danger. Further away from the land the trade wind blows uniform, constant and uninterrupted by squalls so common in tropical seas. With the sailing ships of former days the navigation was compared to a gentle descent down a slow-flowing river. The Spaniards were still more emphatic in their compliment to the genial nature of the mighty ocean that all of a sudden dropped them on the lap of the goddess of fame, wealth, dominion and power. They called it the Ladies' Sea, where the gentle breeze exciting pleasing undulations on its breast might tempt even the timid sex to muster courage and make a voyage to the El Dorado on the opposite side. Oh *Golfo de las damas!* what intoxication didst thou lead the Spaniards and their neighbours to; and oh, what a fall! The sea was calm when we entered the much-dreaded Bay of Biscay. We heard various reports of its boisterous nature, but we had a very pleasant voyage through it. In the Bay of Biscay we saw a whale spurting out water, as also several big sharks which followed our ship a long way. On the 5th of April early in the morning we passed Eddystone Light-house, which is built in the midst of the sea, and shortly after we entered the harbour of Plymouth, a port in the south of England. Here we stayed for a few hours only to deliver the Malta and Gibraltar mails. Many passengers left the vessel at this place to go by rail to London. We however remained in the vessel. From Plymouth to London is twenty-four hours' voyage. We sailed all day along the South Coast of England. In the Indian Ocean and the Red Sea we rarely met with any vessel; in the Mediterranean and the Atlantic the number of such vessels increased, but in the English Channel we found ourselves in the highway of commerce through which numerous steamers and sailing ships were going in all directions. On the morning of the 6th of April we were on the mouth of the Thames. We passed Gravesend and Tilbury, and arrived at the Albert Docks near London in the middle of the day.

CHAPTER II.

FIRST IMPRESSIONS.

At one o'clock in the afternoon I stood on the soil of England. My heart palpitated violently under different emotions that filled it at the time. I was now in that great England of which I had been reading from my childhood, and among the English people with whom Providence has so closely united us. I was thankful that opportunity was given to me to see the British people at home and to study those virtues which have made them the most powerful nation now on the face of the globe. But on the other hand I felt that I was probably an outcast from this moment. The old village where my family lived for the last four hundred years, where I was born, where I passed my early days, will probably be no longer my home. The old stunted mango tree which looks into my room and which always seems to say to me whenever I watch it—"I have seen your father born and die here, I have seen your grand-father, I have seen seven generations of your family," will probably sorrow to see me no more under its shade. The elders of the family on whose bosom I prattled in my infancy will shun me as an unclean thing. But it was not for myself that I was sorry, nor for the lives whose destiny is connected with mine. I was sorry for the unreasonable prejudices of my countrymen. While I respect honest conviction, I cannot but abhor moral cowardice and dishonest opposition. It is a fact that among those opposed to a Hindu's coming to England are well-educated men, who occupy the very highest position in the enlightened native community, and who in India trample under their feet all caste rules and traditions and all orthodox Hindu injunctions. In less advanced provinces of India, in Bombay, in the Panjab, in Rajputana and in the N. W. Provinces, the people have already got the better of this baneful prejudice; the mischievous practice of excommunicating youths returned from England, only prevails in the more favoured province of Bengal. If a century's contact with the English people, and fifty years English education have failed to teach us the primary truth that travelling in foreign countries is highly necessary for the regeneration of our decayed national life, then the English administrators of the country may well feel sad at the slow progress we are making under the most favourable circumstances. I came not to England for any worldly benefit. I came with the express purpose of adding one more drop to the current now set in against prejudice and superstition. The inexorable law of nature is in favour of this current; it is daily gathering strength, and the time is now fast approaching when those who are now trying to turn back this current will be looked upon as the whole Hindu community now look upon those who fifty years ago opposed the abolition of the cruel rite of burning alive helpless widows at the funeral pyre of their husbands.

As soon as we landed we were taken charge of by the official agent deputed for the purpose. He was so clever and so expert! In no time our luggage was passed through the customs office, and we found ourselves on our way to London by rail. In half an hour's time we came to the Liverpool Street Station. Here we took a cab for the " Museum Hotel" at Bloomsbury. In passing through London we were struck with the cleanliness that pervaded all places. Everything was neat and clean—the streets, the shops and the houses. There was no stink in the road, no filth left accumulated in any place. The glass of the shop windows looked as transparent as glass could be, and the wood, brass and iron used in the construction of shops and houses, shone as much like mirror as constant scraping and rubbing could make them do. Frequent use of soap water even imparted a glossiness to the steps leading to doorways. Inside the shops, the articles were tastefully arranged, and everything was tidy and in its proper place. The shops on the Esplanade in Calcutta will give one a little idea of what London is or how the cities of the civilised world are maintained. We have yet much to learn from the Europeans in the matter of general cleanliness. The ordinances of our religion, which in many respects have no doubt made the Hindus one of the cleanliest nations in the world, do not go far enough. Nor are they always consistent with rules which modern science inculcates. Their religious garb often deprives them of the respect they would have commanded in their naked truthful form. Only recently the fact has been put before us in an intelligent form that dust, dirt and unwholesome water have a strong affinity for diseases of the most virulent type. Positive proofs are not wanting to shew that waters, which according to the most sacred books are highly beneficial to the soul, are nevertheless fatally poisonous for the body. By a universalized observance of sanitary laws what a vast amount of misery and sorrow might be averted! If science is true, who can estimate the butchery going on around us? The wholesale slaughter of brothers, sisters, sons, daughters, friends and neighbours goes on daily, hourly, all round us. Could we have saved at least some of those whose loss we now deeply mourn? Ah! teach us to have faith in what you would say for an answer. Would we not then cast our apathy to the winds and with all our heart do for prevention what we now do for cure, often in vain? O for a despot like Akbar or Peter the Great to force us to learn and practise all that we ought to learn and practise! Poor Fate! little dost thou merit the curses of oriental nations unceasingly poured upon thy head as the clouds pour their rain drops on the lofty pinnacles of the Himalayas.

We arrived at the hotel. The same cleanliness pervaded that place. The walls of the sitting room were decorated with pictures, the mantelpiece with specimens of tasteful pottery and glass, the fireplace with grass flower-tops brought from Africa or America. A thick carpet was spread on the floor, ornamental sofas and chairs were scattered in the room, and a massive table with albums, pictures and writing materials stood in the middle. In the bed-room, in the coffee room, and in the dining room, the same refinement was to be seen. Remember, that this was not an exceptionally good hotel. Traders and middle-class country people stay here during their sojourn in town. The landlady and the servants at once took us under their special care, and even the people staying at the hotel felt proud at being taken notice of by us, and were extremely delighted to parade before us all the learning and all the qualifications each possessed. One of these was gifted with the faculty of reading the character of a man from his autograph. He wanted to shew us this special gift of his and asked us to sign our names on a piece of paper. Now, while we were on board the ship on our way to London, we are warned by many well-meaning English friends to take care of London sharpers. We were in utter dismay when our signatures were thus suddenly required; we thought that it must be for some kind of forgery. I asked my Bombay friend, Mr. Gupte, to sign first; Mr. Gupte nudged at Mr. U. C. Mukharji; and Mr. U. C. nudged at me. Seeing our hesitation the autographist, thought-reader, phrenologist, astrologer, or whatever he might choose to call himself, brought out a pocket book in which were many hundreds of signatures. This confirmed our suspicions rather than allayed them. A burglar might as well have shewn his jemmy to prove his honesty. However, in utter desperation we eventually signed our names, but happily no evil has come out of it up to date. Experience has since taught me the necessity of explaining that I have here described our fears in a rather exaggerated form.

Next day we went to the Exhibition. Dr. Watt who had come before us from India kindly took charge of us. He took us home in the evening and showed us over Oxford Street, the Westminster Bridge and the Whitehall Palace. The road, a portion of which is called Oxford Street, stretches under various names from one end of London to the other, and is about 20 miles long. Westminster Bridge is one of the most beautiful bridges I ever saw in my life. We could scarcely realise our own individuality when on that chilly evening of the 7th of April (1886) we looked down from this magnificent bridge into the silvery water of the Thames beneath. The bridge is 1160 feet long and 85 feet wide, with footways on each side 15 feet in breadth. During our stay in London we occasionally read in the newspapers of people committing suicide by throwing themselves into the water from this bridge. We had only a glimpse of the Whitehall Palace, and were shewn a window near which we were told Charles I. was beheaded.

We now daily went to the Exhibition, and spent the evenings in seeing the sights of London. One of these days His Royal Highness, the Prince of Wales, came to the Exhibition; Sir Philip Cunliffe Owen kindly introduced me to him. The Prince was very affable, and made many enquiries about India and ourselves.

We were also introduced to Sir George Birdwood. Sir George Birdwood is one of the best friends of India. He is well versed in our literature, our religion and our ancient philosophical systems. He knows more about our art-industries than perhaps any other man in the world. His book on " The Industrial

Arts of India" breathes all throughout its pages a deep sympathy for the Indian people and their work. This book has done an immense service to India by popularising its art-manufactures among the people of Europe. As for ourselves we were under the special protection of Sir George Birdwood, and I take this opportunity to express my deep gratitude for the kindness he always shewed to us while we were in his country. It was to Sir George Birdwood we owed in a great measure the opportunities given to us to see English society in its best aspects. I understand that he is now engaged in a more comprehensive work on Indian art. I have no doubt his book will throw an immense light upon the commerce and commercial products of ancient India.

We now frequently travelled by the Underground Railway. This railway system is one of the wonders of London. It belongs to two companies, the Metropolitan Railway and the District Railway, and is divided into the Inner Circle and the Outer Circle. The former is carried round the central and thickest part of the town, the line being constructed within tunnels excavated underground and supported by arches. The stations are built in open spaces, but below the level of the surrounding ground, with which they are connected by broad easy staircases. There are 48 stations in the two circles. The trains run every three minutes from 7-30 A.M. to 12-30 or 1 A.M., and every one is thronged with passengers. Some of the stations are very large having three or four platforms for trains going to different directions. Two or three trains can always be seen at a station arriving from different quarters. Engines puffing and whistling, passengers running in and out, guards shutting doors, the faint hum of voices, all combine to create a grandeur of busy life which must be seen to be fully realised. Here passengers do not shout to each other as they do in India. At railway stations or at public places, and even at home, they talk in whispers or at any rate in a low voice. Our habit of talking loud frequently drew upon us the eyes of our neighbours, and though they did not say anything, we soon found that it was better not to attract attention. Boards with " Here wait for first class," " Here wait for second class," " Here wait for third class" are hung at different sections of the platform, where passengers for each class wait and find before them their respective carriages as soon as the train stops.

The stations are full of advertisements; there is hardly an inch of wall not occupied by one kind or other, so that at first we were at a loss to know whether the name of a station was " Pears' Soap" or " Colman's Mustard." The carriages are also full of them. The best of everything that man wants is here offered for sale at the cheapest price, its merits being often illustrated with pictures of fantastic designs. The elixir by means of which poor mortals are to banish for ever all mundane troubles has at length been found in Cherry Brandy, for never was the expression of sublime happiness so vividly depicted as in the face of the Hottentot man and his wife rejoicing after taking this earthly nectar—as shewn in the advertisement. Complaints of injustice done in this world owing to a difference in colour are often heard.

The black races need no longer have the fear of being eaten up by white men for the sake of their complexion, for a single application of Mr. Pears' Soap will whiten the blackest of black faces. Mr. Pears is a master in the art of advertising, from whom even patent medicine-makers may well take a lesson. Wherever you go you meet with " Pears' Soap," even pennies are marked with these magic words. How many people must have gone mad by these words being constantly presented before their eyes! Mr. Pears certainly deserves an extensive sale of his soap. Not only in the railway stations and carriages but wherever you go you meet with advertisements. The walls, where allowed, are full of them, boards are placed in the streets covered with them, sandwich boys carry them on their shoulders, in the omnibuses, in the steamboats, they are everywhere. The advertisers say that their cost is distributed among so many millions that the incident per head of consumers is merely a fraction but what this fraction is, nobody knows. The business of advertising must give employment to a large number of persons. Besides printers, engravers, sandwich boys and others in the regular line, there are agents who undertake to do this work for merchants and manufacturers; then it has also given rise to inventors of new paints, new types, new boards, and new machines, used solely for this purpose.

If one is to find out the name of a station, he must look for it in the lamps, on which it is written. Although so many trains run night and day over these lines, the whole work is so carefully managed that accidents seldom happen. While we were there a German gentleman met with a singular fate in the Underground Railway. He had a habit of thrusting his head out of the carriage window to see what his fellow passengers were doing in other compartments. Once before his head came in contact with something while he was thus looking out. He was slightly hurt, but this did not teach him to be careful in future. The last time his head was almost smashed to pieces by a stone projecting from the arches. He died three days after the accident. Besides the Underground Railway system numerous other suburban and provincial railways traverse all sides of London. There is the Great Eastern Railway which runs from Liverpool Street Station towards Cambridge and other places; the Great Northern Railways from King's Cross towards Scotland; the Great Western Railway from Paddington to the western counties; the London and Northern Railway from Euston Road to Manchester, Liverpool and Scotland; the Midland Railway from Euston Road towards Scotland; the London, Chatham and Dover Railway which connects England with Belgium and France by way of Ostend and Calais; the London, Brighton and South Coast Railway, which goes towards Portsmouth and connects London with Paris *via* Normandy; the South Eastern Railway which runs to Folkestone and Dover with corresponding mail steamers for Boulogne, Calais and Ostend; and other miner lines.

Numerous omnibuses go night and day from one part of the town to another. The omnibuses are big carriages with cushioned seats inside and benches on the top. Like tram cars they run at regular intervals of time and are drawn by horses, but do not go upon rails. While the two Underground Railway companies carry annually about 136 millions of passengers, the omnibuses carry more than 78 millions. Then, there are the steamboats which ply every five minutes on the Thames from one end of busy London to the other, *i.e.*, from Chelsea to London Bridge, touching at various piers erected on either side of the river, which serve as stations. It will be an insult to the London cabs, if in order to explain to my countrymen I call them hackney carriages, for the conception that will be thereby formed of them will be entirely erroneous. In short, cabs are very superior four-wheeled carriages drawn by strong, sleek, well-fed horses, with which the rickety, dirty second-class carriages of Calcutta and their miserable skeleton horses cannot be compared. It gives comfort to an Indian's eye to see the huge sinewy beasts which here perform all the work that bullocks do in India. They do agricultural work, draw trucks (which take the place of our carts), and tow boats in the canals. It would not be respectable for a baker or a butcher to employ in his delivery-truck any but a strong showy beast. Two wheeled-carriages are called hansoms. There are upwards of 13,000 cabs and hansoms in London. In the busy streets they run so continuously that it is dangerous to cross the road. In difficult crossings small spaces have therefore been railed in the middle of the road where foot passengers take breath after running through the first half and wait for an opportunity to cross the other half. With all these means of conveyance which are more than fully utilised, one would suppose that the roads are comparatively empty of foot passengers. No such thing. Go wherever you will, the main streets are always so blocked up with passers-by, who habitually walk at a more rapid pace than we do in India, that two men can hardly find room enough to go abreast. But they always walk side by side, and do not go in what they call the Indian file, *i. e.*, one following the other. No collision takes place. Nor that curious phenomenon which often occurs in India of two persons coming from opposite directions, who suddenly meet face to face and try to pass each other, but with an unanimity of purpose worthy of a better cause they repeatedly move to the same side rendering all means of egress impossible except through each other's body, when at length they suddenly change their mind and shoot across as if by a sudden inspiration. Such things do not happen in London, for the rule is universally followed that foot-passengers should keep to the right. Carriages keep to the left.

But if any one wishes to see what a concourse of active human beings is like, he must go to the City at office time between the hours of nine and ten in the morning. We have fairs in India where thousands and tens of thousands meet and form a motley crowd, but in India everything is inert and dead, even a crowd of living men. The listless indolent look noticed in the face of prisoners while at work, or in the face of men dragged from their homes to work under the forced labour system prevalent in certain parts of India, is merely an exaggerated form of expression natural to the Indian races. The resigned submissive expression of an Indian face suggests to one's mind the idea that the owner has, after a long course of reasoning, come to the conclusion that he had no business to be born, and that he is constantly smarting under the sense of wrong done to him by being sent to this world against his strong wish to the contrary. He therefore goes through life as a prisoner goes through the task allotted to him, and brings the same energy to bear upon his work as does the forced labourer while employed in carrying the *Jhámpán* of his petty Rana or the baggage of a European tourist through the meandering paths on the outer slopes of the Himalayas. In point of fact the high intellectuality of the Indian races, being driven back by the rampant forces of nature to work in an imaginative sphere, has created a diseased state of mind. This disease assumes more and more a virulent form as a man advances in age, and it becomes positively mischievous to the well-being of the nation at large if a man happens to have deserved by his education and abilities to be a leader of men in his younger days. Respect due to age enhances his prestige, and his words are received as gospel by the younger generations, however absurd and antagonistic they may be to all notions of national economy. In short, the whole nation is suffering from a mental aberration which my countrymen fondly call *intense religiousness*. Hence perhaps this vacant look. It is impossible for a Hindu to comprehend the earnest reality of life unless he witnesses that mighty human stream which every morning pours into that little bit of ground, measuring 632 acres, called the "City." Eight hundred thousand human beings and seventy thousand vehicles daily pass in and out of this little space. It is, the centre of the earth, the heart which supplies the life-blood to the commerce of the world, and sends forth the impulse by force of which the Esquimaux hunts the seal among the icebergs on the Greenland coast, the whaler braves the perils of the polar seas, the Chinaman's ape plucks the tea from the steepest hills, and the savage Negro pursues the fleet ostrich in the boundless deserts of Central Africa. Here luck finds its due, merit its reward; fortunes are daily made and lost; hearts elated and hearts broken. In what number? Ah, who can collect such statistics of this microcosm of the world!

Among this flowing multitude may be noticed the rich banker. He began the battle of life under serious difficulties, but his serene face will tell you that he has succeeded in overcoming them. He has been honest, industrious, frugal and methodical, and always knew how to take the best advantage of every opportunity that came in his way. He has risen in life not by chance, but by sheer force of mind. He now occupies a palatial residence in the suburbs with a large garden attached to it, owns a deer-preserve in the highlands and has English governesses for his children and Swiss maids for his daughters. The family lives in a sumptuous style, as may be seen from the variety of food daily placed on the table. One day's bill of fare may be taken as a sample.

For breakfast they had—ham and eggs, sole (fish), mutton-chop, veal cutlets, ox tongue, bread of different sorts, vegetables, tea and coffee. Being a business man, the breakfast was rather early for a rich family (8-30 A.M.), and was somewhat hurried. The banker himself took his lunch at a restaurant in the City. The lunch at home for the family at 1-30 consisted of—Imperial soup; mayonnaise of salmon, pickled salmon, lobster salad; York ham, pigeon pie with truffles; forequarter of lamb, sirloin of beef; Victoria jelly; strawberry cream; French pastry, Venice bread, rout cakes; pineapple and filberts for desert; with hock, claret, sherry and champagne for drink. Afternoon tea at 4 was simple, consisting of tea, bread, cakes and a little cold meat and tongue. Dinner at 7 P.M., was elaborate in which the whole family joined. It consisted of—Clear turtle soup; turbot and lobster sauce, fried fillet of soles; haunch of venison, saddle of mutton, roast sirloin of beef; roast duck, boiled chicken; pine apple cream; macedoin of fruits, savoy cakes, cheese, biscuits; grapes, melons, filberts, walnuts; sparkling champagne, pale sherry, hock, claret and port wine for drink. The ladies pass their time in visiting friends, in needle-work, and in reading novels in English, German or French. German and French are indispensable for a lady's education. He sent his first two daughters to France for education; but a younger one is now in Heidelberg, for Germany is the fashion of the day. One of the girls is a great linguist: besides French and German she has perfect command over Spanish and Italian, as also some knowledge of Greek and Latin. Two aunts of the family can boast of extensive learning and high scientific acquirements. Such women are usually very stiff and they are nick-named "Blue stockings."

The time passed by the banker in the drawing room after dinner is perhaps the most agreeable part of his life. The incidents of one evening may be mentioned. As soon as dinner was finished the whole family repaired there. A cheerful fire was burning which shed a soothing influence all over the room and imbued the mind of every one present with a sense of voluptuous comfort, the charm of which was further enhanced by the density of the darkness outside, where the angry wind with terrific hisses and growls was chasing myriads of cotton-like snow flakes, driving some to seek shelter among crevices of houses, edges of balconies, and hat-brims and pockets of passengers, bringing others to bay under the wall opposite the leeside of the road, and compelling some to rush for refuge into the narrow passage of the bricklayer's cottage close by, as the little girl opened the street door for her belated father. The matron of the house presided over this family assemblage. She sat on her chair with needle work on her lap, surrounded by her young ones, one on the sofa, one on a low chair, while two squatted on the ground near her feet along with a sleepy dog whom they began by turns to fondle and tease. The young Miss of eighteen just returned from the Continent was asked for music. She went to the piano and sang, while a young neighbour, invited to dinner, stood by her side and turned over the pages of the music. Meanwhile the master of the family reclining on his easy chair was enjoying a quiet nap dreaming of the bright faces with which God has blessed him. After the music and the usual compliments to the lady for her performance, a little girl of nine was requested to recite a short poem. She did it beautifully, and the piece she selected was well suited to the time and the weather outside. The story ran thus:—The wife of a life-boat man was ailing for sometime. On the night in question she grew worse. Her husband sat by her side with the palm of her left hand within both of his, and mournfully watched the pale face and the hard breathing which he supposed was getting less and less every minute. He thought she would go with the tide; she herself thought so too. The night was pitch dark and a furious storm raged outside. At this moment, the boom of a distant gun rang above the howling storm and the roar of the waves that thundered on the rocky coast, the signal of distress from a ship about to be wrecked. Another gun signified to him the summons to his duty. He hesitated to leave his dying wife, but she insisted upon his going. "Jack," she softly murmured, "you must leave me to obey the call to your duty. Our Alfred left home these five years. The poor boy may have gone to sea, and, who knows? that in this wild night he may be at this moment in some unknown shore in the same situation as the men in the yonder vessel are. May be, I will be no more when you come back, but, Jack, for this act of yours God will bless you and our dear Alfred. My last wish has been to see my poor boy before I died, but as it is not to be, I will when the moment arrives cheerfully resign my soul to Him who does everything for our good. God bless you." Jack and his comrades bravely rowed the lifeboat to the vessel in distress. It was, however, completely wrecked and all hands washed away except a boy who tenaciously clung to the ropes high up in the mast. Him they saved with considerable difficulty and at great risk of their own lives. Jack found in him his long lost son Alfred. His wife was living when he came back. The sight of her son whom she dotingly loved gave her new life. She recovered, and she and Jack and Alfred were happy ever afterwards. The little girl repeated these lines with such grace and animation that as she sat down shouts of applause from everyone present greeted her ears. This is how respectable Englishmen pass their evenings. Any one who as a guest shared in all these innocent enjoyments will ever afterwards associate the English fireside with one of the most refined ideas of human happiness possible in this world of troubles.

The next unit in the crowd whom I shall notice is a young assistant in a shop. He married a pretty dress-maker against the wish of his father and has therefore been discarded by him. The young pair and the little baby, one year old, live on thirty shillings a week, out of which they pay 8 shillings as rent for two small rooms furnished with their own furniture taken on the hire system now universal in London. It is almost the same system under which a cartsman in Calcutta is provided with money to buy a cart which he repays with an exorbitant rate of interest by daily instalments; with this difference that the furniture man supplies the furniture in kind, the price of which is paid to him by weekly instalments. Furniture to the value of £50 can be had on a payment of 10 shillings per week. This man pays 5 shillings a week for the things he has taken. These consist of—carpets £3, bed £3, wash-stand and mirror £1, sofa £2, six chairs £2. 2, mahogany drawer £5, three tables £7, perambulator £1. 10, book-shelf £1; total £25. 12. 0. The food of the family costs about 15s. 6d. per week, distributed as follows:—Meat 6s., bread 2s. 4d., vegetables 1s. 9d., butter 1s., tea, sugar and milk 2s., oatmeal for porridge 1s. 7d., beer 1s. 2d.; total 15s. 10d. The remaining 1s. 2d. is not enough for coal, soap, washing, clothing and other miscellaneous expenses, but the little wife does some sewing which not only pays the deficit but leaves a slight surplus, by the aid of which the young pair is gradually feathering its nest. She also cooks the food and does all household work except washing. They have breakfast at half past seven, which consists of porridge, bread and butter, and tea. They take their dinner at 2 P.M. On Sunday they have hot joint, the same meat cold on Monday, and the same meat stewed on Tuesday. A new joint comes on table on Wednesday which is made to last till the end of the week. Most people who work far from home take their dinner at eating-houses and restaurants of different degrees of respectability according to circumstances. Such a dinner costs from 6d. upwards. For 6d. a plate of meat and vegetables is given. Some people manage to have a dinner at 4d. for which they get a pork-chop and fried onions. There are shops especially for this sort of dinner. It is difficult to fix the lowest sum on which a poor man can maintain a family in such an expensive place as England. There are men who with a family of five or six children live on £1 a week. This sounds a large sum when applied to India, but it is not so in England. In this country a man can subsist on 1d. a day and can do without many things which in England are indispensably necessary for the maintenance of health. In many parts of the United Kingdom the poor people can seldom afford to have meat. Bread, potatoes and oat-meal are their chief food staples. An Indian student can have board and lodging in England for 30 shillings a week, but he cannot do without another 30 shillings to pay his washing, railway fare, and various other items of expenditure which one does not foresee but are sure to come up. A middle aged gentleman who goes there for sight-seeing cannot do at less then £5 a week.

I shall now notice a young girl of about twenty belonging to a toy shop where she serves as an assistant. She was saying to her friend that she could live on love. Her case is a sad one. One Saturday night three years ago she paid six pence at the door of a public bath and was admitted to a hall where a ball was being held. Such balls take place weekly or bi-weekly in many parts of London and are got up as private speculation by enterprising individuals like the proprietor of the baths. They are largely patronised by young folks of an affectionate turn of mind, who are in quest of worthy objects on whom to bestow their love. The young miss danced with a railway plate-layer, and immensely enjoyed the evening. Next day the plate-layer loitered about the toyshop for two long hours though he knew it never closed before seven. At last he met her on the road, and offered to see her home. She distinctly told him where she lived, yet the forgetful young man lost the way, but why she herself did not notice the mistake it is not explained. There was no help for it now; they took many turnings, crossed the Hyde Park, sat there for a while to take rest, and further refreshed themselves with a glass of port wine each, which the Miss at first declined but was obliged to accept after much pressing on his part. Every day since that time the young man came punctually and escorted her home, not direct of course, but through streets and parks not quite on their way. Once he took her to a theatre and spent 6s. 4d., *viz.*, 2 tickets 4s., ice 1s., two glasses of port wine 8d., omnibus 8d. Matters at last came to a crisis. All day long and in the still hours of night, the sweet face of the young maiden was ever present in the platelayer's mind, and she too wondered if the hour hand of the shop clock now took more time to move towards VII. than heretofore. One Sunday while they sat side by side on a bench in the Hyde Park and watched the sport of wild ducks on the Serpentine, the young man broke silence and in the usual way told her his love and asked her to be his wife. She blushed, and cried, and at the end she laid her head on the broad bosom of the plate-layer and whispered a little " Yes," adding however that she could not consent to be his wife without the permission of her parents. This the young man readily obtained and they were " engaged." For three long years they remained in this engaged state, because in the first place they were too young and in the next place the earnings of the plate-layer were not sufficient to maintain a wife and family. So the parents advised and necessity compelled them to wait. A short time ago, the plate-layer got a more lucrative employment in another railway and then they talked of marriage and their future prospects. But alas, for the treachery and fickleness of man! He went to Margate on a week's leave, " to take" as he said, " the smoke of London out of his system." While on an excursion boat, he met there a young girl with a prettier face, with which he was at once over head and ears in love, she on her part nothing loath to accept his attentions. Their mutual relations did not however assume any precise form, for the law court and breach of promise loomed before the mental vision of the amorous swain, but it was understood that they would meet again in London. On his return his coolness was at once noticed by his forsaken sweetheart. He did not meet her with that warmth natural on such occasions; the breach widened when the indifference developed into studied neglect, and it was a positive insult when the young man one day threw himself in her way in company with his new love. It broke the poor girl's heart, but womanly pride came to her aid, which enabled her to meet the vile conduct of her unworthy lover with supreme contempt. But a woman's love is not effaced in a day; true affection leaves in her tender heart a deep scar which is often carried through life. To one friend only she confided her deep grief, to whom she said sobbing, that she could have lived upon love if they had nothing to live upon.

This was however an exceptional case. Such meetings and such "goings out" generally end in marriage. The time of courtship with its first sensation of love, the earnest longing to see the object of one's affection, the joy of meeting, the pain of separation, the hopes and doubts, and many little things which make one now transcendently happy, now dolefully miserable, they remember in after days as the sweetest moments of life. The mind of an oriental youth can be possessed with a temporary infatuation, but it has really no opportunity to experience the romance of love. The custom of the country has thus deprived him of one of the charming excitements of life.

But the individual who has the strongest reason to curse this custom is the Indian novelist. To write a novel without a love story is to play Hamlet without its hero, or to sing Rámáyana leaving out the name of Ráma. Reluctantly he therefore falls back upon bygone times when lovely damsels were allowed to roam about at their pleasure; or he fabricates far-fetched stories of latter days, when the Muhammadan invaders of India carried their victorious arms from one end of the country to the other; or still later, when in the early days of British rule Dacoits ravaged the villages of Bengal. Charles Dickens has thus narrowly escaped from wholesale piracies being committed upon him, but historical romance-writers of Europe have not fared so well in his hands.

In a sober point of view, the oriental is no sufferer for this want of romance in his life, and in the matter of family happiness at least, he can altogether dispense with the pity which English people often bestow upon him. There is more concord in an Indian family consisting of father, mother, uncles, aunts, brothers, sisters, brothers-in-law, sons-in-law, nephews, grand-sons, grand-daughters and all sorts of near and distant relations, than in an English family of husband, wife, a few children, and a mother-in-law. An Indian husband and wife have no chance of comparing their lot with that of others, so they are content. They grow up together from childhood, and left solely to themselves they learn to like each other, and their affections are soon fixed on the little progeny which come to them at an early age. Besides, it requires a little spirit to quarrel.

But happiness or no happiness, the present state of things shall not continue if India is to take her place among the civilised countries of the globe. Education and liberty among women may jeopardise family peace to a certain extent by creating new ideas and aspirations in their heads and making them impatient of control, but it is the old, old story of the tyrant to disregard the inestimable advantages of knowledge and to lay stress on its little drawbacks. Infant marriage must cease, and women must be fully emancipated not only in India but in all countries of the world. At all events, let China glory in her *patria potestas*, but in no form whatsoever shall it exist in British India. Indian parents must be made to recognise the fact that they have no right to sell for money or to "give away" a helpless human being even to a worthy object. Within the last fortnight a Bráhman acquaintance of mine purchased from her mother a little girl of four years for Rs. 300. Facts like this can be easily gathered which would appal the most ardent admirer of Hindu society. Among the poorer classes thousands of infants are every year bought and sold under the name of marriage. If religion is the root of this evil, no right-minded man can support that religion, for a man has no more right to dispose of an infant on religious grounds, than he has to allow his aged mother to become a *Sati* or to offer a human sacrifice to his tutelary deity.

But the most serious argument brought forward against Zananá emancipation is that education and liberty in women will lead to immorality. I venture to say this notion is entirely a mistaken one. I may not approve some of the European customs and may not desire their introduction into this country, but this I can unhesitatingly assert that with all the education, all the freedom and all the independence allowed to women in Europe there is not more immorality there than there is in India. An opinion of Indian morality based on the conduct of the servant women of Calcutta will be as sound as an opinion of English morality based on the conduct of the street girls of London. An English woman values chastity and honour as much as an Indian woman does. In her strong sense of duty an Englishman has implicit trust; and even if he is otherwise disposed the Englishwoman has the spirit to compel it from him.

With all the meekness and modesty of the Indian woman, her kindly and affectionate disposition, her religious fervour, her strong love of virtue, her sense of self-respect, and all the good qualities with which nature has endowed her, it is very ungrateful on our part to entertain the notion that she cannot be trusted unless she is kept under lock and key. After all, if confidence cannot be placed in the honour of a woman that woman is not worth taking care of. The relation between man and woman was carefully defined by the early sages of India. It was a sacred knot which tied the sexes by the rules they laid down. Duties of human life, not carnality, demanded this blending of destiny with destiny, spirit with spirit. Nobler sentiments have not been uttered in the world than what those sages said about the relation between man and woman. Yet, the light which dimly burnt in the forest homes of a few Bráhman ascetics scarcely cast a momentary flicker on the deep gloom outside. Outside all was darkness, where passions raged strong among the diverse races in all stages of civilization that peopled India then, as now. That light in the forest soon burnt itself out; so that I am now forced to admit that the respectful deference shewn to women in Europe can scarcely be seen in this country, and that savagery not chivalry will as a rule be experienced by a young woman who would dare act against the present customs, and gaily laugh and chat and go about all alone in the streets. The very strangeness of her conduct, and the very fact of such a conduct being hitherto associated with disrespectability, would bring down upon her suspicions of the worst kind and would subject her to all manner of annoyances. Yet, the bright faces of women, the reflection of their pure innocent hearts, freely moving around us, can alone efface the brutal instincts which man has received as a legacy from his primitive ancestor and which still maintains the kinship between him and the lower animals. A period of painful ordeal has to be passed through by those bold spirits among us who dare go ahead of their time, dare ignore the drawbacks of a weakened national character in which their own is included, dare face all the consequences of a sudden influx of light where all was darkness before and dare despise all the evils to be feared from their terrible environments. All honour, therefore, to them. For little do we know what incalculable mischief this anomalous position of women in our society has done to the country! Give us mothers like English mothers to bring up our boys, young girls to spur impetuous youths on to noble deeds, wives to steer our manhood safely through the whirlpools of life, and elegant ladies to refine, revive and invigorate our rotten society—then India will be regenerated in twenty years' time.

The day after our arrival in London, we saw an article in the *Daily News* triumphantly proclaiming to the world that Mr. Gladstone was about to introduce in Parliament a "Bill for the better Government of Ireland," which would for ever set at rest the strifes and dissensions in that unhappy country, make the Irish peaceful and prosperous, and unite them eternally to England in the closest bond of amity and goodwill. Having lost all touch with the outside world for about a month, we could not realise the portentous nature of the news learnt for the first time. There were no outward symptoms to foreshadow any kind of serious commotion, nor were any distant rumblings heard of that tremendous storm which soon threw English society into violent convulsions. But in truth we were deceived. Under that superficial calm, the mind of conservative London was boiling and surging in nervous anxiety about the next piece of wickedness meditated by the Grand Old Man. Rumours of Mr. Gladstone's contemplated proposals had already got abroad, the "Separation" cry had already been taken up by his opponents, and four days before our arrival a meeting was held at the Guildhall protesting against the grant of Home Rule to Ireland. How the Bill was introduced in Parliament, how on that day the House was crowded by members and visitors from early morning, how the Bill was received, how it was defeated, and how Parliament was dissolved, are matters of history with which this narrative has no concern. What struck me most forcibly at the moment was the mistake which Mr. Gladstone made in justifying his Bill almost entirely on grounds of right and justice. His opponents sneeringly said—

"Did ever a politician utter such arrant nonsense before? Right and justice indeed! As if the world is governed by sentimentality! Such noble doctrines should have been reserved for the defence of acts like the extirpation of a patriotic band striving to free their country from the domination of foreign usurers, or the bombardment of an inoffensive town." In such a sweeping measure when self-interest was so much at stake, Mr. Gladstone no doubt overestimated the sense of justice among his people, however strong it may be. But nevertheless it reflects great credit on the English nation that a veteran statesman like him could place such absolute reliance on Englishman's proverbial love of justice in such a momentous question.

Such a thing was unknown in the East. Even in our halcyon days, when on many points we reached such a moral altitude that European nations have not yet been able to arrive at, we never thought of such international obligations. In comparison to the rules of warfare laid down four thousand years ago, just before the battle of Kurukshetra was fought, the results of the Geneva Convention sink into utter insignificance. But our kings never knew that it was sin to rob a neighbour of his kingdom, or to efface by despatches and regulations the physical, intellectual and moral deficiencies of a conquered people, in order to bring them up to a level with the conquerors. Religion permitted a king to make conquests, and there the matter ended. It is solely from English teachings that we have learnt to criticise international politics in a moral point of view. But we go to the extreme. Being weak and powerless ourselves we have found it very convenient to heedlessly criticise the acts of the strong and the powerful. We make no allowance for the imperfection of human nature and expect that Englishmen should always do what is right. This is expecting from them more than what we found in the celestial politics of our gods. Take for instance that shabby swindling transaction by which the gods deprived the Asuras of their share in the spoils of Ocean churned out by their joint labour, to which any lawyer of to-day would say they were legally and morally entitled; or that mean deception which the gods, enamoured of her beauty, tried to practise on poor Damayanti, but in which they most ignominiously failed. If I were an Englishman, I would feel highly flattered by the abuse daily poured upon the head of the English for their proceedings in Egypt and other places, and would modestly take it as a high compliment to the English character which all orientals thus tacitly acknowledge as more god-like than the nature of their own gods. I do not defend a wrong act. I simply take into consideration what the world is, and think what we would have done ourselves had we the power to do what we liked under circumstances in which self-interest required a deviation from the right path. Criticise by all means every public measure, but criticise wisely, soberly and honourably.

In my point of view, even what my countrymen call the sanctimonious way of doing a wrong reflects great credit on the English nation, for it proves the existence in the country of a large body of right-minded people who require to be hoodwinked and deceived. Of all countries in the world, this party is very strong in England, and it gains fresh accession in strength as each year rolls to its end; otherwise slavery could not have been abolished, Catholic disabilities could not have been removed, the Protestant Church in Ireland could not have been disendowed, or the Alabama case could not have been settled without a war. Mr. Gladstone appealed to this party, but either he overestimated its strength or he asked too much of it; for England could not be asked to make a more tremendous sacrifice than to consent to the separation of Ireland from the Empire, as many understood by Mr. Gladstone's Bill. The creation of a little disaffected independent state in such close proximity to England would simply mean the annihilation of the British Empire. But Mr. Gladstone's Bill, with all its defects, never meant separation.

The main strength of the cause espoused by Mr. Gladstone lay in the self-interest of the British nation, the morality of the measure being only a secondary and auxiliary force. Mr. Gladstone did not utilise the main strength to its fullest extent, and frittered away the auxiliary force by making too much use of it. To an outsider, who could watch the controversy in a calm and dispassionate way, it would appear that he could easily have taken the wind out of his opponents' sail, and could honourably, more forcibly, and with a better prospect of success point out in his first speech that it was not separation that he contemplated, but the pacification of Ireland and a cordial union between the sister islands. This object must have to be gained anyhow for the preservation of the British Empire and for the general welfare of humanity; for, the destruction of this colossal power with its ramifications thrown on every quarter of the globe will upset the equilibrium of the world, will produce more direful calamities than what resulted from the subversion of the Roman Empire, and will push civilisation many centuries backwards. Mr. Gladstone and his party subsequently discovered their mistake, but it was then too late; the cry of "Paper Union" was lost amidst the din of "Separation" which resounded throughout the length and breadth of the land. Does a union exist between England and Ireland now, or did it ever exist before? No, never. Ireland has always been treated as a conquered country. She had a Parliament of her own, but it never had any independent power, except only for seven years from 1783 to 1800, when by 23 Geo. III. c. 28, full power was relegated to it in all matters of legislation and judicature; but that was at a time when the world was in an unsettled state from the effects of the French Revolution, which made it impossible for it to get a fair trial. The country has been in a chronic state of rebellion, open or covert, since Pope Adrian IV. authorised the Anglo-Normans of England to partition its lands among themselves seven hundred years ago, and since that time Ireland always took advantage of England's home or foreign troubles. The disaffection of Ireland could be overlooked with safety so long as England was a first class military power, but since the Continental powers have outstripped her in fighting capabilities, England can no longer allow Ireland to remain in her present state. Ireland must have to be thoroughly united to England. Only two courses are open for the achievement of this object: one is to adopt a conciliatory measure, full and complete, like that proposed by Mr. Gladstone, and the other is to treat Ireland just as Germany is now treating the conquered province of Alsace, *i.e.*, to compel the Irish to leave their country and then people it with Englishmen. But before the adoption of such a drastic measure, a chance should be given to the Irish to become peaceful members of the State. Mr. Gladstone's Bill would have given them that chance. If they had abused it, the whole world would have cried, shame! on Ireland, and England for her self-preservation would then have been perfectly justified to denude her of her disaffected population. England is sufficiently strong to do justice to Ireland in the first place, and to punish her for her perfidy if the worst comes to the worst. The third course of half-hearted coercion, and imperfect measures for the settlement of the land question is not only waste of time but highly mischievous in the long run. The people of India are watching with keen interest this Irish controversy; for they know that in time to come, though it may be very remote to-day, England will have to decide a bigger Home Rule question—the Home Rule for India. No Indian dreams of separating his country from the influence of England: the highest aspiration of Young India is to have the privileges of a British Colony. They want to nationalise British Rule in India.

To an Indian on the spot, the political activity displayed on this occasion by the people was a great novelty. In eastern countries the personality of the sovereign was the guiding principle in all matters affecting the commonwealth. The country belonged to the king, who could sell, gamble away or make a gift of it to any one he pleased, along with the people inhabiting it. Instances of this kind often occurred in India in her best days, and on such occasions the people instead of making a manly protest tore their hair and wept like women. It is quite different in England. There every individual is part and parcel of the sovereign power. They feel their own importance, know their responsibility, and are worthy of the trust. The dignified bearing of the people, when the Home Rule discussion was at its height, was surely a treat for an Indian. In theatres, in railways, in omnibuses and in all public places the topic of conversation was Gladstone, Ireland, Home Rule, Union and Separation. Fashionable gentlemen in their clubs, merchants at their desks, traders behind the counters, mechanics in workshops, cabmen sitting on their cabs, waiters and waitresses in the restaurants, roughs in public houses, railway porters, news-vendors, every man and woman freely discussed this important matter, and every one felt that on him rested the responsibility of deciding this momentous question. In London we could hardly meet with a single supporter of Mr. Gladstone; his adherents were in the country, chiefly in Scotland. If we were to believe what half the people of England said about Mr. Gladstone, we would conclude that a more gigantic swindler than he the world never produced; while on the other hand the other half worshipped him as a demigod. One day, as I purchased a copy of the *Pall Mall Gazette* at the South Kensington railway station, a man, who was standing by seeing the paper in my hand, began to abuse Mr. Gladstone most scandalously. Among other things he said for my special behoof that Mr. Gladstone was an " old washerwoman." On this some one said that in that case "his hands at least are clean." Unaccustomed as we are to the subtleties of party politics, we were perfectly bewildered at the excitement Mr. Gladstone's Bill produced in the country. All this will pass away, Ireland will get her Home Rule, instead of the Paper Union there will be a firm union of hearts, and future generations will look back with a smile upon this madness of the time. Grattan said in 1780—"I wish for nothing but to breathe, in this our land, in common with my fellow-subjects, the air of liberty. I have no ambition, unless it be the ambition to break your chain, and contemplate your glory. I never will be satisfied so long as the meanest cottager in Ireland has a link of the British chain clanking to his rags. He may be naked; he shall not be in iron. And I do see the time is at hand, the spirit is gone forth, the declaration is planted: and though great men should apostatize, yet the cause will live; and though the public speaker should die, yet the immortal fire shall outlast the organ which conveyed it, and the breath of liberty, like the word of the holy man, will not die with the prophet, but survive him." Mr. Gladstone may now give expression to similar sentiments.

Just after our arrival I saw in the papers mention of a meeting of the Nihilists held in London. To an Indian a live Nihilist was a sight worth seeing, and I went to the place where the meeting was held, but the birds were flown before my arrival. My mind is never clear on the subject of Nihilism, and I do not know what the Nihilists really want, so I cannot say whether they are a misguided band of fanatics, or some of those benefactors of the human race whose only fault is that they are before their time. At any rate a more determined and disinterested set of individuals the world perhaps never saw. The martyr dies after suffering unspeakable tortures buoyed up with the hope that as soon as his life is extinguished his soul would fly to heaven ; the Gházi rushes to death cheered by the vision of charming houris, crystal fountains of nectar, and other pleasures of Muhammadan paradise; the Hindu woman burns herself with the full belief of meeting her husband in a better world; even the patriot and the warrior dies for his country in full faith in his God and in the justice of his cause. But what has the Nihilist to hope for ? He does not believe in God, nor does he believe in the existence of the soul and the future world. A Nihilist calmly sacrifices himself (or herself, as is frequently the case) for an idea ! It is a pity that such self-abnegation should be stained with innocent blood. To fight or die for an idea is beyond the conception of the Indian mind. It is however universal in Europe where the people are always ready to make immense sacrifices for a principle. The story of the boy who got a black eye is very much to the point. On being asked how he got it, he explained that he fought another lad who said that his sister squinted, and he got the worst of the encounter. "Does your sister really squint?" "Oh no, a'int no sister" was the reply. "Then why did you fight?" "It is for the principle of the thing," was the most conclusive argument set forth for his fighting and getting the black eye.

CHAPTER III.

THE EXHIBITION AND ITS VISITORS.

On the 4th of May 1886, the Colonial and the Indian Exhibition was opened. It was a bright and glorious morning, Queen's weather, as the people of England call it, when we first saw our beloved Empress. No British subject can conceive a higher honour than to have the privilege of doing obeisance to his august sovereign. And are we not the favourite children of our Empress-mother? In all the presentations when one could watch her mild benevolent face as the representatives of the different nations filed past, she had always a special kind look for us poor Indians. The gratified expression on her face when our artisans touched her feet must be imprinted on every one's mind who witnessed the touching scene. I tell this to my people—be he from the rugged plains of Peshawar or the alluvial swamps in the Brahmaputra valley, from the snow-covered Bhot or the scrubby country near Cape Comorin,—that our Empress-mother takes a deep personal interest in the welfare of her Indian children.

At 11-30 their Royal Highnesses the Prince and Princess of Wales, accompanied by Prince Albert Victor of Wales, and the Princesses Louise, Victoria and Maud arrived at the Exhibition escorted by the Life Guards. The other members of the Royal Family invited to take part in the ceremony were the Crown Princess of Germany, the Duchess of Edinburgh, Prince Alfred of Edinburgh, the Duke and Duchess of Connaught, Prince and Princess Christian of Schleswig Holstein, Princess Louise and Marchioness of Lorne, Marquis of Lorne, Princess Beatrice, Prince Henry of Battenberg, Duke of Cambridge, Princess Mary Adelaide, Duke of Teck, Princess Victoria Teck, Princess Frederica of Hanover, Baron Von Pawel Rammingen, Duke and Duchess of Oldenburg, Prince and Princess Leiningen, Princess Alberta of Leiningen, Prince and Princess Louis of Battenburg, Prince and Princess Edward of Sax-Weimar, Prince and Princess Victor of Hohenlohe-Langenburg, and the Countess Theodore Gleichen. At about 12 a flourish of trumpets by Her Majesty's State Trumpeters announced the arrival of the Queen. On entering the main avenue of the Exhibition, she was received by the Prince of Wales as the executive head of the Exhibition and by the other members of the Royal Family. The Queen wore a plain black dress, without any decorations, and unless from her majestic bearing you could hardly realise that you stood before the great sovereign of the vast British Empire. She first made a dignified curtsey to the assembly present and then kissed her relations. The representatives of the various Colonies and India were then presented to her in a body by the Prince of Wales. After this ceremony we were taken to another part of the Exhibition where the Indians waited with an address to be presented to the Queen. In the meantime a procession was formed in the following order

H

—(1) Pursuivants of Arms, Rouge Dragon, Rouge Croix, Blue mantle, Portcullis; (2) Assistant Secretaries and the Official Agent to the Royal Commission and Members of the Finance and Lighting Committees; (3) Heralds: Chester, Windsor, Lancaster, York, Somerset, Richmond; (4) Her Majesty's Commissioners and the Executive Commissioners for the Colonies and India; (5) Garter King of Arms, Treasurer of Household, Comptroller of Household, Vice-Chamberlain, Lord Steward, Lord Chamberlain; THE QUEEN; their Royal Highnesses the Prince and Princess of Wales and other members of the Royal Family; (6) Acting Mistress of the Robes, Lady of the Bedchamber, Maids of Honour, Women of the Bedchamber, Ladies in Attendance on the Royal Family; (7) Gold Stick in waiting, Master of the Horse, Captain of the Yeomen of the Guard, Captain of the Gentlemen at Arms, Lord in Waiting, Groom in Waiting, Keeper of Her Majesty's Privy Purse, Equerries in Waiting, Gentlemen Usher in waiting, Comptroller—Lord Chamberlain's Department—Silver Stick in waiting, Field officer in Brigade waiting and Gentlemen in waiting on the Royal Family.

The Procession started from the main entrance and proceeded through the vestibule where the clay figures representing the various races of the Indian soldiery were arranged in a row. Passing under the carved wood-work on which the Jaipur motto "Where Virtue is, there is Victory" was emblazoned, it entered the Indian Court glittering with the richest workmanship of our skilful artisans, and finally it arrived before the "Indian Palace" where we waited. His Royal Highness, the Prince of Wales here presented us individually to Her Majesty. The Indian artisans who stood in the opposite row were instructed to receive the Queen with the salutation of "Rám, Rám." Among them were some devout Muhammadans, who cried "Rám, Rám," but being unaccustomed to such a strange mode of salutation they added to it the words "Al-Ahmad-ul-illah." So they continually said—"Rám, Rám, Al-Ahmad-ul-illah, Rám, Rám, Al-Ahmad-ul-illah." After this was over an address was read, and the procession then moved on. Not knowing what to do next we followed and passing through the Australian and the Canada Courts, we arrived at the Albert Hall. As we were pushing our way, Sir Phillip Cunliffe-Owen came running to us and with a face full of concern said "What are you doing!" Then we realised our actual position. As soon as the address was read we followed Her Majesty and went on along with the Royal Family. We felt somewhat nervous and asked him, "Shall we go back?" He said, "No, stay where you are." We were very sorry for the mistake, but there was no help for it ; we could not go back even if we would, for the passage behind was entirely blocked up. So we were obliged to stand where we were. The Royal Albert Hall where the ceremony of opening the Exhibition was held is an immense circular building covered by a glass dome, and capable of holding 10,000 persons. It was built by a Company in 1868—71 at a cost of more than 30 lakhs of rupees (£200,000). Every inch of space in this vast building was occupied, and as I stood on the opposite end to that reserved for the public I could see nothing but an immense number of heads before me arranged in semi-circular rows one over the other. The Chair of State was placed on the Dais, in front of which Her Majesty took her seat, His Royal Highness the Prince of Wales on her right, and the other members of the Royal Family standing on either side, with the Great Officers of State and the Ladies and Gentlemen of the Household around them. As the procession entered the Albert Hall, the first verse of the National Anthem was sung in English by the Royal Albert Hall Choral Society. When Her Majesty reached the Dais the second verse was sung in Sanskrit, as translated by Professor Max-Müller. The whole of the Anthem was thus rendered by him:—

Rágním prasádiním, loka-pranádiním, páhíswara!
The Queen, the gracious, world-renowned, Save, O Lord!
Lakshmí prabhásiním, satrúpahásiním, tám dírghasásiním, páhíswara!
In victory brilliant, at enemies smiling, her long-ruling, Save O Lord!
Ehy asmadíswara, satrún pratiskira, ukkhinddhi tán!
Approach, O our Lord, enemies scatter, annihilate them!
Takkhadma násya máyáska pásaya, páhyasmadásraya, sarván ganán!
Their fraud confound, tricks restrain, Protect, O thou our Refuge, all people!
Tvadratna-bhúshitám rágye kiroshitám, páhíswara!
With thy choice gifts adorned, in the kingdom long-dwelling, Save O Lord!
Rágya-prapáliním, saddharma-sáliním, tám stotra máliním, páhíswara!
Her, the realm-protecting, by good laws abiding, her with praise wreathed, Save O Lord!

After the second verse of the National Anthem was sung in Sanskrit, the third verse was done in

English. Madame Albani and the choir next sang an Ode written specially for the occasion by the Poet Laureate, Lord Tennyson. The Prince of Wales then read an address to Her Majesty, and presented to her a Catalogue of the Exhibition. Her Majesty made a reply to it and commanded the Lord Chamberlain to declare the Exhibition open, which being done, it was announced to the public by a flourish of trumpets by Her Majesty's State Trumpeters, and by the firing of a royal salute in Hyde Park.

India formed by far the most interesting section of the Colonial and Indian Exhibition. Passing the vestibule at the main entrance, the visitor would stand before the clay models of the military races which uphold the power of England in the East. He would then be led to that gorgeous display of costly jewellery, gold and silver plate, brass and copper vessels with tasteful designs, minute wood carving, inlay work on metal, stone and wood, lacquered ware of ruby, emerald and golden hues, costly fabrics woven by patient hands unrivalled in the world, and various other articles which from time immemorial excited the wonder and commanded the admiration of the western nations. As the visitor stood facing this vast panorama of India's artistic wealth, he could watch on his right the multitude crowding to the spot where the jungle life in India was illustrated in a rather over-drawn vividness. Within a narrow compass was pressed the sloping section of a low rugged hill, high trees with arms spreading in all directions, bushy undergrowths, clumps of the feathery bamboo, the wild date with stumps of their petioles sticking on all sides of the stem, rank grass, and other accessories of a sub-Himalayan scenery. This miniature representation of the happiest of hunting grounds in India was densely packed with all sorts of big and small game, the sight of which often elicited a sigh from the superannuated sportsman, as the pleasant days of his youthful life rushed into his mind, when regardless of all danger from his ferocious enemy of the forest and the more deadly jungle fever of the Tarái, he defiantly strode through hills and swamps dealing death and destruction wherever he went. Here the mighty elephant was shewn with his uplifted trunk, his mouth open, as if roaring from fear and pain, failing to shake off the royal tiger which had fixed his firm grip upon his huge head, from which several streams of blood trickled down dyeing the yellow grass below of a mottled crimson. The roar of the elephant and the angry growl of the tiger had evidently startled a herd of deer which might have been quietly grazing in the neighbourhood, but had now succeeded by rapid strides to gain the hill opposite the place where the fierce struggle was taking place; all but a brave antler, which after running for a certain distance, now stood still with an inquisitive look expressive of wonder, curiosity and an earnest longing to sift to the bottom the cause of all this tremendous uproar. High up in the tree a herd of monkeys, cowed with terror, crouched beneath every leafy branchlet that afforded a hiding place, while the little babies clung fast to the breast of their mothers as the terrific howl resounded through the forest and echoed by the distant hills. The peafowl had taken shelter among the green leaves, but the vulture had risen in the air exultant at the prospect of the dainty meal which he knew by experience was being prepared by the brave tiger. In another part of the scene, the Bengal tiger was shewn in his attitude of noiselessly creeping through the friendly grass preparatory to that fatal spring on his unsuspecting prey. The jungle scene, though overdrawn, which could not probably be helped owing to the small space at the command of the designer, was altogether highly attractive.

On the left hand of the visitor lay the Indian Economic Court where models of the various aboriginal races were interspersed among the products and manufactures of India. Here could be seen the short-statured Andamanese woman, bedecked with shells and leaves, the white skull of a near relation dangling on her jet black breast. Her husband stood near, spear in hand, his hair frizzled according to the most approved modern fashion. The original of this latter model was no doubt a regular dandy among his people. The Negrito type of the Andamanese bore a strong contrast to his neighbour, the Nicobarese, in whom the Malay element is predominant, although there seems to exist a strong admixture of the Mongolian blood in his veins. The Mongolian element grew stronger as the visitor passed on to the next group of models, consisting of the Burmans of the Irawady Delta and the Karens of the hills. Following up the ethnographical arrangement adopted in this court the visitor would next arrive to that most interesting assemblage of tribes that people the North-east frontier of India, all belonging to the Mongolian family of the human race. There stood the tawny Sinpho, his head adorned with a helmet made of plaited rattan cane, and the everlasting Dáo in his hand, with which he fights, chops off the head of his fallen foe, clears the forest land, cuts his scanty crop on the hillside, and does all sorts of household work. The proud Nágá was there, fully equipped for war, dyed tufts of feather waving over his head, dyed human and goat's hair adorning his breast, a long richly decorated spear in one hand, while the other grasped a large shield made of tiger skin, the first trophy of his youthful ambition. His necklace of human and goat's hair proclaimed to the world, that he the proud wearer received this decoration from his nation for the valour he displayed in the field and the stratagem he employed in securing a number of human heads from his tribal enemy. For none but a man successful in obtaining such a trophy is allowed to wear this much coveted mark of honour. After all, the Nágá is a savage. His insignia of honour are therefore so crude and primitive. Had he been civilised he would have prided in stars and ribbons. His distinction is short-lived too, for it ends with his life. The praise of a hero who has ruthlessly massacred men, women and children, robbed his weak neighbours of their property and carried death and devastation wherever he has gone, is not sung by the bards; nor are there any historians among the Nágás to record with admiration his wholesale butchery of fellow-beings; nor do they possess any moralists to hold up his deeds before the mind of the younger generation to point out to them the noblest course by which a man can achieve everlasting glory. The poor Nágá has therefore to be content with the short-lived honour of being privileged to wear the necklace of human hair round his neck. But he kills not so much for that distinction as for the pleasure which the act of killing affords to most men of all nations, except, all honour to him, the Hindu. The greatest pleasure which wild tribes in all ages and in all parts of the world found in life was in exterminating their fellow-men living on the opposite side of a river or a hill. Civilised men in Europe, restrained from cutting the throats of their neighbours, enjoy *innocent* pleasure by hunting to death the poor little fox, or by shooting the deer, or the pheasants and pigeons specially reared for the sake of being killed. The rich among them go to all parts of the world to kill. They may be seen following the wild deer among the pine forests of Norway, after the chamois in the Swiss Alps, shooting the musk deer in the snowy Himalayas, hunting the Bengal tiger in the Sundarbans, killing the elephant among the dense forests of Ceylon, and pursuing the jumping kangaroo in the wilds of Australia, the camelopard in South Africa and the wild goat among the Rocky Mountains. The religion of the Christian teaches him to pay no heed to the earnest longing to live, implanted in the mind of every living being; he therefore kills, usefully or not, wherever he has the chance to do so. Of all nations in the world, the Hindu alone feels sorrow to shed blood, and is able to realise the fact that such acts are against the dictates of mercy; for *his* religion teaches him to look upon every living thing as his own self. The power to relish destruction of life is developed in the Nágá in as high a degree as it is in the European. Sometime ago a Nágá lad of fourteen acquired the badge of honour. He hid himself with his Dáo in the bush near the spring of a neighbouring village at feud with his own, and he cut off the head of the first woman that came there to take water, which he carried in triumph to his elders who immediately invested him with the insignia of honour.

On the side of the Nágá stood the Hill Miri of Assam. The customs and manners of this tribe agree in many respects with those of the Hindus of Lower Bengal. Like the high-caste Bráhmans their men practise polygamy to a large extent. Wives are purchased, but unlike the Hindu, they pay the price in kind and not in hard cash, the average rate per girl being three buffaloes, thirty pigs and a number of fowls. They also consider it fit to deprive their women of many privileges which the men enjoy, and as in the case of the unfortunate Hindu widows, this tyranny is extended even to the matter of food. In explaining away such injustice to women, the Miri assumes the same lofty moral attitude which is often seen in educated Indians who, afraid of doing what is right against the mandates of the prevailing custom, find excuses for their moral cowardice on grounds of expediency. Thus the Hill Miri disallows the flesh of tiger to women, though it is highly prized by the men, on the ground that it would make them too strong-minded. But in one respect the Miri woman is better off than her sisters of Lower Bengal; she can dress decently, for religion and inexorable custom do not compel her to go half-naked. The Abors of Assam dress like the Indian sages of old, a small piece of a bark of a tree forming their only raiment, which they also use as a carpet to sit upon and as a covering in the night. The great Shan tribe had its representative in the Khampti model. Among other races of Assam were to be seen the models of the Mikir, the Daphla, the Khasia, and the Jaintia in this interesting group of figures. The tribes, inhabiting the mountain and forest regions further west all along the Himalayas up to the Gangotri, are ethnologically related to those above described, and these were represented at the Exhibition by the models of the Garo, Mech, Limbo, Lepcha, Gorkha and Garhwáli, all with flat nose, high cheek bone, and scanty hair on the face to denote their Tartar descent. The Gangetic valley, occupied by a people of more or less Aryan origin, lies as a wedge dividing the Mongolians in the north from the Kolarians and Dravidians in the south. The Santál, the Pahári, the Oráon, the Kol and the Gond illustrated the Kolarian tribes, while the Telugu, the Tamil, the Irula, the Badgar, and possibly the Toda and the Kurg, represented the Dravidian races. From the West of India were sent models of the Thákur, the Katkari and the Son Koli, all of Turanian origin. Central India supplied the Bhil and the Mina to represent its aboriginal population, while the pure Aryan had its representatives in the Pathan, the Jat and the Rajput.

The myriads of visitors that daily flocked to the Exhibition revealed to us the great mysterious cause of European progress. It is discontent. It is the constant search after knowledge and the constant readiness to accept a better state of things, whenever that is discovered and understood. Power and prosperity in a nation depend upon its capacity to change, while its decline may be dated from the time when its glory reaches such a climax as to make it afraid to interfere with the existing order of things lest a false step produces untoward results. From that date the religious, moral and social system of a nation begins to get fossilised, and it soon becomes quite incapable to replenish its diminishing vitality by the absorption of new truths. From such a society the spirit soon departs, and it is the dead body of the nation that remains behind. Blinded patriots and immoderate reverencers of the past hug this nation's corpse with extreme fondness, and vainly try to throw the cycle-hand of the world's chronometer many thousand years back. The builders of the pyramids would sooner rise from their crumbling sarcophagi to make railways and telegraphs than a retrocession to the Vedic life in India, for which my countrymen are so anxious, would revive the glory of the Indian nation. The past is dead and gone; and to be what is past is to be dead. The past has been the builder of the present, and the present is the builder of the future. Every moment of the universal life lays a stone for that edifice—the future. The life of every human being and all creation, animate and inanimate, help nature within their respective spheres in this building operation. Woe to him, who obstructs nature's progress by clinging to that which is past and gone. The fate of all laggers-behind in this inexorable onward march soon overtakes him, and that is destruction. In the history of the world many nations met such a sad fate, and but for the extenuating circumstance of being possessed of a very high order of intellectuality such would have been the fate of the Hindu nation. So far as material condition and intellect as applied to practical life go, the present of the European nations will be our future perhaps many centuries hence, but instead of making rapid strides to regain the lost ground if we choose to go still more backwards, while the whole world will be moving on, then the race for life will be hopelessly lost, for the present is nearer to the future than the past. Such alas! is the will of the nation at the present moment, the effect of a reaction and of the praise bestowed by generous westerners on every thing that is Hindu. A more effective method could not be devised to ruin a highly sensitive and proud people labouring under physical and mental infirmities and demoralised by centuries of foreign domination. Thus the difference between the European and the Indian is very marked on this point. The former is always on the look out for new things. He is constantly striving to make new contrivances and to discover new ways and means to enable him to move on to a higher plane in the sphere of his own pursuits. Not so with the Indian. He will not easily accept any new knowledge even if it is forced down his throat with a hydraulic hammer. It is certainly not the fault of the Indian if the irresistible force of western civilisation has somewhat relaxed the stiffness of his mind, elasticised his character and expanded his ideas of the world, for he has always done his best to shut his eyes against the influence of modern enlightenment. An *Ekka*-man in the Northwest would not introduce the innovation of spring wheels nor would a peasant cultivate potato in Etah, for such daring rebellion against the established custom would at once bring upon him the thunderbolt of excommunication. In fact that was the reason given to me sometime ago by an *Ekka*-man and a peasant for their inability to try the improvements suggested in their respective lines. Under such encouraging circumstances it is very surprising indeed that a host of Indian Stephensons and Edisons are not produced on all sides!

It was therefore very refreshing to us to turn aside from our national torpor, and witness the all-absorbing enthusiasm of the European for progressive advance. We, therefore, constantly watched with pleasure the anxious inquisitive scrutiny to which the various raw products of India were daily subjected by thousands of visitors at the Colonial and Indian Exhibition. Merchants, manufacturers and scientists flocked there to see what new sources of wealth and human comfort had been brought within their reach from her Majesty's distant dominions. Even the natives who came from villages took an unusual interest in the most trivial objects, such as leaves and barks, and exhibited intelligence of a superior order in mastering the details of the various uses to which they are put in India and other parts of the world. Parents explained to their children, and young men to their sweethearts, the various points of interest found in the innumerable products and manufactures which India sent to that Exhibition from her different provinces. The late Reverend Mr. Long and myself often stood for hours together behind these people to hear the remarks that fell from their lips.

This old friend of the Indians used to come to me punctually every Thursday morning and heard with interest the progress which India had made since he left the country. He was never tired of this theme, and every morning he came he had some new point ready on which he sought to be enlightened, and which evidently he was revolving in his mind during the week. "Do the vernacular newspapers now really discuss politics and not fill their columns with abuses of each other as they used to do in my time?" was the question he once asked me after reading through a copy of the *Sanjibani* I gave him. He felt so glad when I assured him that such was the case. At another time I gave him a copy of another vernacular paper. The next time I saw him he was very downcast. He had evidently read the paper and had seen the opinion strongly expressed there adverse to a Hindu's going out of India. He wondered how any one could for a moment doubt the advantages of foreign travel. He asked, "Have not the railways in India shewn that?" At another time he asked, "Why do they abuse the British as a nation? They should know that they have sincere friends among us, who wish them well, and who constantly watch over them with a paternal care.

Look at Lord Northbrook, John Bright, Sir George Birdwood, Miss Manning, Miss Florence Nightingale, and others whom you know; are they not your real friends? Oh, how I wish to see you a great nation!" I said that both in good and evil the vernacular papers generally took their lessons from English periodicals conducted by Englishmen in India. On the vernacular newspapers, the village schools, the caste rules, indigo cultivation, and on various other subjects he wanted the most detailed information. He often expressed to me his regret at not being able to procure Bengali books and newspapers, and his joy knew no bounds when I gave him the papers mentioned above. He often expressed a childish delight at the admiration which the magnificence of the Indian court excited in the mind of the natives, I mean the natives of England. On such occasions his face beamed with pleasure and seemed to say—"My beloved India has done all this." Once, after he had heard me explain to the late M. Eugene Rimmel the various sources of perfumery found in India, he asked me whether there were now many people among the Indians who took an interest in the development of the raw resources of their country. I answered that a sentiment was growing among a few that at least for some time to come our chief hope of bettering the national prospects lay in this direction. He was very glad to hear of the establishment of the Scientific Institution at Calcutta by Dr. Mahendra Lál Sarkár. "Do you mean to say that it is founded and maintained by voluntary contributions?" He asked. I said it was so, though the contributions did not pour in as readily and abundantly as in the case of the Patriotic Fund started in Lord Lytton's time.

Knowing me to be a Hindu and a Bráhman, in all the conversations he had with me he would never enter into the controversial question of religion, Christian Missionary as he was, and I fully appreciated his kindness in this respect. As I write, the benevolent face of my departed friend is present in my mind, and I sadly remember the last leave I took of him at the South Kensington Station before my departure from England, never again to meet in this world. His soul was a heaven by itself, the abode of everything that was noble and good. His love of God made him love all creatures, and he must have now attained that blissful state which we believe to be the destiny of every good man be he Hindu or Christian, white or black, civilised or savage. How can we help loving the nation to which he belonged? That is our humble offering to his memory, and our gratitude for the noble deeds of his life.

The economic products of India attracted the attention they deserved. People who deal in gums critically examined the specimens we sent, for their supply from Africa had considerably diminished owing to the Soudan war. But our gums are not of such good quality as those brought from the arid regions of Arabia and Africa. Our gum acacia, the product of *Acacia arabica, Willd.* (Báblá), is not so white and clear as the product of *Acacia vera*, imported into this country from Aden, and neither is it so abundant. But even the inferior gums of India, tons and tons of which every year rot in the jungles and villages, would find a market in Europe and sufficiently remunerate those who would take the trouble to collect them. The gums of *Acacia leucophlœa, Willd.*, sent from Bombay, and of *Acacia Catechu*, sent from Upper India, were considered suitable for use as substitutes for the true gum acacia. The gum of *Odina Wodier, Linn.* (Jibal), a tree reared as a hedge-plant all over Lower Bengal, would, if collected with care and at the proper season, answer the same purpose. The reaction against the gaudy aniline dyes invited attention towards our vegetable substances which, from time immemorial, yielded under the skilful manipulation by Indian hands the most beautiful sober colours, and the use of which is still unknown in Europe. The roots of *Morinda citrifolia, Linn., Oldenlandia umbellata, Linn.*, and of the different species of *Rubia* received commendation. England annually imports extracts and barks to the value of several crores of rupees for dyeing and tanning purposes. India has a very insignificant share in this important trade. Is the vast continent of India, with its forests and mountains extending from the arctic climate of the Himalayas to the torrid zone near the equator, so poor in astringent barks and leaves? Most decidedly not. But who is there to study the question, collect facts, make trials and offer sufficient inducements to merchants and traders to make it worth their while to move out of the present groove? Centuries ago the fiat was sent forth that every Hindu should be nailed to the spot where he was born. He must therefore leave to foreigners the development of new lines of trade, the discovery of new sources of national wealth, the utilisation of the soil for more profitable crops, the substitution of modern discoveries for old methods, the building of ships, the construction of railways and various other matters which should have been the first duty of a much less pretentious nationality. The Hindu considers his duty well-performed when he has inveighed against the injustice of not appointing a larger number of Indian clerks in offices, and guards in the railways made by Europeans. I have often expressed in strong terms my feeling on this subject, but it is not want of sympathy for my countrymen that wrings out from my mind hard words; it is the shame that I feel for the artificial barrier we ourselves have raised against our advancement, for our weakness and impotence, and for the wilful waste of mental faculties which stand second to none in the world, that compels me to emphasize the language of condemnation. The resources of India are unlimited, which, if intelligently utilised, would give employment to thousands, raise the standard of life and, if wealth is power, would enable the people to command the respect of other nations in the world. It is not so very difficult, as one would suppose, to divert England's money towards India from foreign countries in the welfare of which Englishmen have not the least concern. Englishmen are very partial to India, and I am sure they would a good deal go out of their way to help their fellow subjects. Besides, the benefit will be mutual. The money thus sent to India will be returned to England for her manufactures. Half of India goes half-naked for want of means to purchase the necessary clothing. Increase the means and a large part of the money will find its way back to Lancashire, Birmingham, Sheffield and other manufacturing centres, for dress, finery, cutlery and crockery. My wanderings through the London market, where the products of the world were displayed for sale, taught me the lesson that India could do many times better in the matter of foreign trade than she does now. But it was impossible that in the few hours I could snatch at different times to visit the produce market, I would be able to collect such reliable information as to warrant any one to embark on a new venture without a more detailed enquiry and preliminary trial, for theory requires verification by practice. What is required now is careful and continued investigation, trial consignments to verify the facts thus obtained, and removal of difficulties as they appear. It is by such means that the Australians have found in England a profitable market for their meat, which formerly they used to throw away, and for the fresh fruits of which they grow more than they require for home consumption. I would not blame Government for not taking energetic action in this direction; I would rather turn to my countrymen and say that if any of them wish to do anything in the line indicated above, I would gladly place at their disposal all the information I possess, but they must come prepared for preliminary trial and arduous and expensive experiments.

My friend, Mr. Thomas Christy, of 25 Lime Street, London, has laid the world under a deep obligation. His peaceful arbour at Sydenham reminded me of that quiet hermitage where my great ancestor, Bharadwáj, instructed his disciple, Charak, in the subtle properties of officinal plants, long before Æsculapius sat at the feet of Chiron, the Centaur. What Charak and Susruta in the prehistoric times and Dioscorides in a comparatively modern age, did for the exploitation of vegetable medicines, Mr. Christy and his coadjutors are doing at the present day. With the aid of that systematic generalisation to which the vegetable kingdom has now been reduced and the facilities for analysis afforded by modern chemistry, the products of the whole world are being thoroughly ransacked for the discovery of new medicines capable to cure disease, alleviate pain and prolong human life. The same spirit of restless enquiry which led the Arab physician, Ahram, to introduce into Europe the use of rhubarb, cassia, senna, camphor and other eastern medicines, and effected in later times the discovery of quinine, morphia and strychnine, has enabled Mr. Thomas Christy to add many powerful medicines to the British pharmacopœia, some of which are valuable remedies for obstinate diseases which hitherto baffled all human efforts to cure or control. Thus in the seed of a fruit tree, common all over India, Mr. Christy has discovered an active principle which, I am told, exercises a beneficial influence on diabetes. The seed lies in heaps under the tree, unused and uncared for, waiting for the rainy season to germinate and form a thick undergrowth, breathing miasma, until the leisurely browse of a herd of goat opens the way for the purifying rays of the sun to reach the damp soil beneath.

Another small plant, a common weed all over the country, has been proved to be an effectual remedy for a still more terrible disease. More brilliant results can be achieved if Mr. Christy's exertions are supported by the knowledge accumulated in India by observation and practice extending over hundreds of years. Old oriental and modern European knowledge should meet and mingle here and generate new forces for the conquest of that dire enemy—Disease—which is a constant cause of unhappiness to humanity at large. In such work the co-operation of men like Dr. Kanai Lall Dey, Dr. Nobin Chandra Pal, Dr. Mudin Sharif, and the late Drs. Sakhárám and Udai Chand Datta would be extremely valuable. India has an especial interest in the success of Mr. Christy's efforts, for it would turn to gold many things which are at present totally useless, or even injurious to health, owing to the poisonous gases they generate by their decomposition during the rains.

Mr. Christy is one of those men in whom I found united the most leading characteristics of a typical Englishman. The ideal Englishman, as I conceive him, is strong and stout in physical make, generous, open and stern in mind, and unrelenting in his aversion to all sorts of humbug and nonsense. He is the essence of action, as contrasted with the Hindu, the essence of inaction. In the former, both the mental and physical faculties are fully developed, in the same way as in the ancient Aryan before climatic and other influences upset the equilibrium of his system by the deterioration of his body. John Bull may be taken as the representative of vigorous manhood in the humanity of the present day; the savage of the childhood; and the Hindu of a moribund condition of decrepit old age. John Bull is therefore able to educate his internal forces for the subjugation of external forces; while the Hindu, after passing through different stages of idealism and becoming the fountain-head of Neo-Platonism, has at length totally ignored the presence of external forces, and fixed for the aim of life the education of intellectual faculties for the attainment of a state of imaginative ecstasy resulting from a complete cessation of action. However poetic and subtle such an esoteric doctrine may be, the hard and unpliable realities of the world are a little too gross for its adoption in the ordinary practices of life.

So far as the short time at my disposal permitted, I carefully examined the London drug market to see what substances England gets from foreign countries. Among the articles now brought there from eastern Asia, Africa, America and other parts of the world are many substances which can be easily supplied from India. The pods of *Cassia fistula* (Sondál), thousands of which dry on the trees all over the country, tamarind, the yellow powder obtained from *Mallotus Phillippinensis* (Kamilá), the root of *Hemidesmus indicus* (Anantamúl), were the articles I saw in the London market which might be cited as examples. The Indian specimens of such articles were placed before the merchants assembled at a conference held in the Exhibition. They expressed their willingness to give Indian consignments a careful trial. An examination of prices prevailing in the London market showed that these could be made paying if the preliminary difficulties were removed. Similarly there is ample room for the expansion of trade in other articles, of which the most important are fibres and paper-materials. That Indian enterprise can produce excellent results was shewn from the attention which a fibre, sent by Raja Kristendra Narain Roy of Balihár in Rajshahi, received at the Exhibition. The fact is there is no one in London or any where in Europe or America to look after the commercial interests of India. All civilised countries have consuls in different parts of the globe to watch over such interests, but the vast continent of India, with its enlightened administration, has none.

The late M. Eugene Rimmel was one of the numerous friends I had the good fortune to make in England in connection with the question of development of trade in Indian raw products. He undertook to experiment with substances used in perfumery and in essential oils. He wrote—"I left at your office to-day my Book of Perfumes. I wanted to ask you for the list of sources of Indian essential oils which you promised, and which would much interest me. If you have a moment to spare to make it out, I shall feel much obliged by your forwarding it to me." The list was sent, but to my great sorrow, I received the news of his death before he could be put in a position of commencing the work in an earnest and business-like manner. Mr. Cross, the renowned chemist, undertook the examination of fibres. A fibre was once placed in my hands and I was asked to name it. I immediately pronounced it to be Tasar silk—it was so soft and glossy. It was however jute reduced to that condition by a chemical process discovered, I think, by Mr. Cross. By another process a brown coarse fibre, that of *Bauhinia Vahlii*, had been transformed into a soft white stuff hardly distinguishable from pure white wool of a very superior kind. A trade is already springing up in this article as will be seen by the following extract from a letter written to me by an English friend residing in a place not 150 miles from Calcutta :—" Messrs.———applied to me for a sample of *Bauhinia Vahlii* fibre which I have sent. I have promised, if they wished me to do so, to collect fibre for them. * * *Bauhinia Vahlii* grows plentifully in the hills here and at a small cost for protecting it from fire, &c., any quantity could be procured. Messrs.———said you had recommended them to write to me. I have therefore taken the liberty to write to you and explain." I have treated these matters in detail, hard and dry as they are, in order to show to my countrymen that independent livelihood, wealth and prosperity are within their reach if they would only move out from that baneful atmosphere of superstition and prejudice which stifle the breath of national advancement,—if they would only open their eyes and put forward their hands to grasp the benefits of civilisation. One thing more I must add. It is we ourselves that can be most useful in this matter. I think that in these experiments merchants in England will, as a special kindness, pay more attention to "turbanned gentlemen" than to their own countrymen, for they care very little for small consignments, and traders as a rule are extremely averse to move out of old channels.

For the common people the Indian Art-ware Court was a centre of great attraction, and it was chiefly around the glittering cases, that displayed costly jewellery of antique patterns and rare workmanship, the crowd largely congregated. Sweet little cherubims with yellow hair flowing in profusion on their backs; pretty maidens just out from school, whose lovely timidity and bashfulness gave to their face a heavenly charm; young girls who came to the Exhibition with the pleasant prospect of receiving from their accepted lovers the first instalment of that life-long tribute, which alas! in after days, when the spell of early love is broken, becomes too often an extortion against which a Socrates might rebel; and sober matrons on whose face sat a dignified expression of care and responsibility, examined with wistful eyes the bracelets, bangles, chains, necklaces and lockets sent from Trichinopoly, Cuttack, Dacca, Delhi, Lucknow and Jaipur. Poor little Swamy! When, in his humble cottage in the far south of India, bending before his primitive anvil which his father and forefathers used before him, he lovingly stroked a rough piece of silver with his short hammer, little did he know what those playful strokes of his subsequently produced in the far West, where young women of angelic beauty and men whom precept and example, honour and prudence, have taught to curb their passions—have taught to adore love and abhor lust—sanctified their devotion to each other by fervent kisses, under the spreading boughs of the broad-leaved chestnut, the evergreen pine, the bending willow or the stout-hearted oak as the sombre shades of the evening closed round to screen them from the impertinent gaze of the outside world. Those little strokes of the Swamy let loose a tremendous force under which beat many a heart in a way that would make even Vulcan pause and stare in astonishment, generated tempests in family circles which swept away for a time all peace and contentment, and above all produced sadness on faces on which to bring back their wonted sweetness the Swamy would have given everything that he possessed in the world. Could the most delicate tracing of the conventional lotus, impressed by tradition on Indian gold and silver workmanship, the deep-red ruby enamel worked out by the most expert hand and the master-mind, the glorious blue of the lapis lazuli, the pale green of the torquoise, or the brightest diamond that Satrájit possessed in days of yore add to the charms which kind nature has so lavishly showered on the English woman? Might not the radiant spring, though washed and cleaned by an early shower, droop and sigh and shed tears, jealous of the freshness of her blooming face? Might not the unblemished snow, that wraps the northern zone with a sheet of white, covet a little transparency from her soft smooth skin? Or might not the red rose, always glowing with vanity, wish to steal a little tinting from her ruddy cheeks? The most bigoted ascetic could not blame appreciative youths snatching a kiss from those moist crimson lips, at the sight of which the bright red coral would wish to lie for ever and ever under the deep. An oriental, however, prefers a different style ; unless keen in observation, he sees nothing in English beauty to admire except the complexion. He likes a symmetrical face, chiselled out to geometrical nicety, but a close observation would show that a statue-like countenance only appeals to the eye, while the influence of the fresh expressive face of the English woman penetrates the mind. The defects in her beauty are in her eyes which might have been a little blacker, in her hair which where not golden might have been a little darker, longer and more abundant, in her general make which might have been more slender, supple and lithe, and in the expression of her face which might have had a little more mildness and less of that rebellious spirit which seems to lurk within. But these faults are so trivial that they only serve to set off to greater advantage the grandeur of her beauty, of which Englishmen might well be proud, and the worshippers of idols might take patterns for the images of their goddesses. Indeed many Madonnas, notably the Madonna of the Chair, must have been conceived from a style of northern beauty, for it has little resemblance to **La Fornarina** or to the Jewish cast of face, while on the other hand it possesses in a high degree that inexpressible refinement that adds womanliness to woman, which is not very common in the Continental woman. Although I would give preference to English over Continental beauty chiefly for this reason, I would hesitate to judge if American ladies came to the field as competitors. With all her charms, the English woman would as much sigh for glittering trinkets, as the Dyak lady of Borneo for cane-bracelets, the Tamil girl of South India for lacquered palm leaf to fill the huge holes made in her ear-lobes, and the peasant woman of the North-West for ten-pound brass anklets, which she painfully drags through life and bequeaths on her death to successive generations.

The jewellery and most of the superior kinds of Indian art-ware were sold within a few days after the opening of the Exhibition. Besides jewellery, other articles that found most favour are pottery, metalware and lacquered-ware. The glazed pottery of Bombay, Halla, Multan, Jaipur, and Khurja were all immediately sold. A happy adaptation on the Bombay pottery of scenes depicting Indian life two thousand years ago, painted on the walls of the Ajanta cave temples, lent an additional interest to the plates and jars made in the "Wonderland Pottery Works." The realistic nature and the artistic value of these paintings can only be expressed in Mr. Griffith's own words who, admiring a scene known as the "Dying Princess," says that—" For pathos and sentiment, and the unmistakable way of telling its story, the picture cannot, I consider, be surpassed in the history of art." The Khurja pottery of *terra-cotta* ground with green ornaments was universally liked. Benares brass-ware, shining like gold, made a very picturesque show, and their low prices placed them within the reach of poorer visitors, who wanted to carry away with them a token of their visit to the Exhibition. Nor was the sober-coloured ware made in Moradabad less in demand. The lacquered wooden articles of Pákpattan, Derá Ismail Khán and other places in the Panjáb found a ready sale. But ivory work, embroidery, shawls and textile fabrics did not find much favour. Immense quantities of bead bracelets and necklets *(Rudráksha)* were sold to ladies. Many visitors, who came late and found everything worth having sold, were most disappointed. Among them, I am sorry to say, Professor Max-Müller was one.

I saw this world-renowned Sanskrit scholar, dear to every Indian heart, at Oxford, in the latter days of my stay in England. He had lately suffered deep sorrow from the sad bereavement of his beloved eldest daughter. At that time he kept himself quite secluded to mourn his deep loss in private, but when he heard that a Hindu from that far country, which is more beloved to him than any worldly tie, came to pay his homage to him, his heart at once warmed up and he prepared to receive him with open arms. So one day in November, when a thick fog cast a gloomy mantle over the shades of the evening, I rang the visitor's bell at the door of his cottage in the suburbs of Oxford. Mrs. Max Müller herself opened the door, of whom I enquired, " Is the Professor at home ?" She answered in the affirmative and bade me come in. An elderly gentleman of venerable appearance soon appeared in the passage who received me with the utmost kindness. It needed not an introduction to tell me that I stood in the presence of the man who would vie with Sáyana and Yáska in his profound love of Vedic learning, and with Pánini in his power of critical investigation and intelligent collation of facts. Still I asked: " Have

I the honour to speak to Professor Max Müller?" He quietly said: "I am that individual." Then we sat for a long time in his cosy drawing room where a cheerful fire was burning, but alas! deep sadness reigned over the whole house. The Professor constantly talked of India and the Hindus for whom it is needless to add he has the deepest sympathy and love. He told me that although his body lived in England his mind and soul were in India. He therefore surrounded himself with what little Indian objects he could secure. He went to the Exhibition to buy a few little things, but he could not get them as most of the good articles had been sold. He shewed me a few Indian articles which he had collected from time to time, and which he cherished with the greatest care. Among these was a brass jug, which he as a Sanskrit Pandit received as a present from a Calcutta gentleman on the occasion of the Sradh ceremony of his mother. The Professor attaches great value to this little present and keeps it in a place of honour. He kindly introduced me to Mrs. Max Müller and Miss Müller. He spoke very strongly against the marriage system prevailing in Europe. As far as I can remember he told me he would prefer early marriage arranged by parents, but of course not so early as is practised in India. Thus passed away one of the most delightful evenings I spent in England. He asked me to see him again, but unfortunately press of public duties deprived me of that pleasure.

Indian silks had a separate court at the Exhibition, presided over by Mr. Thomas Wardle of Leek in Staffordshire. Few people have studied the subject of Indian silk so carefully as he. Year before last he came out to India, and saw with his own eyes the present state of the industry and its future prospects. Its decline has brought ruin to the peasantry of Birbhum, Murshidabad and other silk-growing districts. My friend is however sanguine in his hopes of resuscitating this dying industry. Indeed his efforts have already proved successful, inasmuch as he has been able to wrest from China an appreciable portion of the ground lost by Bengal in the English market. While I was in England the demand for Bengal silk and cocoons suddenly revived, the price rose and every ounce available was taken up, so that in a very short time the supply totally failed. Large orders were however registered for the next year's crop. Among other measures to further the cause of Indian silk trade, Mr. Wardle adopted an improved process of reeling by means of a machine invented by himself, which was worked at the Exhibition by a French woman from Lyons. The silk thus reeled was well received in the market, and it commanded a higher price than that ordinarily sent from this country. The machine is portable, simple in construction, easily worked, and cheap, the price being about £12. Meanwhile, the indefatigable exertions of Mr. Wardle interested Government in the matter, which ordered a thorough investigation of the causes that led to the deterioration of the Bengal silk. In this work, the Government is fortunate in having secured the services of Mr. Woodmason, and I am glad that an Indian gentleman, Mr. Nitya Gopal Mukharji, is in active co-operation with him.

The whole subject will be no doubt thoroughly overhauled. Preparations are going on to enslave Bombycidæs and Saturniidæs which, happily ignorant of their impending danger, creep, crawl and writhe through leaves and branches, and spin their webs on slender twigs among their jungle fastnesses. Ruthless man is about to sacrilegiously invade the thready home, shut up in which the ugly chrysalis lead the life of a contemplative recluse, before it bursts its case and comes forth to the world, lo! a fluttering little object charming to behold. The anxious zeal, beaming on the face of the man of science as he peers through the microscopic lenses on the flexible larvæ placed on the stage beneath,—with the object of enhancing the blackmail now levied on the *Bombyx mori*, that feeds on the dwarfed mulberry, carefully cultivated on the alluvial lands of Central Bengal; the *Antherœa mylitta* (Tasar), tended by the Kol lad in the highlands of Chota Nagpur; the *Philosamia ricini* (Eria), which gorges itself with the castor-leaf in damp districts shaded by the eastern section of the Himalayan wall; the *Antherœopsis assama* (Mugá), nourished on the cellular tissues of *Machilus odoratissima, Nees;* and various other domesticated Lepidopteras reared all over India,—can only be compared with the enthusiasm displayed by the young, energetic officer, who, examines, in the presence of the terrified Zamindár, the capabilities of soil and the trace of a half-effaced watercourse from a concealed well, with the object of increasing the land revenue of a village on the expiration of the thirty years' settlement.

In one of the conferences held at the Exhibition, Mr. Wardle gave a lecture on Indian sericulture. When he finished, I said that as an improvement in the quality of the Bengal silk was desirable so was the lowering of the price, in order to better enable it to compete with the China article. This could only be done by a reduction in the cost of production. Somebody's profit must be cut down to meet the emergency. The grower, the middleman, and the merchant have all been shorn close to the skin, and even deeper; it is the Zamindár alone (permanent farmers of land revenue) who has hitherto eluded the shears and who still goes on in the world with the superabundant fleece on his back. In short, it is his covetousness that has ruined the silk trade. The item of rent of land, on which the mulberry plant is grown, has room for considerable reduction as compared with that paid for other crops. The present rate is an abnormal one which was possible when the profits from the silk trade were large, but it must go down under the altered state of things. If, however, the readjustment of rent is left to be worked out by the natural law of supply and demand, it will not come to pass until the silk trade has been totally extinguished; for, as a rule, our people do not know what is happening in the world, their eyes have not yet learnt to take survey of a wider surface of the globe than what could be done by their walking and cart-riding forefathers hundred years ago, they are not aware that misfortunes are the effects of causes which in most cases are capable of being remedied, and lastly they are totally incapable to organise a combined action in a common cause. Compulsion is therefore necessary to make the Zamindárs submit to the inevitable. Mr. Keswick who was present at the meeting disagreed with me and, in a neat little speech of considerable ability, propounded his views on the subject. Mr. Wardle nicely arranged the various kinds of Indian silk fabrics in his court, with which Her Majesty was so pleased that on one occasion she graciously expressed her satisfaction at the way Indian silks were displayed.

Another place of considerable interest to the natives of England was the Indian Bazar where Hindu and Muhammadan artisans carried on their avocations, to witness which men, women and children flocked from all parts of the kingdom. A dense crowd always stood there, looking at our men as they wove the gold brocade, sang the patterns of the carpet and printed the calico with the hand. They were as much astonished to see the Indians produce works of art with the aid of rude apparatus they themselves had discarded long ago, as a Hindu would be to see a chimpanzee officiating as a priest in a funeral ceremony and reading out Sanskrit texts from a palm leaf book spread before him. We were very interesting beings no doubt, so were the Zulus before us, and so is the Sioux chief at the present time (1887.) Human nature everywhere thirsts for novelty, and measures out its favours in proportion to the rarity and oddity of a thing. It was from the ladies that we received the largest amount of patronage. We were pierced through and through by stares from eyes of all colours—green, gray, blue and black—and every movement and act of ours, walking, sitting, eating, reading, received its full share of "O, I, never!" The number of wives we left behind at home was also a constant theme of speculation among them, and shrewd guesses were sometimes made on this point, 250 being a favourite number. You could tell any amount of stories on this subject without exciting the slightest suspicion. Once, one of our number told a pretty waitress—"I am awfully pleased with you, and I want to marry you. Will you accept the fortieth wifeship in my household which became vacant just before I left my country?" She asked—"How many wives have you altogether?" "Two hundred and fifty, the usual number," was the ready answer. "What became of your wife, number 40?" "I killed her, because one morning she could not cook my porridge well." The poor girl was horrified, and exclaimed—"O you monster, O you wretch!" Then she narrated the sad fate of a friend of hers. She was a sweet little child, when an African student studying in Edinburgh came and wooed her. They got married in England and fondly loved each other. Everything went well as long as the pair lived in England, but after a short time he took his fair wife to his desert home in Liberia. Not a single white man or woman could she see there, and she felt very lonely. But the sight of her mother-in-law, who dressed in feathers and skins came dancing into the house half-tipsy, was more than she could bear. She pined for a short time and died.

Of course, every nation in the world considers other nations as savages or at least much inferior to itself.

It was so from the beginning and it will be so as long as human nature will retain its present character. We did not therefore wonder that the common people should take us for barbarians, awkward as we were in every respect. They have very strict notions of dress, manners and the general bearing of a man, any deviation from which is seriously noticed. Utmost indulgence was however shewn to us everywhere. Her Majesty was graciously pleased to lay aside the usual rules, and this favour was shewn us wherever we went. Gentlemen and ladies of high education and culture, however, honoured us as the representatives of the most ancient nation now existing on the face of the earth. They would frequently ask us home, get up private parties and arrange for all sorts of amusements. In other houses we grew more intimate and formed part of the family party. To these we were always welcome, and could go and come whenever we liked. We got some friends among them, and these gentlemen would often come and fetch us home if we absented ourselves for more than the ordinary length of time. I fondly remember the happy days I passed with them, and feel thankful for the kindness they shewed me during my sojourn in their country.

In public matters non-official gentlemen were also very partial to us. "We want to hear the turbanned gentleman" was the wish often and often expressed. But we ceased not to be a prodigious wonder to strangers and to the common people. Would they discuss us so freely if they knew that we understood their language? It was very amusing to hear what they said about us. Often when fatigued with work, or when cares and anxieties cast a gloom upon our mind, we found such talks about us more refreshing than a glass of port wine. I wish I had the ability to do justice to the discussing power of these ladies and gentlemen exercised in their kind notice of us, for in that case I could produce one of the most interesting books ever published. Or if I had known that I would be required to write an account of my visit to Europe, I would have taken notes of at least some of the remarkable hits on truth unconsciously made by ignorant people from the country, which are applicable to all nations and which set one to philosophise on the material difference that exists between our own estimate of ourselves and the estimate which others form of us.

If we were interesting beings in the eyes of the Londoners, who had oftener opportunities of seeing their fellow subjects from the far East, how much more would we be so to the simple villagers who came by thousands to see the wonders of the Exhibition. Their conduct towards us was always kind and respectful. They liked to talk to us, and whenever convenient we tried to satisfy their curiosity. Men, women and children, whose relations are in India serving as soldiers or in any other capacity, would come through the crowd, all panting, to shake hands with us and ask about their friends. Many queer incidents happened in this way. " Do you know Jim, —James Robinson you know of———Regiment?" asked a fat elderly woman, who one day came bustling through the crowd and took me by storm, without any of those preliminary manœuvres usually adopted to open a conversation with a stranger. I expressed my regret in not having the honour of Jim's acquaintance. The good old lady then explained to me that she was Jim's aunt, and gave me a long history of her nephew, and the circumstances which led to his enlistment as a soldier. If the truant nephew lost the golden opportunity of sending through us his dutiful message to his aunt, she on her part was not wanting in her affectionate remembrances of him. Among other things, most of which I did not understand, for she did not speak the English we ordinarily hear nor was her language quite coherent at the time, she begged me to carry to Jim the important intelligence that Mrs. Jones' fat pig obtained a prize at the Smithfield Agricultural Show. I shewed my alacrity to carry the message right off to Jim in the wilds of Upper Burma by immediately taking leave of the lady, who joined her friends and explained to them that I was a bosom friend of her nephew.

Once, I was sitting in one of the swellish restaurants at the Exhibition, glancing over a newspaper which I had no time to read in the morning. At a neighbouring table sat a respectable-looking family group evidently from the country, from which furtive glances were occasionally thrown in my direction. I thought I might do worse than having a little fun, if any could be made out of the notice that was being taken of me. I seemed to be suddenly aware that I was being looked at, which immediately scared away half a dozen eyes from my table. It took fully five minutes' deep undivided attention to my paper again to reassure and tempt out those eyes from the plates where they took refuge, and the glances from them, which at first flashed and flickered like lightning, became steadier the more my mind seemed to get absorbed in the subject I was reading. The closer inspection to which I submitted ended in my favour. Perhaps, no symptom being visible in my external appearance of the cannibalistic tendencies of my heart, or owing probably to the notion that I must have by that time got over my partiality for human flesh, or knowing at least that the place was safe enough against any treacherous spring which I might take into my head to make upon them, or owing to whatever other cause, the party gradually grew bolder, began to talk in whispers and actually tried to attract my attention towards them. The latter duty ultimately devolved upon the beauty of the party, a pretty girl of about seventeen. Of course it was not intended for my ears, but somehow I heard her say—"Oh, how I wish to speak to him?" Could I withstand such an appeal? I rose and approaching the little Curiosity asked— "Did you speak to me, young lady?" She blushed and hung down her head. Her papa came to the rescue. "My daughter, Sir, is delighted with the magnificent things brought from your country to this Exhibition. She saw some writing in your language on a few plates and shields, and is anxious to know its meaning. We did not know whom to ask, when we saw you. Will you take a seat here, and do me the honour to take a glass of something with me? What will it be? Sparkling moselle I find is good here; or shall it be champagne or anything stronger?" He said. The proferred glass was declined with thanks, but I took a chair and explained the meaning of some of the verses damascened on the Koftgari ware. The young lady soon got over her bashfulness, and talked with a vivacity which I did not expect from her. She was delighted with everything I said, expressed her astonishment at my knowledge of English, and complimented me for the performance of the band brought from *my country, viz.*, the West Indian band composed of Negroes and Mulattos, which compliment made me wince a little, but nevertheless I went on chattering for a quarter of an hour and furnishing her with sufficient means to annihilate her friend Minnie, Jane or Lizzy or whoever she might be, and to brag among her less fortunate relations for six months to come of her having actually seen and talked to a genuine "Blackie."

On another occasion in a poorer place called the Grill Room, where less elaborate food and cheaper refreshments were sold, a sailor came up to me and begged hard for the favour of my speaking to his wife. He said that he had returned from Australia the day before, and obtained a day's leave to bring his wife to the Exhibition. He wanted to please her and to satisfy her wishes as far as it lay in his power. The woman took into her head the fancy that she would not be happy nor would she enjoy the sights of the Exhibition unless I spoke to her. In utter vexation at the absurdity of the request I cried—"Nonsense, I can't speak to your wife?" But the man would take no denial, and his pleadings became more and more importunate as now and then he glanced at his petulant queen, who with downcast eyes gloomily sat at a distant table. Well, her ambassador succeeded in his mission, and I had to carry balm to the mind of the unhappy lady. She cheered up at once, and as a reward allowed her husband to have another glass of whisky. That settled him. With the assistance of his wife I had soon to pack him off to his home in a cab or otherwise he would have got into trouble.

How did the Anglo-Indians treat us? I am sure my countrymen would want to know that. They treated us as gentlemen would treat gentlemen. What kinder and warmer friend could any man hope to get than Sir George Birdwood? A fellow-feeling existed between the Anglo-Indians and ourselves as if they were our countrymen in that strange land. Here inequality of official position separated us, there we were guests. Their sojourn in an oriental land would have been for nothing if they had not learnt how honoured a guest is. Occasionally, however, we met with some queer characters who, specially if they had ladies with them, pompously displayed their acquaintance with the Hindi language, however slight it might be, and their power and superiority over us. That was as much as to tell the ladies—"Look, how great I am!" So far it was all right. And we did our best to look surprised at his unlimited command over the vernacular languages of India, and to look submissive before him to help him to be the Great Mogul he wished to look in the eyes of the ladies. The ladies would smile and giggle, his face would be all animation with pleasure and pride, his urbanity would know no bounds, and at the end, ten to one, it would end in an invitation. Lord, what villains we thought we were! But it was all done in charity. At any rate here is a hint for one or two swindling Indians we met in London, whose business was rather slack. Once, but once only, I met with a little rudeness from an Anglo-Indian. I do not give the *exact words* he used, but I give his meaning and materialise his tone into words. He majestically stalked towards me and said—"Slave, show me ———'s office." "I am sorry I cannot obey your command just at this moment, Sir, as I am engaged, but if you go straight, turn to the right and then to the left, you will find yourself before that office," I replied. He got angry and said—"You must, Sir; who is your master?" "My master, Sir, is the Government of India. I cannot go with you for the reason that I am engaged with this gentleman, who is the Reporter for ———." His rudeness did not annoy me more than his servility to the gentleman I named.

Outside the Exhibition we never experienced a single act of unkindness. We travelled alone in the East End, the West End and everywhere, and frequently got ourselves lost. Boys and girls would gather round, but they never molested us in any way. Beggars and bad women would no doubt be bolder with us than with the natives (of England), but they never gave us any trouble worth speaking of. No street Arab or London ruffian ever took advantage of our inexperience. On the other hand men who idly lounge about public houses in low quarters, were always ready to help us, and frequently shewed us the way when we got lost. Places where even cockneys would be afraid to go in the day-time we went to in search of adventures, but no adventure will happen to one who would keep clear of disreputable enticements. Once a villainous-looking Jew tried to cut a practical joke upon me. More than a dozen hands were at once raised in my protection, those hands belonged to English roughs, perfect strangers to me. At another time somebody called me a foreigner. "He is no foreigner!" cried several voices, "He is a British subject as you and I."

Speaking of British kindness, I may as well mention a little incident which happened to my friend, Mr. Gupte. He and Sir Edward Buck one morning went to the Covent Garden Market, where fresh fruits brought from all parts of the world are sold in prodigious quantities. In this place in all seasons of the year the finest flower and the most delicious fruit which man can produce can always be procured. The busiest time in this market is six in the morning, especially on Tuesdays, Thursdays and Saturdays. Sir Edward asked my friend whether he had ever tasted raspberries. On his answering in the negative, Sir Edward tried to procure some, but it was then too late, all were sold and none could be had. A retail stall-keeper, however, bought some baskets earlier in the morning with which he was preparing to depart. Sir Edward asked him for one, but he would not sell. It was then explained to him, who it was wanted for, and without a word, he instantly handed over a basket. He would take no price. "He is the guest of my nation, Sir, and I make a present of it to him," said the patriotic fruit-seller.

I had a notion that tropical countries were the place for fruits, and that mango was the best fruit in the world. I found that these notions required some qualification. There is a soft delicacy in the flavour of hothouse fruits which in vain you seek in the open air products. Mango of superior kinds is no doubt good; it is *one* of the best fruits, not *the* best. Without the slightest hesitation I would give equal rank to peaches, nectarines, pineapples and strawberries, but not the worthless sorts you get in India. How scientific treatment in hothouses improves the fruits may be seen from the splendid grapes sold in first class shops. Ordinary grapes brought from the Continent are like those we get from Kabul, but hothouse grapes are five times bigger and ten times more luscious. I did not much care for English apples, but English pears are infinitely superior to our pears and guavas. Cherries, gooseberries and greengages and other plums have nothing special in them to mention. Hothouse fruits are necessarily much dearer than those imported. Peaches and nectarines of the best sort would cost three to eighteen pence a piece; hothouse pine-apples a guinea, those imported from the West Indies sell at about 4s. each; imported grapes sell at 5d. a pound, hothouse grapes of the best kinds 5s. a pound. No mango can be had in England. I heard of several attempts made by private persons to take them from Bombay, every one of which failed. Good plantains cannot be had, but a variety of green bananas, somewhat like those sold in Bombay, Madras and Burma are brought from the West Indies. A fortune awaits one who would discover a profitable way of keeping fresh fruits in good state for a length of time, just as they have done in the case of meat by freezing it in refrigerating rooms. Oranges are imported to England from Italy, Malta and Spain. A hothouse is a shed roofed, and more or less enclosed, with glass in which the temperature, required for the growth of plants and the development of flowers and fruits, is kept up by means of pipes containing hot water or steam supplied from a boiler placed at a short distance. The supply of light, heat and moisture can thus be regulated at the pleasure of the producer, and not only can the natural climate of a plant of any zone in the world be artificially produced, but the production of flowers and fruits of both native and exotic plants can be retarded or accelerated at will. Thus flowers and fruits are produced in and out of season. Every mansion in England has a hothouse attached to it. I am of opinion that many Indian fruits and vegetables can be profitably forced in hothouses or at least improved by protecting them from climatic rigours by means of glass sheds.

This digression may be continued further with advantage. My countrymen must be anxious to know what vegetables can be got in England. First and foremost is of course the potato which, together with meat and bread, is the staple food of all classes of the people. The Old World will be for ever grateful to the New for the two valuable food substances she has given her—potato and maize. We are also indebted to America for the pine-apple. And, well, I do not mean to disparage tobacco. Just as we did ourselves, the English people would not at first eat potato, for they said it was not mentioned in the Bible. The next important vegetable in England is the cabbage. Cauliflower may also be seen, but not in such large quantities. Green peas come into season in summer, but they keep it tinned all the year round. Tinned green peas are also imported into England from France, and large quantities of it are brought to India from Europe. I wonder whether we cannot prepare it here, considering green peas sell so cheap in season. I have, however, been told that the Indian article lacks the delicacy of the European produce, although by careful comparison I could detect no difference. A gourd, called the vegetable-marrow *(Cucurbita ovifera)*, is a favourite food among them for its mild agreeable flavour. They are also fond of cucumbers, which they eat raw cut up into thin slices, with or without the skin, and plentifully flavoured with vinegar and pepper. Pumpkins (*Cucurbita Pepo*) of large size are grown in England and also brought from the West Indies, but they do not much care for them. Their radishes are not so big as ours, but they have got very good turnips and carrots. I think many of my countrymen have not tasted English carrots now grown solely for European use around large towns in India. I would recommend them to do so. In its raw state, it is sweet and crisp like a half-ripe papaya fruit. Its cultivation may be advantageously substituted for that of our watery untoothsome indigenous variety, only I am afraid its outturn will be less in quantity which is an important consideration with our peasants. Spanish onions of enormous sizes are eaten boiled; smaller ones are sliced and fried. They are very fond of mushrooms, which they gather in their wild state or very carefully cultivate them in dark cellars with plenty of manure. Some of these *Fungi* are poisonous, but they cannot be distinguished from the harmless ones. The English also eat truffles, generally the variety called black truffles (*Tuber cibarium*), which lie about a foot under the ground, leaving no trace above to show where they can be found, and it is said they have trained dogs to search them out. Jerusalem artichoke and parsnips are also eaten in small quantities. Spinach is cut quite fine and eaten simply boiled. The consumption of tomatoes is very great, which they think are good for liver. They are very fond of green salads, *i.e.*, uncooked leaves or herbs (generally lettuce) with pieces of boiled eggs and slices of beet-root, dressed with salt, vinegar, oil and spices. If boiled lobster, chopped fine, is added to it, it is then called lobster salad. Water-cress is also eaten raw. Another succulent shoot-like thing comes on the table boiled, of which they bite off only the tops, as the lower portion is tough. I forget its name. Asparagus ? I have seen rhubarb cultivated in some parts of England and Scotland for its leaves which are eaten as a potherb. These are I think the principal vegetables to be found in England.

While I am on the subject of vegetarian food, I may include in it what I have to say on the subject of English milk. I visited a few dairies in England

and Holland, and from what I saw there I can well understand how loathsome and repulsive must be Indian milk to Europeans with the slightest touch of daintiness in their constitution. In no point are the Hindus more shamefully degenerated than in their treatment of cows. The sight of half-starved skeleton-like beasts, with scarcely any strength in their body to whisk their tails to drive away the flies tormenting them from all sides, is little calculated to impress a European, new to this country, with the seriousness of Hindu belief in the sanctity of this animal. He would think it a shame that men who find fault with the politics of Bismarck, criticise Herbert Spencer, correct the errors of John Stuart Mill and view with indifference the researches of Huxley, Tyndall and Faraday, could soberly, earnestly and enthusiastically agitate in order to prolong the torture of these miserable beasts. "Why, would it not be a happy release for them to put an end to their wretched existence?" he would naturally ask. "Hush," his friends would cry, "you are talking sacrilege." India has much to weep for; the delinquencies of her children are numberless and the cruelty to cows which the Hindus as a race practise all over India is only one of them. This inhuman treatment of a most useful animal ought not to be permitted to continue under a humane Government, and it is high time the Hindus were restrained by repressive measures of the most severe kind. The cowhouses I saw in Europe are spacious well-ventilated buildings with verandahs, and are as clean as a dwelling-house. The floor is paved with brick, over which a quantity of litter is strewn on which the cow stands or lies as she pleases. The litter is removed once a day and carried to the dunghill at a distance. Every time the litter is removed the floor is swept clean, and in summer it is washed with water. All the liquid runs into the gutter sunk along the wall towards which the tail of the cow is kept. The gutter is washed clean twice a day. Considerable attention is also paid to the food and drink of the milk-cow. They give her for food a considerable quantity of albuminous materials and phosphates to increase the flow of milk, but they take care not to convert into milk the flesh, fat and blood of the cow as the Hindu milk-sellers of this country generally do. In England I saw acres upon acres of turnips, swedes and mangolds which they grow there exclusively for their livestock. I do not think a single acre of land is devoted to that purpose in Bengal Proper; in Upper India they cultivate a little *Sorghum vulgare* (Joár) for cattle-food. Great care is also taken to supply the cow with pure water. Typhoid fever in children has often been traced to milk obtained from cows drinking unwholesome water. In this country milk is frequently adulterated with all kinds of foul water. How many children in this country annually die after taking this kind of milk? Then the dairy itself, where milk is kept and cream made, is worth seeing. It is a place with a lofty room and free ventilation, where cleanliness is scrupulously observed to the minutest details. The neighbourhood of a sewer, pigstye or anything that can give out an offensive smell is carefully avoided in the construction of a dairy. No meat, cheese or any kind of animal food (except fresh milk) is allowed in the premises; not even a drop of spilled milk permitted to remain long on the floor. Daily the floor and the shelves are most punctiliously and sedulously scrubbed and washed. The utmost care is also taken to maintain the purity of air in the dairy. Even the dairymaid going into it should at all times be extremely clean in her person and should not remain inside longer than is necessary. I have also seen dairies kept by rich gentlemen. The arrangements there are more elaborate and, besides what is requisite for the constant maintenance of absolute cleanliness in the premises, wealth is profusely lavished in the beautification of the whole concern. I have been told that Rs. 75,000 (£5,000) is not quite an unusual price for a cow! Not for any special quality or quantity of her milk, but for her beauty according to the standard fixed in Europe. The back straight as a rod, neat tapering head, large bright eyes, short narrow neck, large udder of good shape, and soft silky hair are among the qualities of a handsome milch-cow. The Ayrshires, Alderneys and the Channel Island cows are among the noted breeds in Great Britain. Considering all the care I have mentioned, no wonder that milk in England is particularly good as compared to the Indian article. Even in London good milk is available, specially when the milkman himself is a cowkeeper. Even in the ordinary shops, where it is sold a penny a glass (about half a pint), I found the milk very good, at least better than the best milk usually obtainable in India. I also saw one or two dairies near London. Cows are not ordinarily slaughtered in England, but from what I saw and heard in these town-dairies, I strongly suspect that they are in the habit of selling the cows to the butchers when they are dry and of obtaining fresh ones in their place. This is just the practice with Hindu milkmen in Calcutta. Although as a rule in England they do not slaughter milch-cows for beef, yet the number of these animals does not outgrow the food-supply available in the country. Just the number of calves for which food is available is allowed to grow up to be cows; the rest are made into veal. I noticed an inhuman practice in England of bleeding poor little calves slowly to death in order to make the veal white in colour.

It will be seen from the above that a Hindu in England, if he so chooses, can keep his caste intact. He has rice there and wheaten flour. Lentils are brought from Germany and Egypt of which he can make his soup. He has plenty of fruit and vegetables, good milk and any amount of butter and sugar. The sale of butterine, *i. e.*, artificial butter made of fat is prohibited by law. As for water, there is pipe-water everywhere, even in the smallest towns, which neither in England nor in India is raised by Bráhmans with any particular share of sanctity ingrained in their system.

To revert to the treatment we received in England. My countrymen would think that the shopkeepers at least must have cheated us when we wanted to purchase anything from them. We had no such experience. Not only did the English shopkeepers not cheat us, but they often allowed us a liberal discount, of their own accord, without our asking for it, at the last moment, after the price was settled, the article purchased, and just when we offered to pay in full.

A few of my countrymen have by this time found out the disadvantages of incessant haggling and higgling. But we have yet to learn the new system of trading as of every other occupation. The British by their trade and manufactures are amassing one hundred millions of sterling pounds every year. India saves annually about ten millions, even that is doubtful. Compare the annual saving of the two countries with their area and population.

Thus what I have said above about the kindness of the British people to strangers, and specially to the Indians, corroborates what has been often said on the same subject by other Indians who lived for a time in England. The British people take a pride in being kind to strangers who happen to be in their land, they consider it mean to be otherwise, and they feel it their duty to resent on their behalf any unmannerly conduct that may be shewn towards them by the rude and the rough who are to be found in all countries and among all nations. The manners of an Englishman, however, undergo some change when he is outside his own country, whether it be in France, Germany or Italy. Outside his own country, he is proud, somewhat disdainful, and not too anxious to conceal in his breast that opinion which every nation in the world entertains—that all other nations are inferior to itself. Not only with him, but as a rule with every man, this feeling of superiority is intensified when he finds himself amongst a people manifestly and vastly inferior to his own. He finds it impossible, for instance, to be on equal terms with a people whose low organization permitted their being reduced from time immemorial to the position of cattle, and who has been rescued from this position solely by his clemency. That portion of the human race which gave such a signal proof of its low organisation was always distinguished by the colour of its skin; and the universal decadence of *all* coloured races in the present cycle has in the eyes of the Europeans effaced all nicety of distinction among them, has divided the human race by one broad line into two main classes—the white and the coloured—and has established in their mind the idea of a more or less close consanguinity between the Chinaman and the Hottentot and between Kálidása and Hiawatha. The actual condition of things in a non-European country,—acting on the mind of a European predisposed by traditions, tales and historical teachings, prepared by examples set by others before him, and narrowed by caste-rules already established around him,—leaves no room for the full play of that broad sympathy which is a prominent feature in the character of an Englishman in his native home. He is therefore often judged by the non-European races among whom he lives under very unfavourable circumstances. A fish *out of* water is not exactly the fish *in* water.

In India we see very little of the English people. Neither do we know them nor do they know us. So in England we found ourselves entirely among strangers, of whom practically we knew nothing except the language. Eight months' time is too short a period to study a people, and whatever opinion I formed of them I state with great hesitation, specially, considering how very soon a change, pleasurable though it was, came over my first impressions with the rapid expansion of my experience of English life. At first I took the English to be a selfish people, but when I considered the noble sacrifices every day credited to Englishmen all over the world, I abandoned this idea. History has related a thousand instances of their self-sacrifice for public good, and thousands occur every year in private life which are not cognizable to history. While I was there a case of this kind came before the public. When the excavation of a tunnel under the English Channel was taken in hand, very powerful opposition was raised against it, which eventually succeeded in stopping the work. Among other opponents of this scheme to destroy the insular position of Great Britain was a gentleman in affluent circumstances, a painter by profession. Not content simply with delivering speeches, writing newspaper articles and drawing up memorials, as we do in this country, he gave up his profession in order to be able to devote his whole time to oppose any further progress in the tunnelling work, and spent all his fortune in organising the opposition against it. The projectors of the scheme were compelled to abandon it, but the victory was dearly won so far as this gentleman was concerned. At the end of the fight he found himself a pauper. Instead of trumpeting to the world his losses and grievances and posing as a martyr before his countrymen, (which, by the way, he could not have done with any chance of success where so many do the same kind of thing), he quietly hid himself from the world by taking refuge in a Workhouse, the greatest misfortune which can befal a respectable man or woman in that country. Such instances of self-abnegation are common among European nations. People who can so forget their private interest can hardly be called selfish.

Then I thought the English uncharitable. But who support thousands of schools and dispensaries in England, subscribe princely sums to famine funds, establish scientific institutes, found libraries, endow museums and bequeath large fortunes for the benefit of future generations? These are, generally, private persons. The same man, who would not only refuse a penny to a hungry beggar but hand him over to the police, would the next day give a hundred thousand pounds for the foundation of a hospital for the blind and the infirm. A principle guides an Englishman in all his actions and he firmly adheres to it. The Indian people are equally self-sacrificing and charitable, if not more, but these qualities are exercised in such a blind meaningless way that they often become childish and ridiculous. A man of the hunting caste catches a cageful of small birds, which he carries to a fair and patiently waits for charitable Hindus to come and release them at the rate of one pice a bird. Pious men are not wanting in this country, *that* I can assure our revivalists of the present day, who deplore the decadence of Hinduism as practised in the early part of the present century, for often and often have I observed crowds of people around these cages, every man and woman waiting with an eager anxious face for his or her turn to purchase a farthing's worth of piety by releasing a bird. How many millions are spent every year in India to feed, not the poor, but men who do not want a feeding. Go to the man who the day before spent a thousand rupees to feed such men to beg for a little subscription for a school, and you will find ready for you a pair of ears hermetically sealed against any such petition. Such is the difference between charity as practised in England and that to which we are accustomed here. No wonder then we thought the English people very uncharitable.

The English people appeared to me to be wanting in family affection. As soon as a person attains majority he or she leaves the paternal home to seek his or her fortune in the wide world. Not encumbered with relations out of number, the young man enters upon the battle of life free and self-reliant, and if he is not successful he has nobody to blame but himself. Separation and distance weaken the family tie, and on many occasions I saw Englishmen receive the news of the death of a very near relative with perfect indifference, when on a similar occasion we should be killing ourselves with inward grief and loud lamentations. It appeared to me so strange! Once I was standing in a shop where a man came and told the shopkeeper that he had been " for a bit of ground for the old one, who went off like a shot last night." It was his father whom he wanted to bury. It is not true though that as a rule Englishmen do not take care of their parents in their old age. In the first place their parents are very independent, who would prefer to work for their own living as long as they could. We had an old man at the Exhibition serving as an attendant, while his son held a high position in the Metropolitan Police. It was not because his son would not support him that he kept the place at the Exhibition, but he would not take his son's assistance. In the second place it is so very difficult to bring up a family in that country that if the son is married his first care will be to maintain his own children. The Workhouse will open its doors to the old folks and the law will not compel him to support them, but he cannot so easily shirk his duty to his children. To maintain poorer relations a Hindu will often make large sacrifices which an Englishman will not hold himself bound by duty to do. But whenever circumstances permit, Englishmen *do* make great sacrifices for the sake of their helpless relations. The mind of the European is however not yet sufficiently developed to appreciate the virtue of supporting big burly relations, with their sons and daughters, their sons-in-law and daughters-in-law, their grandsons and granddaughters, their grand sons-in-law and grand daughters-in-law, *i.e.*, the family of men who would not stir a finger to help themselves. On the whole, however, my impression is that European nations are more hard-hearted in comparison with the Hindus. A Hindu would commit the most flagrant acts of cruelty in a moment of frenzy just as the French did during the Reign of Terror, or under a religious impulse like those committed by the Christian fanatics of past days or the Muhammadan Ghází's of the present day, but he can never do what Cortez and Pizarro did in America. Systematic, determined, long-enduring cruelty a European is only capable of. His heart knows no mercy; no earnest supplication softens his mind. The heart of a Hindu is naturally more divine than that of a European, but the divinity of the former is polluted by mischievous social customs, baneful early teachings, low surroundings, and the most absurd practices sanctioned by long usage which now go by the name of Hinduism.

As yet I have said nothing of other parts of the Exhibition, those occupied by the youthful progeny of Britain growing to maturity in distant lands all over the globe. Colonies in all stages of development, from Canada and Australia of exuberant boyhood to the baby settlement of North Borneo, all proudly placed their offerings at the feet of the great mother who clasped them to her bosom with a fondness which did good to our heart to behold. But full-fledged colonies could only shew reproductions of articles daily bought and sold in England and Europe, and objects of interest furnished by minor settlements could hardly compete with the variety and novelty of articles sent from India. In point of show and curiosity, therefore, India threw them all into the shade. Her dazzling trinkets glittered forth ridicule at the trophy of produce erected by Canada, and scornfully peeped through costly cases at her monster apples, pears and grapes, pickles and preserves, starches, meals and extracts, cabinet work, musical instruments, printing presses and agricultural machinery of automatic construction, which worked night and day to show how to dig and drill, reap and gather and bind into sheaves the luxuriant crops raised on the virgin soil of the boundless prairies of northern America. Before the shining baubles of the Indian court, which people anxious to be reckoned as fashionable admired and fostered, in vain did the golden trophy of Australia raise its gilded head, and her silver, copper, zinc, tin and coals, her piles of new wines, specimens of her agricultural and pastoral wealth, and the collections of her forest timber all shrank into insignificance. The people of England and the Continent, wearied of the monotony of bottles, tins, iron, steel and the prosaic products of mechanical contrivances, and surfeited with pigtails and waggish whiskers of plump mandarins and the comical winks from flat-faced ladies on Japanese screens, sought relief in the fanciful handiwork of India. The collection of Maori relics, displayed in the New Zealand Court, the Zulu weapons in the Natal Section, the fetishes, implements and wearing apparel of the inhabitants of Western Africa and the Ashantee gold ornaments, were objects of some interest, but the chief attraction in the Colonial Section was the model illustrating the diamond industry in the Cape of Good Hope, and the practical demonstration of the way to cut and polish the stones with the aid of electrical machinery. However commonplace the Colonial exhibits might have been in English eyes, they formed a subject of deep interest to us.

My countrymen should think and ponder over the wonderful progress which Australia has made during the last thirty years. It was only in 1788 that the wilderness of New South Wales received on her bleak bosom the first batch of English life convicts. In 1803 Van Diemen's land (now Tasmania) was similarly taken up, and in 1835 the descendants of these men crossed the channel and laid the foundation of the now prosperous Colony of Victoria. The magic wand of British pluck and enterprise waved over the gloomy land and joyous smile instantly beamed on its face. The extemporised shed of green boughs, under which shivered the half-famished aborigine, made room for palatial mansions filled with the melody of chubby little rowdies, the Marsupia retreated before the useful Capridæ and Equidæ, the Dingo before the greyhound, and shot and spear took the place of bomerangs and stone implements. *That* wilderness now cheers with bread and meat the humble table of the poor in the distant north, clothes and warms the honest labourer who drudges in frost and snow, supplies fiery steed to the gaudy chariot of the rich, and exchanges for the hitherto valueless myrobalams of Indian forests the shiny metal which glitters on the sweltering body of the sable Hindu. Populous towns and villages have sprung up like mushrooms all over the fertile waste, and grim, smoky vessels of huge dimensions from all parts of the world rip with powerful screws the capacious bosom of well-protected harbours, whither also their swanlike sisters, with out-spread wings fluttering in the air, softly glide, welcomed by the gentle ripple of the sea and the hum of human voice wafted from the approaching shore. Bridges of iron and mortar span the impetous mountain torrents, roads and railways traverse in all directions the inhabited part of the continent and the telegraph line has crossed the dreary desert in the interior where bleach the bones of many a hero who boldly plunged into the waterless *terra incognita* as pioneers of exploration. O for a fraction of that indomitable spirit which animated the face of Edward Kennedy when he launched himself with his dark friend Jacky Jacky into the trackless country of York Peninsula forty years ago, or of that unflinching perseverance with which the lonely squatter chased the Emu far away from Gipp's land before his own flock had multiplied and supplied him with the necessaries of life, or of that intelligent diligence with which Hammond Hargraves triumphantly ended his search for gold among the auriferous regions in the vicinity of Bathurst !

If we could only bring a fraction of those sterling qualities to the aid of British administration in its struggles to subdue the wild forces of tropical nature, to utilise its blind unguided energy for the benefit of man, to wipe away all trace of savagery from the country, to cleanse the land of filth and dirt as old as the Himalayas, to stamp out preventible diseases which cut off vigorous manhood and shock civilised humanity, to make roads and railways, to impart the benefits of education to the ignorant masses, to shew them the road to wealth and prosperity, to teach them to eat. dress and live like men, and generally to bring this interesting people within the pale of modern civilisation, then in a couple of generations

India would wear altogether a different aspect. How many English lads, burning with enthusiasm to rush into this struggle, must allow their minds to revel in hopes of victory and glory on sleepless nights just before their departure for India! Vain hopes! They counted only on battle with inanimate nature and not with the intellectual darkness that has shrouded the country from time immemorial. To awake the sleeping Himalaya and to make it walk bodily to Land's End would be an easier task than to open the eyes of 250 millions of human beings, to invest them with the power to discriminate good from evil, to instill into their weak heart the courage to do what is good and to shun with loathing what is evil, to shake out from their system all dreaminess, indolence and apathy, and to infuse into it the life and vigour of a youthful nation. The disappointment of noble-hearted Englishmen may be great, but *our* disappointment and *our* impatience are acutely painful. They feel the same sympathy as a doctor feels for the sufferings of a child after his fruitless ministrations for its relief, but *we* feel the keen nervous longing of the mother for the power to wipe away with a brush of her hand the agonies of her beloved offspring. In my own humble way I have worked for the benefit of my nation for the last seventeen years, in new lines which I could never have dreamt of but for the example set before me by English friends and superior officers, and I speak with that authority which practical experience gives, when I say that the greatest difficulty one has to meet in this country is from the opposition of those forces of intellectual darkness I have just mentioned. The people of the country, the material with which and for which, you have to work are not fit or yet ready to receive and assimilate to any appreciable extent innovations, however profitable they may be. Their deep-rooted confidence in the existing state of things, their disbelief in the efficacy of change, their sentiment of human helplessness to contend with natural evils and to surmount difficulties, their short-sighted covetousness that prompts them to kill the goose that lays the golden egg, their habits of slovenliness, indolence and procrastination, their careless talk and reckless promises and assertions, all combine to make earnest work slow, exasperating and very often abortive. So we have now a treble duty to perform; first, to conquer the natural shortcomings of our own character, to extirpate from our mind the deep-rooted effects of early teachings and to withstand the baneful influences of our every-day surroundings; second, to teach and help those elected to co-operate in the work to do the same; and third, to organise the work itself. Generations will pass away before the country will attain the state of a thorough working order, but nevertheless it behoves each individual to do however little he can to pioneer his nation in its march to that state, first by working in his own person, second by working on those with whom he comes in contact.

Vanity, undue reverence for the past, and reluctance to alter the present, seem at present to be serious obstacles in the way of our progress towards a new national life. Pressing needs of life are however too strong for such sentimentalities. Vain now we are no doubt, full of conceit, the result of imperfect knowledge. We hold that with our present acquirements we are capable of those deeds which make the English great; only opportunity is wanted, forgetting that if we were really worthy of those deeds opportunity could have been made, with the start that we have got and under the causes that are working around us. But we are not worthy. Our presumption is due to the fact that the conception we have formed in our mind of those deeds is superficial and vague. Nor have we rightly understood the necessity that led to their accomplishment in Europe, nor the circumstances which begot the power to perform them and favoured their being built one over the other. Neither have we yet formed a clear conception of the diverse and complex manifestations of human faculties which in the same regions have further differentiated man from the lower animals. In a transition like ours, conceit must have its course. It is the pride of ignorance, which can only be dispelled by the influx of additional light. Our past has long since gone, as it must; and its work is in ruins. We do not quite know what that work was, in all its details; nor do we pretend to make that the guide of our life. We fall back upon a vague surmise of it owing to vanity and ignorance, and bewilder our mind with a sublime mysticism borrowed from that unintelligible mass of gloomy ruins, among which historians weep, antiquarians grope, philologists feel for clues, and dyspeptic dreamers find solution of all doubts. It may deceive and lead astray the national mind, but only for a time; for hard facts are immediate, positive, solid and incontrovertible, and wants of life will not be put off or put down. This clamourous noise, therefore, about Vedas and Yogas, esoteric and exoteric doctrines, denotes merely an expression of regret for the decay and disintegration of things existing. Such regret often dooms a nation to destruction; but happily we have been at the bottom of the wheel long ago; it is now turning round, forced by English education and English example, and we are rising. As a first step, we have acknowledged the superiority of western civilisation. We have accepted from that source a well-organised Government that has verified the wildest hyperbolical proverbs of old about peace, justice and safety of life and property, and we have gazed with wondering idiotic eyes at its railways, telegraphs, postal arrangements and steam-ships. We have humbly bowed before its mechanical contrivances that with gigantic powers spin and weave more ingeniously than he with hands, feet and brain who, fanned by the blossoming *Pipal* tree, wove under its shade of a wet summer evening the delicate muslin, which even aided by the early sun no eye could perceive as it peacefully lay on the grass wet with the dews of overnight, and hence the name *shabnam*. Moreover, we have paid the highest tribute to western civilization by our willing bondage to nearly everything connected with it in the supply of the minutest necessaries of life, from nails, hinges and locks, knives, scissors and razors, needles, thread and sewing machines, to clothing, doctoring and educating materials. Above all, we owe to it that perception which is slowly taking a definite shape in our mind of the rights and duties of man.

Thus vanity and conservatism can only retard the nation's march; yet sometimes a moderate pace is necessary to allow new ideas to take root. At any rate they do not establish the *unfitness* of a nation for a higher destiny. But other things or want of other things do. For instance up to this time we have not displayed much solidity of character, or discernment, or tact and power to give cohesiveness to loose floating ideas, and to discover and invent, wisely plan, arrange and organise ways and means and to work them out for our material good. Prophets innumerable we have had since the British came to this country, not to speak of former times, who added to content where discontent was wanted, and prophets of the most recent fashion too, who in search of light lead their countrymen to pursue the will-o'-the-wisp that dances fitfully among the pool of Indian ignorance, where the putrid mass of ages has been stirred up by a freshet from the West. If we go on working for shadows and sentiments, as we have been hitherto doing, then I would despair of a bright future for India. My hope however, rests in the great intellectuality of the Indian races which will not allow their being killed off the face of the earth. This fact is sometimes forgotten by a certain section of Englishmen, and that forgetfulness is proving to be a strong, very strong incentive to bring out all the forces of the Indian mind, to bring about a common understanding among Indians of all creeds and nationalities. What a world of meaning, for instance, does that word NATIVE contain in it? Like one of those magic words of old it is performing wonders in all parts of the land wherever its true significance is understood. For Sir, we are all "natives." We were never "natives" before: we might have been *Gabars* which signified a difference in religion, but did not carry with it any humiliation or disabilities; not even anything like those to which enlightened and liberal England subjected her "Papists" only a short time ago. We are all "natives" now—We poor Indians, the aborigines of Australia and the South Sea Islands, the Negroes, the Kaffirs, the Hottentots and other races of Africa. The Egyptians have lately become "natives." The Chinese, the Japanese, the Persians and the Turks are not "natives." While I was in England, the English people came to see the "natives" at the Exhibition and often asked me where the "natives" were working, and English papers wrote about "natives." In England a French, German or Italian is a "foreigner," an Indian or an African is a "native." Colour has much to do with the making of a "native," but as Harris of "Uncle Tom's Cabin" found to his cost, human beings of the "native" kind are not always distinguished by colour. Fair or dark, we in India are all "natives." The Kashmiri is a native, the Madrasi is a native; the Muhammadan is a native, the Hindu is a native; the Bráhman is a native, the Sudra is a native; the prince is a native, the peasant is a native; I am native, thou art native, he is native. Sir, we are all natives. O Muhammad, Muhammad, thou the destroyer of all mockery in God-worship, thou, who established in the actual practices of life the fundamental principle of all religions—The Fatherhood of God and the Brotherhood of Man—thou, the great redeemer of coloured races, O Muhammad, well art thou rewarded by the gratitude of millions of souls who even to this day come flocking into thy fold in countries of Africa, where, if I am rightly informed, Christianity, with its sublime doctrine of "Do to others as you would be done by," but unhappily associated with brandy and gin, unheard—of diseases, rifles and bayonets, rapine and spoliation, and other ordinary dealings with the "natives," cries in vain, as in a wilderness!

The word "Native," or rather all that it signifies, is having a miraculous effect in India. For, if we cannot cease to be "native," as we could cease to be *Gabar* or Hindu and become one of the imperial race in the Muhammadan times, we can now make "native" command respect. With a people who pay such high honours to Mammon, wealth alone can do that. Every one of us cannot have Mammon in his house, and so cease to feel the humiliation of being a "native," but our people can be ardent votaries of his heavenly counterpart and so practically become co-religionists of those that look down upon them. We have no Mammon in this country, but we have a lovely little goddess in heaven, benevolent and kind, who presides over wealth and prosperity and who occupies a foremost place among our three hundred and thirty millions of gods including their wives and children, and we have allowed her to usurp a day of the week, although it properly belongs to Jupiter, and we worship her many times in the year. For all that we have lost her favour. Her affection must have to be won back, by worship according to western method. But remember it is not for us Bráhmans to do that. We care very little whether they call us "natives" or "niggers." Our ambition should be always higher. It is to make the nation rich, whole humanity powerful, comfortable and happy. Our duty is to teach the people how to achieve these objects.

The real inequality between Europeans and "natives" rests not on the fact of the former filling a few high posts in this country, but the difference is in the race which the whole world is running ever and for ever. The great question will not be settled by the settlement of the minor and consequential question—who is to fill this post or that post? The great question is, who is better capable of reducing the devastating cyclones, the destroying floods of our mighty rivers, the hot blasts of the summer, the parching rays of the sun and other uncontrolled forces of our wild nature to the submission and service of man? These are for time to come. But now, answer me the question, who of us two is better able to disembowel the earth for her hidden treasures, to span mighty rivers, bore mountains, and bring to the service of man the various substances which lie in all parts of India? The answer is that the European is able to do these things and the native is not, and practically for that very reason he is "native." We have not yet the preliminary knowledge necessary for the attainment of such power.

The European knows more of our mountains and rivers than we do; he knows more of the seas that girt our land on three sides; he knows more of the plants that grow around us, their names, their properties even to the size and shape of their leaves; he knows more of what is interred in the bosom of our earth; he knows more about the capabilities of our land; in everything he knows more than we do of our own country. Then he knows better how to use that knowledge for the benefit of man. We do not know these things, hence we are "natives." And necessarily the only way of getting over being a "native" is by our being equal to the European. I say again that our people have that high order of intellectuality which if rightly directed will enable them to equal if not to surpass the Europeans. No doubt like the power of the Niagra Falls in America various forces of nature are lying unused in this country, but those are insignificant when compared with the vast intellectual force of the most brilliant type that goes waste in every part of India, in search of miserable clerkships, for want of proper guidance to better things. Our honour, our safety, and our salvation lie in the ardent pursuit after knowledge and wealth. Weightier words have not been spoken on the subject than what Cuvier said :—

"Se succédant dès lors sans interruption, des espprits méditatifs, dépositaires fidèles des doctrines acquises, constamment occupés de les lier, de les vivifier les unes par les autres, nous ont conduits, en moins de quarante siècles, des premiers essais de ces observateurs agrestes, aux profonds calculs des Newton et des Laplace, aux énumérations savantes des Linnæus et des Jussieu. Ce précieux héritage toujours accru, porté de la Chaldée en Egypte, de l' Egypte dans la Grèce caché pendant des siècles de malheurs et de tènébres, recouvré à des époques plus heureuses, inégalement répandu parmi les peuples de l' Europe, a été suivi partout de la richesse et du pouvoir : les nations qui l'ont recoueilli sont devenues les maîtresses du monde ; celles qui l' ont négligé sont tombées dans la faiblesse et dans l'obscurité.

"Succeeding one another without interruption, thoughtful spirits,—faithful depositaries of accumulated knowledge, constantly occupied in augmenting and vivifying it,—have brought us in less than forty centuries, from the earliest efforts of rude observers to the profound calculus of Newton and Laplace and the learned classifications of Linnæus and Jussieu. This precious heritage always accumulating,—brought from Chaldæa to Egypt, from Egypt to Greece, hidden during the ages of darkness and misfortune, rediscovered in more happy times, unequally spreading among the peoples of Europe,—has been followed everywhere by wealth and power : *the nations who have cultivated it have become the masters of the world : those who have neglected have fallen to feebleness and obscurity.*"

In addition to sentimental incentives, we have now chronic hunger too in our midst. O Chronic Hunger, how much man owes to thee! All the sharpening of man's intellect, all the conquests which man has made over nature are due to man's everlasting struggle with thee. If thou hadst not been so vigilant, and hadst not paraded the streets night and day, requiring ceaseless efforts to shut thee out, man never would have been the master he is to-day. We had Hunger, sudden, violent and overpowering, that occasionally took us by surprise when we were little prepared for it, and left us as sudden to return nobody knew when, so teaching little except the baneful lesson of our utter helplessness to wage war with it. It is just like our wild mother nature whose spoilt children we are, always indulgent, but capricious and fitful in the use of the rod, which brings no amendment but spoils us the more. Not so where she has not been so lavish of her gifts. There the child man forced out nourishment from her flinty bosom; the child man grew to be strong, self-reliant adult man, and the adult man grew to be the master, for he learnt that he had the power and how to exercise it. Thus wherever he goes he is the lord of land and water, and it is he who talks of using the sun for fuel and the Niagra Falls to drive his engine. And it is he who is teaching us that we, "natives," too are masters and not slaves of wind and tide; for are we not brother-men, his kith and kin? A priceless idea! for which alone we cannot be sufficiently grateful to the English. There is the idea and there is the necessity for working out the idea too; for has not chronic hunger come amongst us? Not necessarily that hunger should be for food only; it is the feeling of want, for better dwelling, for better clothing, and for luxuries which by habit become necessaries. It is discontent; of which we never can have enough. Let moralists and philosophers preach contentment, but the law of God and nature teaches quite a different thing. Who can separate discontent from exertion, and where is evolution without exertion? Stop a while, to allow the idea of our power over nature to take root and our hunger to intensify, and you will see. You will soon see whether we do not cast to the winds our false pride and our foolish objection to manual labour (for are we not getting to be monarchical radicals of the most scarlet type?), dig earthen wells on the corner of our fields to raise two crops where we get only one, take basket on our head and spade in our hand to throw metal and earth on the village road through which we now wade in knee-deep mud, whether we do not weave from Anona and other wild fibres carpets soft and beautiful to lay on our floor, bid our bamboos yield us comfortable chairs and sofas, and from our jungles get, only for the gathering, materials for clean healthy residence to take the place of miserable pig-styes as meet your eye in passing through the Chord Line of the East Indian Railway. Have care, O Hukka, the days of thy glory and monopoly of time are numbered! The exercise by each individual, in whatever capacity he finds himself, of all his faculties to their fullest extent, makes a nation great. The disuse or abuse of such faculties is to despise the gifts of God, which makes him fit to be reckoned among those creatures that are devoid of such faculties. This is modern science rightly understood; this is the religion of sages of all times rightly interpreted.

CHAPTER IV.

NOTES AND OBSERVATIONS.

We saw the General Election of 1886 take place. Chelsea was close by, and here we keenly watched the contest between Sir Charles Dilke and Mr. Whitmore. Chelsea became Eatonswill all over for the time being. Large placards stared from everywhere, calling upon the people to "Vote for Whitmore" or to "Vote for Dilke." These placards seemed to say "Short is your friend not Codlin." A black board put up in the Kings Road proclaimed to the world the various good works performed by Sir Charles Dilke. While, outside Mr. Whitmore's office in Fulham Road, caricatures, verses and other incontrovertible facts represented Mr. Gladstone as the greatest of traitors. If an outsider were to believe what, roughly speaking, one half of the English people said of the other half, he could not help taking both the halves as extremely selfish and immoderate lovers of office and power. Leaders of both parties fought as desperately as the gladiators of old fought in the arena of a Roman amphitheatre. Next to religion, politics have always been the hotbed of enmity between man and man. In most cases political faith is hereditary in England, as trades and professions are in India. "We have always been conservatives," or "we have always been liberals," they say with pride. And practically it makes very little difference what they have been or what they are. For no hard and fast line demarcates the two parties. Both parties follow close at the heels of public opinion, as it is created, educated, expanded and consolidated, and woe betide the one that lags behind or goes too far ahead. The path is thus first cleared before every step is taken in the onward march. It is quite the opposite here in India. Leaders here run by themselves, like a locomotive without the train, and when they look back, they behold the sleepy masses in the dim distant horizon fast fading from their view. They do not restrain their impatience and impulsiveness. They do not first hammer the people into a higher organised body, before they cry for things, of the use of which the millions have not the faintest conception. In vain did we look for "Compulsory Education" among the resolutions passed by the National Congress. I must stop, lest I say more. A conservative family in England always supports a conservative candidate, so does a liberal always vote for a liberal. The mind of men, conservatives or liberals by caste, is as hard as the rock of Gibraltar, on which the reasonings of the opposite party make not the faintest impression. They count among them numerous bigots who would gladly make you taste the pleasures of *auto-da-fe* for what to them are your heretical opinions. We were too green to note the intensity of caste and political prejudices in England. To us all Britishers (including the Irish) were alike, high or low, conservative or radical. We knew not that friendliness for the low was a sin against the high, sympathy for the radical an offence against the conservative. Even in private quarrels you must unreservedly choose your side. If you speak to the one, you must not expect to be spoken to by the other. It is to be feared that our ignorance and sometimes our vanity prevented us from exercising due caution and prudent reserve in such matters. The new-born chivalrous independence of the Bengali lacks worldly wisdom. Over and above the families whose political creed is irrevocably fixed there is a body of the people whose opinions fluctuate now in favour of this party, now in favour of the other. The conservative and liberal families practically pair off, leaving this fraction of the people to decide the destiny of the nation. What a tremendous power this fraction wields in its hands! At Chelsea, the electioneering operations conducted on the part of Sir Charles Dilke seemed to us somewhat lacking in enthusiasm. Mr. Whitmore however was all vigour and energy. The polling took place at a house in Kings Road. All day long the neighbourhood was thronged by voters, sympathisers, idlers and sight-seers. Accompanied by an English friend I went there at 10 in the night to see the fun. The votes were then being counted. An eager expectant multitude filled the Kings Road from one end to the other, and straggling bands of men promenaded the neighbouring streets. A row was expected, for Chelsea and its neighbourhood abound in choice spirits who, it was thought, would improve the occasion by a few broken heads. At 2 o'clock in the morning the result of the election was declared. Mr. Whitmore, the conservative candidate, won the seat. Deafening cheers at once rose from the crowd followed by equally enthusiastic groans from the opposite party. The result of the election was a surprise to all. Sir Charles Dilke sat for Chelsea for upwards of 20 years, and his name was a tower of strength to his party. Soon after the result of the election was declared, both Mr. Whitmore and Sir Charles Dilke appeared on the balcony above. Mr. Whitmore thanked the electors for the honour done to him, and Sir Charles Dilke congratulated his opponent on his success, declaring at the same time that the battle was fairly fought out. They shook hands and parted. But the excitement among the crowd did not cease for a long time. The roads remained full till late in the morning, and cheers were met with groans and groans with cheers. No serious fighting took place.

Although I did not see a fight here, I saw one elsewhere in one of the election meetings. A friend who perhaps knew something of what was expected to happen took me there. By his advice I put off my turban and put on a workman's hat. I was rather late, for when I came I found the place quite full. No sitting room was available. A large number of people stood at the back part of the hall, among whom I quietly placed myself. More men came, so that at the end we were packed very close. The meeting was to be addressed by the candidate selected by one of the two parties in the borough. When the time came to open the meeting, he rose to speak, and was met by enthusiastic cheers from all sides. He patiently waited for the cheers to cease. The front seats took the hint and stopped, but continual thumping of sticks and soles of thick boots, not unfrequently ironed at the heels, was kept up in the lower part of the hall. An incessant rattling noise was maintained here, and when the party at one end grew tired it was relieved by the party at the other end. The front seats turned round with angry eyes, but no heed was paid to them. Once or twice the gentleman on the platform essayed to speak, but his voice was completely drowned and not a word could be heard. Many cried "Silence," but it was met with loud "Boo, Boos." Presently there was a hustle and all was confusion. Men on the front seats put on their hats and rose to their legs. A few chairs came flying through the air and fell among the crowd where the battle raged fiercely, but the men were so closely packed that none was knocked down. In a moment the legs and backs of the chairs were wrenched asunder, and thus armed the maddened crowd fought more fiercely than ever. Some big fellow tried to raise a bench, it got upset, and down went a number of heads, making a gap in the compact mass of black hats. A whiz through the air with a train of water drops, like a big comet with its tail! It was the glass tumbler that stood on the lecturer's table, containing the crystal liquid from the pipe. The meeting thus progressed delightfully well. Men went at it with a heart, and seemed to thoroughly enjoy the fun. Soon it warmed up their blood which burst all barriers and overflowed through the nose, the head and other parts of the body. Those, thus cooled, stepped back and their place was eagerly taken by other warm-blooded warriors who pushed themselves in from behind. Up to this time I watched the fight from a safe distance, but now fresh recruits came from outside, and like the wolves in Robinson Crusoe, tried to push me and my neighbours to the front. But as I am not particularly fond of a broken head, a flattened nose, or an eye a shade or two darker than it is, I did my best to dodge and slip my head under the elbows by the aid of which big burly fellows made their way to the scene of battle. It was a struggle though, to keep one's ground in that bustling and pushing and swinging backwards and forwards. The place grew too hot for one peacefully disposed, having no share in the work, which he could not help feeling as quite a profitless affair. I now repented of my having left my turban behind. If at this stage of red head excitement the people would not respect my nationality as they did on all occasions, the turban would at least have been a better protection for my head than the hat I wore. At least I was so taught by the man in my village who hurriedly wound up a sheet on his bald head, when his hairy comrades were one by one getting a little thrashing for having stolen wood from the garden of a neighbour. He was pardoned, as also his other comrades who were waiting for their turn, when the bald man provided his head with the cotton helmet. There was no getting out now. Even if there were any means of egress, which there was not, the door being entirely blocked by an anxious multitude heartily enjoying the fun, it would be the height of cowardice to turn one's back when all eyes were towards the front, and when every body seemed to feel it his duty to fight somebody else, be he a friend or a foe. Who knew, who asked, what the politics were of his neighbour in the crowd, and who cared for them? It was not of the slightest consequence. It was sufficient that he stood near and handy, and had a heart to notice the attentions paid to him, and the immediate neighbours polite enough to shrink and squeeze themselves a little to make room for the two friends to exchange a few commonplace civilities. They fought gaily, like school-boys, while bystanders watched that no unfair advantage was taken by either party. As soon as one was knocked down and gave in, another came forward out of the lookers-on to take his place and have a turn with the victor who had just earned his laurels. These were bye-combats, skirmish-like affairs, little sports, got up for the occasion to divert people at a distance who were tired of waiting for an opportunity to make their way to the actual field of battle. In one of these knots a big bully gave a *casus belli* to a plucky little fellow, who immediately got ready to have it out. But at the very nick of time an individual of great stature, probably from the north of Scotland, elbowed the little man out, and covering him by his capacious wings, told the first one, "I am your man, come on." The fight was short but decisive. In no time the bully got a black eye, a bleeding nose, and was four times knocked down. But he would not give in. Every time he was down, he would be up in an instant and goaded by the people around he would go in for it again. "Well done, Rob Roy,"—this probably in allusion to the red hair which the north-man had; "Try again, Billy,"—this to the man as he got up a second time. He had to be helped up the fourth time he was down. He said that he would have it out on another occasion. While these bye-fights were going on, the battle on the front raged more sanguinarily than ever. All of a sudden, and without any cause that I could assign, the crowd as if made of one body swung back, and with sheer force of weight cleared the door and the passage in the staircase. Before I could count ten I was landed in the street below, where I found fighting going on within different rings, organised by individuals for their own special amusement, quite independently of that just ended in the meeting-room upstairs. But things were managed in a more business-like way upstairs, where they had the special advantage of arms, offensive and defensive, afforded by the broken chairs.

I thought, after all the British are civilised savages. But stay, are they not animate humanity, like our earth with its tides and floods, typhoons and cyclones, active volcanoes and earthquakes; while we its inanimate counterpart, like our moon over there with, for all we know, its vacuous envelope, its dead mountains, its waterless deserts, treeless plains, and lifeless silent surface? It must be remembered too that in a highly-civilised country, like England, you must expect to find the best and worst of everything. The most generous and the most mean, the most benevolent and the most niggardly, the most pious and the most vile, the most ferocious fire-eater, and the most strict follower of their great Teacher who taught them to offer the left cheek to one who had just slapped the right. Then the English Dictionary does not contain a word significant of more bitter insult than the word "Coward." Almost all Britishers would prefer death to being taken for one by his fellows, far less to act like one, of course in the sense the word is generally understood by the world, *i.e.*, entirely physical. To be a Christian and yet not practise Christianity, to be a non-Christian and yet go to Church at the bidding of one's wife, and other acts of a similar nature, are not there, as they are not among my countrymen here, considered acts of cowardice. Another moral. In all the fights that I witnessed in that country I never saw two or more men combining to waylay and strike at one. It is often done in this country by my countrymen who as often or not call themselves "gentlemen." I would have given the British very great praise for their mode of fighting, but for the cases that happened in this country of late years in which certain individuals maltreated and beat to death feeble and weak-bodied Indians, who would not for their very life return the blow, and who, if I have heard aright, were often kicked when they were down, and that in a bad place of the body. I have heard that in England too people of certain counties end a combat in this dastardly fashion. But I must say that such conduct is considered by the Britishers in general as cowardly, as well as the act of striking a man when he is down, or a man perceptibly weaker than one's self, unless he shows fight. As regards international warfare the European nations would do well to study a little of the Mahábhárata and learn what was done in India some four thousand years ago. They of Kurukshetra fame would not send a rifle bullet into the heart of an unarmed or unequally armed savage, would they? Aswatthama after considerable hesitation threw something like the Greek fire on foot soldiers and other common warriors, but he was by no means a reputable character, though the son of a high-caste Bráhman of that age. Even there are savage nations in India among whom it is a point of honour not to use poisoned arrows against human beings. Modern civilisation has developed destructiveness at the expense of honour.

Boxing, fighting and other occupations of a like nature give the greatest enjoyment to an English public. They begin it at schools, in the gutters, among the fields, wherever their life is cast, and carry it on till they are old. Of course gentlemen, after their school-life is over, do not indulge in pugilistic encounters, but yet not even a lord would consider it disreputable to give battle to a low caste man on a good cause, or to be beaten by him in fair fight. But people often fight for the sake of fighting, and of course drink has often a great deal to do with it. A man on the war path lays his coat on the road, and just as Ráma and other heroes of the great Horse Sacrifice challenged the world to lay hold of the horse, he howls to the passers-by—"Who would dare tread on my coat tails?" If the police were not too near or if they winked at it a little, he would soon find that many dared do so, and that it would have been better for him had he left his coat and his face at home. Boxing matches are prohibited by law, but still they are frequently held in secrecy. While I was there, an encounter took place, and one of the boxers was killed on the spot. When I heard of it, I remarked to a friend that the man should have cried " enough " after the thirtieth round when he felt faint and almost unable to stand, but it was simply outrageous that the people present allowed him to continue the fight in that condition. The answer I received was— " Look at his pluck !" This people seem afraid of nothing, neither man nor woman, child nor adult. They court danger, to have the pleasure of overcoming it. They drift in baloons over lands and seas. They cut their way through the adamantine ice of the arctic regions to find the little point where the North Pole lies. They go headlong in casks down the Niagra Falls merely to be able to brag that "I have done it." How many people get killed every year in the Alps merely for the sake of " I have done it ! " And their exploits in the dark continent ? Air or water, heat or cold, fever or cholera, lion or tiger, they brave everything.

They are not even afraid of ghosts now-a-days, nor of witches, imps or fairies. Even the shoeless little urchins that waddle in the mud on the side of Loch Awe care not for these frightful things. How dreadfully pernicious these ghosts and witches are to village life in India, specially to boys ! Government ought to set a reward to hunt them down, just as it does for tigers and serpents. We have very worthy men amongst us quite competent to take care of them. To corroborate my statement with facts and figures I would cite the man who the other day killed an evil spirit at Howrah. The boy afflicted by it died too in the course of his curative operations, but that is of no consequence. If any one wants a milder treatment, I have got the man for him: he lives in my neighbourhood. I also know many ghost-catchers all over the country, in the South, in the North, in the Himalayas, in the Central Provinces. In the last Province there are 70 witch-drivers as the census of 1882 showed. There are other august personages in that part of the country: for instance, there are 954 hail-averters who hold a perfect command over the climate and the weather, rain and sunshine, thunder and hail. All that is required is a suitable budget provision for the development of this indigenous merit, lying latent, alas! unknown and uncared for, like "Full many a gem," &c., &c. But this cruel Government of ours has "no eye for our tears, no ear for our sobs" as a certain vernacular paper in this city would say. I am against ghosts, live or dead, in body or out of body, male ghost or female ghost, child ghost or adult ghost, Bráhman ghost or Islamite ghost, land ghost or water ghost, cow ghost or horse ghost, against all manner of ghosts. I have very nearly been tempted to give a full description of the different kinds of ghosts found in this country, arranging them under classes, sub-classes, orders, genera and species, in a separate chapter, entitled the "Ghostial Kingdom," like the "Mineral Kingdom," "Vegetable Kingdom" and "Animal Kingdom" of topographists. But I forbear, and enjoy the self-satisfaction of having performed a good deed, quite indifferent if my readers thank me or not for having saved them this infliction. A good deed is its own reward. The fear of ghosts, witches, and the whole brood of them is instilled into the tender heart of our boys and girls from their very infancy, which, acting on their mind like the iron shoe on the feet of a Chinese girl, warps the natural courage inherent in human beings. In after life these curdle-blooded men and women quiver with terror at the fall of a leaf or the rise of an owl when the evening shade has fallen upon the haunted garden. Whatever might have been in former times, the English children of the present day are free from such fears. If a lad meets a ghost face to face getting ready to wring his neck, when he is high up a cherry tree in a neighbour's orchard, I would not be surprised, if he coolly asks him not to be so rude or so mean as to peach, but to come down and give him a fair chance on even ground, if he is really minded for business.

I was well acquainted with many English boys belonging to some of the best families in the country. What I admired most in them is their sense of self-importance, their sense of honour and their independence. What I missed in them is the natural liveliness due to their age. They seemed to be all prematurely grown wise. They were boys without boyishness. Their gravity and the solidity of their words made me afraid to look upon them as boys. So I registered them in my mind as miniature men. Whatever might be their grammar, boys of humbler origin were not far behindhand in their conception of the awfulness of the world they were about to enter.

Street Arabs have a bad name, but for my part I would not like to hear anything said against them, for many of this class of gentry honoured me with their friendship. If anything is rare and dear in this earth of ours it is this precious commodity. Would you reject a gem because it lies embedded among the decomposed deposits in the caverns of earth? A little chap of six years was particularly attached to me. This gentleman had great talents, my friend had. He could walk at a time twenty yards, upon his hands with his legs straight up towards the skies. Even at the risk of being accused of partiality for my friend's high attainments, I must state that I never saw a more expert hand-walker than he was. He could beat every one of his age in that performance. He gave lessons to every one who wanted it. Terms moderate, a penny a lesson measuring about ten yards, often gratis. I was also very popular with my friend's friends, who always received me with cheers and acclamations. "Hullo, the Shar! there is the Shar coming! hurrah for the Shar!" greeted my ears as they saw me approach, meaning probably the Shah of Persia, of whose great doings in England they must have heard from their elders. What was it to me if more than one of them got themselves weighed for a penny by the weighing machines placed at railway stations? What was it to me either if they applied unpatented inventions for the extraction of chocolates and cigarettes from the machines containing them? If boys will not do such things, pray, who will? Did you fill your machines with golden sovereigns that a scientific burglar would visit them with his jemmy? If you did not, then do not consider yourself aggrieved if humbler individuals racked their brains and invented means to extract a few chocolates and cigarettes from your ill-devised machines. Accept our best thanks for the stone you placed so handy on which my friends could sharpen their wits and their inventive faculties.

I forget if I have said anywhere that such machines are kept at railway stations and other public places. Standing on a weighing machine you drop a penny through a slit, and immediately the hand on the dial moves round and stops at the number indicating the exact weight of your body. Put a penny into a chocolate machine, and a chocolate stick comes to hand; into a cigarette machine, and you get a cigarette. Hospitals and other public institutions solicit subscriptions by the aid of mechanical contrivances. "Pray give, Pray give, Pray give" says a card to all passers-by as it rises up and down in a glass-fronted box containing the name of the hospital for which help is asked. You drop a penny into it, and, look, there rises another card to "Thank you" for the gift. They do everything by machinery—from the rolling up of cigarettes to the boring of a tunnel under the sea. They also tell fortunes and invoke spirits by the aid of machinery. Happy land! And happier is America, so I have been told.

All boys and girls now go to schools. In England education is now compulsory. Parents are compelled by law to send their boys and girls to school. Children of the humbler classes are taught reading and writing, geography, history, arithmetic, &c. Girls learn needle-work and plain cooking in addition to these subjects. Children apprenticed to any trade go to Sunday schools. In the schools for the poorer classes the fee is one shilling per week and upwards according to the respectability of the institution. The respectability of an institution is determined by the class of people by which it is patronized—people with an income of £50 a year, £75 a year, £100 a year, and so on, all make separate castes, provided that a proportionate amount of money is available for outward show in each case. High caste people do not send their children to such schools. They must send them to Harrow, Eton or other aristocratic institutions. The cost of keeping a child there is simply ruinous.

England is not a country for gentlemen of good family with small means. Poverty is a crime everywhere, but in India, thousands and thousands of the high caste people choose to remain poor by giving away all their savings, and poverty is not therefore so very much looked down upon in this country. I may say with perfect truth that in this country though wealth is respected, poverty is not despised. Not so in England. There it is a crime of the deepest dye. The comparison between the wealth of his relations and his own indigence makes the life of a gentleman there insupportable, especially when the world about him always takes care to remind him of his humiliating position. What a struggle, therefore, it is there to keep up appearances ! In this country you have only to look very pious and your poverty will be forgiven and society will worship you from the next day. The market for piety is extremely dull in England.

There is very great difference between the education of a gentleman in England and that in India. The standard of gentlemanly accomplishments is much higher there. It is impossible for a gentleman in Europe to maintain his footing among his equals if he does not know a great deal more than our independent gentlemen know here. He may not be a scholar, but he must have a general knowledge of *all* things which man cared about in past ages and does care about at the present time. He does not seem to do very well in school, but in after life the tone of his mind undergoes a rapid change when he moves about among refined and cultured ladies and gentlemen of his class. Newspapers and travel are invaluable aids in the formation of his mind. He must know a little of French, must have an elementary knowledge of the sciences, must draw and paint a little, and besides a general acquaintance with music must be able to play on some kind of instrument as a speciality. I do not mention riding, driving and shooting, in which of course he must be proficient. The days of buffoonery are past in England. Nevertheless he has the highest respect for it if it is associated with rank and wealth.

A large number of boys were looking at the fight going on in the street below the meeting-room, fully bent upon making the best of the fun, clapping their hands and otherwise applauding and encouraging the fighters. I requested one of them to take me to a Coffee-house. I asked him on the way to guess what country I came from. He at once said "India." "How do you know that?" I enquired. He simply said "I know." After a short silence he asked me— "Are the Muhammadans in India a bad lot?" "Why?" I enquired. "Because they made the mutiny," was the answer. "Who told you about the mutiny?" I asked. "I have read a book all about the mutiny," he replied. "Did you read any other book about India?" "No." Now, this answer was rather suggestive. I came across many people in England who knew nothing else of India except the mutiny. I felt sorry that the Indians should be known among the common people of England only in connection with the most deplorable incident in their history, for which they feel the deepest humiliation. Connected as we are with England, it is wrong to place a popular narrative of those times in the hands of the English people. Ah, those times! when no frowns of Azimullah, no threat of being blown off from the mouth of a gun, could compel a single "Babu" to serve the mutineers against the English, when the infuriated British soldiers respected nothing but the placard "Calcutta Babus" placed on the doors, and when pensions and grants of land were being showered on the "Babus" as a reward for their daring exploits in the service of the English. And these men who proved so loyal to the British Government in time of need are abused to-day and sometimes their loyalty questioned! If vernacular newspapers abuse the English as a race I can pity their ignorance, but what can I say of English newspapers and English politicians who abuse the forty millions of ignorant peasants in Lower Bengal who know no more of what is going on in this world than the hippopotamus in the sluggish rivers of Central Africa? I hang down my head for shame. In waging this crusade against the Bengalis, I grieve to say, Englishmen often come down to the level of the "Native."

The lad took me to a Coffee House of a very humble description. Things are very cheap here. Tea, coffee or chocolate, a penny for a cup; ices, two pence; bread and butter, two pence; cakes, two pence; soda water, lemonade, ginger-beer, two pence per bottle; eggs, a penny each; sliced ham or pork, three pence a plate. Double or treble this price is charged for such things in a more respectable place. No spirituous liquors are sold here. In London, prices do not always depend on the quality of articles, but on the kind of establishment one goes to. For 7s. 6d. one would get as good a dinner as would be given for a guinea in a more aristocratic place. The same rule holds good with regard to wearing apparel and household necessaries. So, unless guided by an old hand, cheap living has to be discovered, which in that world of a town is not an easy matter. An elderly woman is in full command over this establishment.

In England wives take upon themselves far greater responsibility than they do here. The husband there only earns money and does all heavy work. All details are taken care of by the wife. She manages the household, looks after the family property, does the marketing, keeps the accounts, cleans the house, cooks the food, looks after the washing, tightens loose buttons, mends and sews her own underclothes and those of the children, keeps a vigilant eye on the health of the family, and nurses them when they are ill. In the country she also helps in field work. But an English wife is a great help to her husband in travelling, instead of being an encumbrance of the most trying description, as Indian ladies are. She neatly folds the clothing and makes a trunk take in more than what he himself could put in two. She can easily get the tickets in a crowd, and all through manages much more economically than a single man can do. This is possible because Europe is inhabited by a civilized people, where every MAN feels it his duty to sacrifice his own comfort and convenience in order to help a lady. In brief, an English wife is a help-mate of her husband in the strictest sense of the term. A man is naturally careless of himself, and of all petty details of life. She supplies this want in him, and in all such matters she takes care of him, not he of her. It was a pretty sight to watch the anxious face of young wives waiting for their husbands coming home from office, or going half way to meet them on the road.

Ladies of course do not do any work, nor are they so useful to their husbands. They leave every thing to servants. They dress themselves nicely, return visits, read novels, play at the piano, sing songs, go to churches and theatres and sometimes take interest in some charitable object. What an amount of money they spend every year on their dress! And what a tyrannical sway fashion wields over both men and women in Europe!

This subject of fashion often set me wondering. It impressed me with the thought that the human race is a race of slaves. Men and women in all ages and in all countries have been and are born slaves. I wish Mr. Herbert Spencer or some one would write a big book to shew how from the earliest times, when life was easy, our chief occupation has been to forge chains for our own limbs, how men from time to time obtained greatness by patenting newest improvements in these chains, and how humanity often and often struggled out of old worn out fetters and gleefully put on those of the latest fashion. What would life be without its ceaseless struggles for emancipation? So old traditions, newest fashions, and established conventionalities as much keep leonine England under subjection as they do the elephantine India. True, the western world is preparing to bring about a great social cataclysm, but, what of that? Out of all such deluges come a new set of well-furbished fetters, beautiful to look at in their fresh state and quite effective to enchain humanity for the ensuing epoch. My strong condemnation of the absurdities and abuses in our society has led many to suppose that I advocated the substitution of the social chains of Europe for those of our own. They are very much mistaken. I simply meant to tell them either to keep still or to begin reformation in the right direction. A field produces crops as well as weeds. Should you not take out the weeds? So Time is a field on which humanity grows its crop of good. Should you allow the negative side of good, the evil, the weed, to draw to itself all the nourishment from the field and choke that for which you till and toil? I never asked you to admire the chains which bind Europe, but to admire the wings by the aid of which Europe soars so high.

It is very amusing to see how the English people follow what they call fashion. Some big personage wears for the first time a certain kind of collar or a coat, and immediately all follow him. Many tailors complained to me of the insecure nature of their position. "Now, we have laid stock of these things here," they would say, "these are now in fashion but may go out of it the next year, and then we must sell them off at half price, or keep them by for some years on the uncertain prospect of their again coming into fashion." But the greatest torture is reserved for ladies of limited means. They find it very difficult to move on equal terms with those who have more money than is wanted to meet the most liberal requirements of dress, as well as finery of the costliest description. How to expend the surplus? Accommodating Paris kindly shews them the way. English weather which is notorious for its fitful, treacherous, ever-changing habits, is not so fitful, nor so treacherous, nor so changing as fashion in dress. How many dresses costing from 50 to 100 guineas have to be made in the course of a season and discarded as they get out of fashion? It is all very well for rich ladies to change as the moon changes. But what about their poorer sisters? They would as soon think of going to a drawing room in dress out of fashion as a Hindu woman would think of bedecking herself with the leaf garment worn by the Joáng ladies in the Keunjhar Hills. Wistful looks, long-drawn sighs, and never-ending efforts to make £1000 × 1 equal to £2000, are, in such families, not the least important of the items that go by synthesis to make up human life. Do men who have to earn this £1000 × 1 = £2000 ever think that their lot is not far removed from that of the tiny little worm which with voracious eyes wriggles through the green leaves of the mulberry, and anon makes round itself the glossy globe we call a cocoon? Even after all I would greatly prefer the simple habit, neat and trim, of an humble English woman to the costly, pretentious resplendent dress of a lady. And, Oh the trains! You had better put a gorilla, fresh from the African wilds, among the thousand and one things collected for the worship of your goddess Durgá, than this savage, your humble servant, among the gorgeous trains that on a festive evening move with the faintest rustle, like huge leviathans among reeds and rushes, on the soft thick carpet in a nobleman's house in England. If I did not commit the looked-for havoc, it was because I never took my feet off the ground. A full set of female clothing, of a simple description, costs about £5.

My countrymen little know what importance the English people attach to their dress. They take it for an insult, if a guest comes to their house in a suit which differs from the one custom has prescribed for the time of the day. Even in theatres nobody is allowed to go to the stall if he is not in evening dress. One not decently dressed is not allowed to enter Gardens, the stalls in theatres, and other public places. Perfectly right too. How do you like to sit by a filthy creature in the tramcar? So do not raise a howl when they prohibit you, with your light *dhoti*, to go near the band-stand in the Eden Garden where the ladies wait to hear the music, and if you wish not to be looked down upon with contempt, do not go in such dress to meet English gentlemen invited to a private party. Nobody asks you to adopt English costume, which by the way I do not fancy as just the sort, specially the meaningless, unartistic, rice-washer-like tall hat, but there is such a thing as decency accepted by the civilised world, and you are bound to follow that. A beauty priding in her vermilion-dyed *Pandanus* leaves would better coy among the nimble youths of her forest home in the Andamans, than impudently strut up to the brightest star in a French salon near the Palais Royal. That is all. They did a great kindness by allowing us to go to all places in our native dress. Fashion in dress is not the only thing which keeps the English people under a ludicrous system of subjection. The wheel of fashion raises or grinds works of art, toys, soaps, patent medicines, trading establishments, actors, actresses, singers, dancers, horses, jockeys, poets, novelists, exhibitions, Bufflalo Bills, the Zulus, the Colonials and Indians, and all manner of things. In some lucky moment, somebody, somewhere, somehow, whispers something into the ethereal ear of that wayward Fairy, Madamoiselle Fashion, she feels the tender concussion, a lightning-smile plays on her derisive lips, she raises her flowery wand and away goes the ecstacy to fill the mind of the world, to make it dance in joy at the rise of that little silvery moon yonder who ere long will spread a soft limpid light over the dramatic firmament of Europe. Thus it is now the fashion to abuse the Bengalis. Some great man says an angry word against them, and it is immediately echoed from all sides. Nothing on earth has a stronger sound than a human reverberator. Ah Madamoiselle Fashion! Why frownest thou upon us, my sweet fairy? Oh Madamoiselle, Madamoiselle! why hast thou sent forth the fiat that it is not respectable not to cry down the unconscious millions that dig and delve in the aguish swamps of the Gangetic Delta, and their brethren just opening their eyes after ages of torpitude? Fie, Fie, thou naughty little Fairy!

The woman to whose coffee-house I went had six children, of whom two were twins. In another coffee-house I saw four twins. The last two were babes in arms, whom the good woman brought to me and explained how they had arranged a division of labour among themselves, for one of them could talk, while the other could walk. Since that time I came across many twins in all parts of the country. They are quite common there. The British seemed to me more prolific than the Indians, and owing to the excellence of the climate, the superior physique they inherit, and their better mode of living and better system of nursing, infantile ailments do not end so much fatally there as they do in India. So notwithstanding the fact that a large number of men and women do not marry for prudential motives, or for the sake of a more exalted notion of the duties and responsibilities of life, the population goes on increasing and something like six hundred thousand little Anglo-Saxons are every year brought to the world with no provision for their sustenance. This is not a place to discuss the various causes which contribute to keep the lowest ranks of the people in a chronic state of distress. My countrymen are however surprised that there should be so much distress in a country reckoned as the wealthiest in the world. In the first place there are the bad characters, the idle and the good-for-nothing people, who in all countries and in all ages must suffer. In the second place, when the resources of a country have been developed to their utmost extent, it cannot provide for more than a certain number of people, and distress and disease must come among the unfortunate overflow to weed it out of the land by death or by driving it away to seek a new home in distant regions beyond the sea. No amount of charity can remedy such a state of things. The English people already pay a poor tax, and if by an increase on the tax one year's surplus population is provided for, another addition to the tax will be required next year for the next year's surplus. So long as a country goes on producing more population than it has food for, the surplus population must always remain in a chronic state of distress. The radicals however contend that England ought to support more population than she does now.

They say that the land belongs only to a few landlords, who take a large portion of the produce from the cultivators and spend it in England and out of England just as they please. Then the larger capitalists in trade have swallowed up minor establishments, thus crushing all competition in the demand for labour and reducing the labouring classes to the position of white slaves. I do not know how far they are right, and what remedy they propose for such a complicated state of things. The labouring classes have however formed "Trade Unions," members of which bind themselves not to work under a certain rate of wages. But these Trade Unions do not always work well. They are very much hampered by the competition of foreign labour. The higher rate of wages prevailing in England and the various ways by which money can be earned in such a wealthy country bring to it a large number of Germans and other Continental people. They consent to work for lower wages than that fixed by the Trade Unions. Then the higher rate of wages in England increases the cost of production of her manufactures, thus enabling America, Germany and other countries to oust English-made articles not only from India and other English colonies but from England itself. Thus England's unbounded wealth, her colossal power, her world-wide dominion, her equality of laws for individuals of all nationalities who set foot on her soil, and her free-trade policy, have their advantages as well as their drawbacks, and it would be a great misfortune to the world if dire necessity compelled her to adopt a retrogressive policy.

America and Europe are thus gradually ousting England from the nests which she with rare good sense and luck has built for her commerce in every part of the habitable globe. The teeming barracks of Europe may some day, as the result of a great war, restore—to the peaceful plough, the hammer, the chisel and the loom—the mighty legions on whom the early sunshine now flashes, before it reaches the trampled dews on the parade grounds near the Seine, the Rhine and the Danube. Those funnels which now proudly rear their heads in Lancashire and at Birmingham and scatter to distant lands the glad tidings of a cheap protection from inclement weather and of pretty cutlery, light and strong, may have their rivals at Lille, Dresden and Prague. Thus those who can live on less may produce at a less cost things in which England had hitherto almost a monopoly all over the world. If she is placed at any great disadvantage, self-preservation will compel her to take measures to put a stop to unrestricted importation of foreign labour into her manufacturing industries, just as Australia and America have done with regard to Chinese immigration, and to give up free trade and adopt what is called a fair trade policy, not for herself alone, but also for India and other not self-governed dependencies. It will be a long time before we can take advantage of such occurrences, and establish new industries or improve our existing manufactures. In the meantime we will have to buy things not at their legitimate prices fixed by free competition, but at prices fixed by English manufacturers. Connected as our destiny is with that of England, her prosperity or adversity will materially affect our own fortunes. But apart from such considerations, it will be a great misfortune to humanity at large if England is compelled to adopt a retrogressive policy. She alone stands in this wide-world as the great stronghold of liberty. United States, Belgium or Switzerland are mere satellites which receive their light from this great sun of human freedom. All other civilised states creep far behind. I have swept my mind from China to Peru and feel the assurance to say that I would rather be among the Irish roughs in the border districts of New Zealand or Texas than make my home in any of the most civilised countries of Europe, and speak in hushed voices, cultivate feelings of hatred for my neighbours across the river, waste the best part of my life working as a slave to learn the newest method of destroying humanity, and live under the constant apprehension of a national annihilation. It has often been said with truth, which my own experience has confirmed, that we in this country enjoy more freedom than what the European nations do under their own governments. It would therefore be a great loss to human progress if the light which England now sheds upon the world is allowed to get dim. Mankind, specially the coloured races, have suffered immensely from the extreme of rationalism, just as in times past it suffered untold miseries from the extreme of religionism. The fact of a life, as we see, being a compressed and continuous use of force for the destruction of lives, has created rationalistic superstitions, which are the more demoralising because they are supported by the highest knowledge human mind has been able to grasp up to the present time. The most striking difference between the philosopher and the fool is that the one knows his ignorance while the other knows it not. Does knowledge reveal more than rectify our ignorance? Does every discovery throw open a new America in the boundless world of our ignorance? It is one thing to enquire after the unknown: it is another thing attempting to lay down infallible dogmas about the unknown. They are too impatient to wait. So we have now rationalistic fanaticism to ignore truth, justice, mercy and all other higher attributes which distinguish human beings from the lower animals, to subvert moral laws by inductions and deductions from imperfect half-way facts, which to these blind eyes only make the forces working around us darker and still more incomprehensible, and to preach among the powerful nations of Europe a national and rational Thugeeism more systematic than that under which the Spaniards spoliated the empire of Montezuma, or the Arabs ravaged the climes from the banks of Tagus to the banks of the Irrawady. Yet in this age of barefaced rationalistic spoliation England alone has been able to temper conquest with justice, moderation and civilising influences. Not only is she the home of freedom, but from *her* radiates the blessings of freedom to north, south, east and west, everywhere.

My countrymen may not see anything to boast of in the equality of laws on English soil for men of all creeds and colour, and in the free interchange of commerce which England by her own example asserts as a principle for other nations to follow. For the

CHAP. IV.   FREEDOM IN INDIA.   169

Hindus practised such things long, long ago. They did not swerve from this duty even at a time when degeneration and decay had loosened the fabric of Hindu national life (as it was), and when it was crumbling to pieces by the mere touch of a new upheaval in the west. That it was so I can prove from the testimony of a man who was not over-friendly towards us, *viz* of Kamál-ud-din Abdur Razzák, the son of Jalál-ud-din Ishak of Samarkand, who was born at Hirat on the 12th Shabán, Hijri year 816 (6th November, 1413, A.D.), and who undertook a journey to India in the year 1441 A.D. He says of Calicut, the capital of Samari (Zamorin):—" Kálikot is a perfectly safe harbour, and like Harmuz merchants of all parts of the world come here, and bring abundance of rarities, particularly from Abyssinia, Zirbad and Zanzibar. Ships come here now and then from the abode of God (Mecca) and other parts of Hijjaz, and stay here as long as they please. This is a city of infidels, and therefore a lawful object of our conquest. Many Musalmans live here. They have got two mosques, where they pray on Fridays. They have got a Kázi, a pious man, and most of them are of the Shufi sect. Absolute security and justice reign here. Merchants bring their goods and deposit them in the streets and markets for any length of time, and go away without leaving them under any one's charge or placing them under a guard. The custom-house authorities look after them and guard them day and night." I can also quote Abu Abdullah Muhammad Al Idrisi, the great geographer of Morocco, who flourished in the 11th century of the Christian era, to shew how the Hindus of even those times were celebrated for their love of justice. Al Idrisi says :—" The Indians are naturally inclined to justice, and never depart from it in their actions. Their good faith, honesty and fidelity to their engagements are well known, and they are so famous for these qualities that people flock to their country from every side ; hence the country is flourishing and their condition prosperous."

For this reason my countrymen are slow to give credit to the British for the freedom and justice that prevail in their country. They view this as a matter of course, as the normal condition of things. But we forget that our lot has been cast in an age when rationalistic fanaticism is gaining the upper hand, when philosophers openly teach those doctrines which hunger-blind savages unconsciously followed in the primitive world, that civilised nations should practise Thugeeism on less advanced races, that right should give way to might, that the strong should prey upon the weak, and that the most successful murderer should alone live in the world. With the strength of the lion, with the craftiness of the fox, and with knowledge and power that might have been reckoned superhuman a few centuries ago, these doctrines are being applied on inferior races all over the globe. Thus we see the hand of Spain deeply dyed with American blood, but yet " the transatlantic history of Spain has no case comparable in iniquity to the act of the Portuguese in Brazil, who deposited the clothes of scarlet-fever or small-pox patients on the hunting grounds of the natives, in order to spread the pestilence among them; and of the Europeans in North America who used strychnine to poison the wells the Redskins were in the habit of visiting in the deserts of Utah; of the wives of Australian settlers, who, in time of famine, mixed arsenic with the meal which they gave to starving natives; or, finally, of the English colonists in Tasmania, who shot the natives when they had no better food for their dogs."* Every Bengali, however black, feeble and cowardly he may be, can say with pride that he belongs to a race which never in its history so degraded the image of God after which man is made, and never heaped upon the heavenly soul such an amount of moral filth. Yet, to me it seems that in England alone justice and mercy have now more adherents than in any other rationalistic country upon earth. To me it seems that but for our connection with England we might have been like Turkey or Persia, but certainly not like Japan. England is not so much the home of Englishmen, as it is the home of imperialism, liberalism and human freedom. It is practically the home of all races, as any one can testify who has seen the large number of foreigners marrying and intermarrying there—the pigtailed Chinese, the dark lascars, the wooly-headed Africans, the straight-nosed Jews, not to say of Germans, French, Italians and other people of Europe. For a long time to come, England by her position and circumstances, is destined to remain an imperial country by whatever race of human beings she may be inhabited. Why

---

* The Races of Man, from the German of Oscar Peschel. London, 1876.

should we not accept that little strip of land as the great metropolis and common property of the empire of which our continent of India is an important part, and take pride in it just as we take pride in Calcutta, and help always to keep it in the vanguard of human progress? Ah! If only the thoughtless thought-reading-Cumberland type of men would cease to create race animosities! The empire is large, my friends, and there is room for each to work for his own good, for mutual good and for the good of the whole. Said the glowworm to the nightingale about to pick her up:—"If you admired my lamp, as much as I admired your ministrelsy, you would be as unwilling to do me injury, as I would be to spoil your song; for it was the same divine power who taught you to sing and me to shine, that we might beautify and cheer the night, you by your music, and I by my light."

We can help the people of England materially by cheapening the cost of living in that country. In this vast continent of India we have numerous food substances on which the poor of England can live as well as the Hunias in the high altitudes of the Himalayas, the Badagars among the forests of the Nilgiri hills and the Kurumbás in the Mysore plateau. We have millets and seeds which yield as nutritious a food as wheat, rice, the pulses and the potato. Create a demand for these, and the vast expanse of land now lying fallow in Chota Nagpur, the Central Provinces, Central India, Mysore, Assam and Burma will smile with a verdure through which will peep the white bunches of *Sorghum vulgare* (Joár) the golden spikes of *Paspalum scrobulatum* (kodo), the red heads of *Amarantus Blitum* (Chua), and the brown claws of *Eleusine coracana* (Rági) and its kindred. I would not think of the advantage that the success of an effort to introduce cheap food in England would bring to India. He who has seen with his own eyes the sufferings of the needy when famine raged in India, or the chronic hunger that prevails among the poor classes in Europe has no room in his mind for any other feeling than the ardent wish to alleviate human misery. It is very well for English philanthropists to shed tears because natives of Upper India eat but once during the day, forgetting by the way that their one meal is nearly equal to the four meals of a man who takes food as many times during the day. It is all very well for my countrymen to sit down and cry because European philanthropists sit down and cry. By this I should not be understood to say that the condition of our peasantry is as it ought to be. If you wish to ameliorate their condition, devise means for a reduction of rent in temporarily-settled districts, ask Government to take a sliding revenue in kind or its equivalent in money, create independent peasant-holdings, make the permanent settlement of revenue with the tenants, forbid sub-letting and subdivision of a farm, reform social customs specially with regard to marriage expenses, and educate the people to appreciate a higher standard of living and to work for it. What I mean to say is that the distress prevailing in this country in ordinary times is not so excruciatingly painful as what prevails among the poor in Europe. The utter helplessness in which a man without means of living finds himself in England makes his situation doubly insupportable. No river has been left for him where he can try to catch a fish, there is no jungle where he can dig for a root or pluck the tender leaves of a tree, he has no neighbours who would share with him their scanty meal, and he has no home where he can lay himself down and die. The land in that country belongs only to a few individuals and they have all enclosed it with hedges and wire fences, so that he has no place like our mango groves where he can lie down and rest his weary body. And consider what his misery would be if he had little ones depending for their food upon the fruits of his labour! Do you ever hear in this country of people drowning themselves to save themselves from such misery? Such things happen in England. After the late Midland Railway strike, an Englishman, who sought re-employment, but could not get it, drowned himself with his whole family to escape starvation. True, they have got the workhouse to go to. But people with a little self-respect prefer death to going to a workhouse. Another very distressing case occurred while I was there. A poor widow had three children, the eldest, a daughter, 7 years old, and the youngest a baby in arms. The widow worked very hard to win the bread of the family. She went out to her work at 7 in the morning and came back at 11 in the night, often at 12, not unfrequently at 1 the next morning All this time the baby was left in charge of the eldest girl of seven years of age, with whom she could leave only a farthing's worth of milk for the little one. That was all she could spare, poor woman! for she must eat something herself to keep up her strength for her hard work. The baby died, and the doctors found that it died of starvation and neglect. It occurred to me that the baby would not have suffered such misery, would not have died, if it had half a farthing's worth of Rági *(Eleusine coracana)* meal mixed with its half farthing's worth of milk. Now we lose nothing if we work to educate the English palate to Rági meal, to Bajrá *(Pennisetum typhodeum)* bread, and to the use of rice and pulses. If we have our own poor, let us work for them too on the lines I have suggested above. We are used to do charitable things in such a concrete form, that we often fail to grasp the idea of working out a principle in abstraction.

Although charity is practised in this country in a very concrete form and is not always well-regulated, we in this country know better how to treat our poor than the people of Europe. There is more brotherly feeling in the East among the different castes than in the West. We have an active religion here, which teaches the Indians to look upon charity as an act acceptable to God, and not as a social obligation. The piety and learning of the Bráhmans, who are in most cases very poor in wordly goods, have compelled kings and princes, the merchants and the opulent classes, to bow their head to poverty. Wealth and landed possessions in this country have not therefore been able to secure that monopoly of worship as they have done in Europe. Notwithstanding our caste-system, there is a thousand times more sympathy between man and man in this country than there is in England. In a village inhabited by different castes, high and low, we feel such love and respect for each other as is unknown in Europe. The wealthy landlord and the sacred Bráhman have a hereditary and complimentary relationship with the poorest of the poor and the lowliest of the low. There is uncle Ahmad the Musalman, brother Rám the shoe-maker, and nephew Nobin the milkman. If Rám the shoe-maker's son is ill, brother Gopál the Bráhman goes to his house, feels his pulse and helps him to the best of his power. After he has done this duty he may go and bathe and purify himself for having touched a shoe-maker. If brother Gopál, the Bráhman, is ill, all the village people flock to his house in the same manner and try to help his family in every conceivable way. One runs for the doctor, one goes for medicine, another goes up the palm tree to procure certain things from its top which the doctor has prescribed, another looks after the diet, and a large number sit down and wait for something to do. Nobin, the milkman's father is dead, and he is poor and he has no money to feast his caste-men in memory of his father. The rich land-lord gives him money, the poor cultivators give him rice and vegetables, his caste-men give him milk and curd, and in a short time he finds himself supplied with everything he wants. There may be ill-feeling between two members of a village community. In such cases one usually says to another—" Brother, you have done me wrong, I will not come to your house when you invite me to your feasts ; but if I hear that you are in distress I will run to your house without any invitation, and try my best to help you." And so he does. If Englishmen want to see how human beings differing in education and social position can yet live harmoniously as members of one family, they must come and live for a certain time in an Indian village. We have no life assurance, no poor-house, no professional nurses, no undertakers. We have no secret from our neighbours. We do not know the meaning of the "Skeleton in the cupboard." We need not hide our tattered rags or our broken pots from our neighbours.

It is different in England. People there do not much trouble themselves with their neighbours' affairs. It would be considered rude for one to shew an inquisitiveness about the private concerns of his next door neighbour. "It is *my* business," is a time-honoured reply they have for the inquisitive in that country, the like of which we have not here. For, John's business is not Tom's business there, whereas, more or less, neighbour Rám's business is neighbour Sám's business here. The individuality of Self is early developed in the European mind, and in this matter they follow nature more closely than we do. They borrow a simile from the habit of birds to describe young people coming to age and entering into the struggles of life. We do not "fly from the paternal nest." We bring our wives to the old family nest. When we go to marry, our mothers ask us—"where are you going, my son?" We answer —"to fetch a servant, for you, mother." This is form. The bride really comes to the old house to the old people as a daughter. She has no idea of a home without the aged folks, which she can call entirely her own. Our little Alice or Agnes does not, since she is five years old, pick up tiny pieces of straw and feathers and lay them by for the nest which she hopes to build for herself after she has learned to fly. Did you ever see parent birds pecking away their grown up young ones to tell them to go and seek their own grub? That gives an idea of parental duty in Europe, at least so far as the body of the people is concerned. Both boys and girls, when they have passed the age of twenty-one, prefer leaving the paternal home, to take up lodgings of their own, and to work for their own living. The duty of parents to their children and their legal authority over them end when they have brought them up to that age and given them what education they could within that time. The paternal door is however always open to lads and lasses who have chosen to live separately. As long as they are not married that fire-side is still their "home," and they have great affection and reverence for their "home," and if possible they spend their Sundays and holidays at "home." Thus they gradually wean themselves away from parental supervision. When married the paternal roof ceases to be their "home." The case is somewhat different with the genteel classes, specially with regard to their daughters. The duty of parents among them does not end with bringing up their children to age and giving them a liberal education, but they must also provide them, or put them in the way of providing themselves, with sufficient means to maintain the position in which they are born. Among these classes, daughters generally live with their parents until they are married, and among them happen those cases of rebellious sons and daughters marrying against the will of their parents of which novelists are so fond of making thrilling narratives. Daughters of gentle families but poor circumstances accept service as companion to a lady or as governess of children.

It is not possible here to further elaborate the outline I have given above of the growth of social units in Europe. There the fission of new units from the parental body is smoothly effected as in most of the Vorticellas, while here the new units stick to the old system until it becomes one unwieldy mass as in an overgrown Myriana, and when at length the rupture comes it comes in the midst of violent convulsions. In England such disintegration is looked upon as the natural result of growth, in India it is looked down upon as unnatural and selfish. I have praised my countrymen for the sympathy they have for the poor. But, however I disapprove certain aspects of the English social system, the result has shewn that the formation of our society is not what it ought to be. The fact is patent to every thinker that our social system has not worked well. Starting with such a basis what other moral can I draw? In the case of one, *viz.*, of England, I gather in my mind the various clues of a glorious national life and induction leads me up to what is right. In the case of the other, *viz.*, of India, I start from a huge failure and deduction brings me down to what is wrong—to the various wrongful circumstances that accumulated their evil effects and at length contributed to bring about the downfall. Often, our virtues have been turned into vices, and their faults into merits. It may be that a faint streak of light is perceptible on our eastern horizon. Shall we hide the gloom, that darkens our world, in the deepest recesses of our heart and not shew it up to our bright friend over there to chase it away or consume it by his fierce glory? Vanity, false Patriotism, frenzied Religionism, shall not be allowed to cherish in our bosom the serpent with milk and honey. It may be that I saw clouds in the firmament of England, some with a threatening look while others in the act of skulking away, some gathering strength while others just dissipating. This is nature, and it will always be so. The ever-present forces of Decay will have to wait a long while before they can eat into the British national body, for, as far as I could judge, the vitality of this body is still working its way forward in its fullest vigour. The people there are perfectly alive to their faults, they are acquiring more and more power, they are not afraid of change, and they can organise for common action. On the whole, the condition of things there is integrating and not disintegrating. Intellect and talent are getting a more honoured place in the estimation of the people, the absurdities of caste-system are being gradually removed, monopoly in land is in the course of being broken down, and the condition of the poor is receiving the most careful attention. No doubt there remains much to be done: in many things only a beginning has been made; but yet one cannot but view with approbation the work of the giants who have manfully put their shoulder on the national wheel.

The existence of self as a separate unit in the creation is thus early and keenly felt in Europe. It has its merits as well as its drawbacks. While it teaches one to put one's own self to the best use for one's own benefit, or in other words, while it trains up a lad to be an independent and self-reliant man, at the same time there is always the fear of love of self being unduly developed. It is this fear that prompts me to advise my countrymen to smooth matters and to be as little as possible in the way of English interests. In the uphill struggles of life in that country the good friends of a man help him to rise higher if he has already risen high, or shoves him further down if he is already down. So partly for vanity, partly for this apprehension people carefully keep their affairs secret from their kindly neighbours. So neighbours do not come to each other at all hours, and when they come on a visit they do not go to all parts of the house, they do not go to the kitchen, and they do not tell each other what they cooked and ate on that day. They only go to the drawing room or the dining room. They only talk of the habits of their husbands, the doings of their children, or of any sensational incident that might be engrossing the attention of the public at the time. They only shew to their neighbours the bright side of things. Life with them is one continuous struggle to beat their neighbours in the possession of such bright things, or—to take a charitable view of it—an emulation to make their affairs brighter than those of their neighbours. Do the " At homes," Tea Parties, Garden Parties and all those costly invitations have anything to do with show? Whatever it may be, many things no doubt are formal and ceremonial in that country. There is first of all duty, then there is business, and lastly there is ceremony, but there is very little of sentiment. To sacrifice sentiment to duty is English character, to sacrifice duty to sentiment is Indian character. At least in Europe there is not that impetuosity of sentiment as we have here. Whatever there is is hard and tough like the iron we get from that country. It breaks, but bends not. They call love, affection, charity, and piety soft things? Well, perhaps I am wrong, but I thought that tender cellular plants transplanted in an arid region get hard and develop spines. The strong sense of individuality in man and woman, the hard formality that surrounds English life, the iron caste-system that prevails there, and the constant danger confiding people are exposed to from thieves, swindlers, card-sharpers and other human brutes, that prowl in all parts of the country in search of prey, render it extremely difficult for English people to know each other so much as we know of each other in this country. Charity in such a concrete form as we have here is simply impossible in Europe. In the first place it would be difficult to find out the real object for charity, and in the second place the life of a man disposed to practise charity in such a form will in no time be made insupportable. Thus happens it that while a man may be subscribing hundreds of pounds for the relief of the famine-stricken people of Madras, a baby lying a few doors from his mansion may be dying of starvation. Charity cannot but take a hard or abstract form in that country, and in this form, any subscription list will shew, it has more votaries there than elsewhere.

I have often had occasion to allude to the English caste-system. Trade and religion have not however so clearly demarcated the different castes there as they have in this country. There they so over-lap each other that it is difficult to say where one caste ends and the other begins. The system there is like the course of our river Ganges which, issuing forth from the gorge at Hardwar, imperceptibly glides over the different levels in the Middle Country, in Benares, in Behar, in Bengal, until it smoothly mixes its water with that of the Bay. Ours is like that of the Ganges Canal with well-defined elevations, lock-ups and cascades. Nevertheless the caste prejudice there is stronger than it is in this country. It is hardly credible that such a thing is possible in a Christian country, yet it is so. Owing to this caste prejudice of Englishmen, and partly of my countrymen too, good social feeling between the two races has hitherto been found impossible. In this country the caste of a European is chiefly based upon position and wealth, so far at least as he is concerned with the natives of the country. These form an insurmountable barrier between the two. Disparity of civilisation, of culture and refinement between them does not count much, for this is remediable, and the European is not undisposed to pass it over in the case of a Rájá or a wealthy man. Necessarily his social dealings with the natives of the country must therefore be confined to a few Rájás, or to that small number of them who have no objection to mix with a European, or in other words his social relationship with the people of the country is practically *nil*. Another great difficulty in the way of a good social feeling between the two races is the difference in the conception of a gentleman. Formerly in this country, piety, learning and birth were the three things any of which made a gentleman; now to these must be added wealth, landed possession, a high post under Government, or a very successful career in a genteel profession. The first three are oriental passports for gentility, the four modern requisites are European and are the only ones recognised by the European. I have said elsewhere that the present caste-system in Europe is gradually breaking down. In the meantime I am tempted to hope, that, in his social dealings with a European in this country, no Indian would so far forget himself as to compromise his native dignity. It is as much the paramount duty of every Indian to do away with the absurdities in his caste-system—those absurdities that are against the dictates of human duty, charity and common sense, and that stand in the way of his national progress—as it is his duty to deserve and maintain the dignity and position he has inherited from his fathers. Self-respect demands both. Only, there should be no mistake about what is true dignity.

The morning after the Election meeting I went to the police magistrate's court of that quarter where the meeting took place to see whether any complaint was laid for assault or hurt. No such complaint was made. They have no time there for litigation. Necessity drives them to law; they do not go to it for the sake of pleasure. The luxuries of litigation, its excitements and moments of depression, its joys and sorrows, its triumphs and defeats, are unknown to this benighted people. Long live our law courts, the source of consolation and pleasure to thousands of our poor peasants on whose hands time sits heavy, on summer days, after they have reaped their rice in January and gathered their winter crops in March. In England, they have got gambling, a poor substitute for litigation, with its varied amusements lengthened along the intricacies and mazes of three solemn courts. In the neighbourhood of the magistrate's court to which I went I saw no seemingly listless persons who, in India, would sit patiently under the trees and cast furtive glances on every new comer to enquire whether he would require their valuable services to prove or disprove an *alibi*, an assault or a murder. This new profession in India is entirely the product of the British judiciary system. Besides professionals there are amateurs too in this line of business. Is there a magistrate, a barrister or a pleader who can assure me that perjury is not committed in one single criminal case in which rich people are concerned? I was going to ask if any single case, true or untrue, goes through the court without a certain amount of hard swearing. Rájás and Zamindárs, high castes and low castes, they all more or less, directly or indirectly, connive at it whenever they think necessary. What a terrible instrument perjury is in the hands of the rich and powerful to coerce their inferiors to submission! It is so common and so universal that an honourable barrister would feel no compunction to argue a case and a just magistrate to convict an accused on the strength of false evidence. I remember the time when the simple village-men (going to the opposite extreme) ran away from their homes, when called upon to give evidence in a court, lest by inadvertence they said anything not strictly true. No doubt our present judicial system is answerable for this state of things, but I do not thereby mean to condemn it, for I cannot suggest a better one. I often despair of our new national life when I ponder upon all its frivolities. National pride should precede national life. What pride is that which dare not manfully face the sources of national shame? Complain of acquitals of European accused! Why not seek remedy for the canker at the root from which grows the tree that bears the evil? National honour requires an unremitting unrelenting crusade against perjury in this country. No repressive measures can be too severe to put down this cruel and disgraceful practice. The demand for false evidence is very small in England at the present time, and whatever demand there is is supplied from more respectable quarters. That cheaper and more abundant supply would be forthcoming if the demand arose can be safely inferred from what happened during the Catholic scare in Charles II's time, or when in the last century the operation of the Licensing Act (9 Geo. II. ch. 23) for arresting the sale of spirituous liquors by prohibitory licenses was in full force. The rudiments of all crimes are present in every nation; impunity, opportunity and sufficient remuneration bring them to full development. Private honour is however too strong in England to create a demand for such an abominable article, and public opinion is too powerful to allow such a trade being practised with impunity. As I have said the people there have no time for litigation. A fight on the spot, with a glass of something strong at the end, settles a dispute in England, and entirely effaces the memory of a real or fancied insult. The cases that usually come up in the London police courts are mostly of a trivial nature, of which drunkenness forms a large percentage.

No doubt the vice of drunkenness is very prevalent in England and in all European countries. It cannot be helped where alcoholic drinks of one kind or other are the recognised beverage of the country. Among the millions there must be a large number with constitution specially fitted to be the home of this vice. From mild bitters they take to strong ale and stout and then to ardent spirits. The habit of taking spirits grows upon a man, it becomes a disease, which is as difficult to shake off as the habit of using opium. This deplorable habit is the cause of much misery and unhappiness in that country. Such a habit in a man is very much to be deplored, but it is shockingly distressing to see woman, the mother of humanity, the object of worship in Europe, her who ought to be the embodiment of all that is good, meek and modest, rendering herself incapable in the public streets and the next day figuring in the police court. Vice of any kind in a woman looks so unnatural that it becomes doubly painful to one not accustomed to such sights. What a home is it of the man whose wife drinks? What a home is it for the children? The less said about it the better. Happily such cases are rare.

These sights have created in Europe a strong revulsion of feeling against the use of spirituous liquors. As is usual in such cases, anti-alcoholists have gone to the opposite extreme, and if they had their way they would put all the men and women in that country under lock and key lest they took anything with even the faintest scent of alcohol in it. They prove by facts and figures how many millions of money are wasted every year for the purchase of spirituous liquors, and how many thousands of human beings die every year from the use of alcoholic drinks. We have prophets to foretell the approaching dissolution of the universe, we have astronomers who constantly quail under the apprehension of the earth being brushed to atoms by the tail of a comet, we have microbists and bacillists to wrangle about the germs of destruction and to keep us in a state of nervous excitement, and we have philosophers to tell us that humanity is getting animalised by the use of meat. Are they getting vegetalised too by the use of corn and vegetables? So we have anti-alcoholists, anti-opiumists and anti-tobacconists to point out to us signs portending evils of the direst kind. Yet the world goes on. Mankind has used spirituous liquors from time immemorial, yet the human race is not extinct, nor short-lived, nor decrepit, compared with what it was in ages past. The bravest, the strongest, and the most intelligent races used it before, and use it now. Yet they live and thrive now as much as they did before. Drunkenness is to be condemned in the strongest of terms, not less the habitual use of ardent spirits, but it has yet to be proved that a moderate use of wines and beer is fatal to human constitution. A glass of beer and a pipe of tobacco afford pleasure and rest to millions of men after their hard toil of the day is done. Thousands of old men, who cannot take to rosaries or books, warm up their cold enfeebled body with a glass of wine. Shall we deprive the sons of toil and old age of the only enjoyment they have in life, because a few men choose to make of themselves abject beasts by making a bad use of this means of pleasure and rest? Bitter experience has made us shy and suspicious of enthusiasts, however their decrees and denouncements may appeal to the vanity and patriotism of my countrymen. We in this country are often heedless of the fact that virtue when carried too far becomes, in its own way, the very opposite of virtue. Most of my countrymen are probably not aware that "taking" wine or beer and "drinking" have entirely different meanings. It is not their fault that they do not know it, for in this country whoever uses wine or spirits uses it for the sake of intoxication. Their taste is not educated to relish such liquors as beverages—beer is bitter like infusion of chiretta, port wine is too sweet and pungent, dry champagne is acrid, and whiskey is smoky.

They hastily gulp these down, as a child does a solution of quinine, for the sake of immediate effects, *viz.*, intoxication. It is quite different in Europe. People take a glass of wine or beer there as any one would take a glass of water here. Costly wines are consumed every day in every gentleman's house all over Europe. Nobody gets beyond the bounds of propriety on such occasions. It is not gentlemanly to do so. He would at once lose caste. No gentleman thinks of going to another gentleman with the smell of brandy about him. It is considered abominable. *Main kih badnám kunad ahle khirad rá galatast; Balkih main khúd shaod áz dast harifá badnám.* "That wine brings bad name to wise men is a mistake; on the other hand, wine itself gets bad name by falling into the hands of low people." So said Háfiz. It is necessary that one should pause before pronouncing the act of taking wine as a sin and a crime.

Anti-alcoholists trace a large number of deaths in Great Britain to the use of spirituous drinks. I should rather think that they generally die of old age, gout and pulmonary diseases. Fever and cholera of the kind prevailing in this country are almost entirely absent there. The ailments which keep the people in a chronic state of painful excitement are cold, dyspepsia and toothache. Both males and females begin to have their teeth taken out from a very early age, seventeen, even earlier. So a large amount of thinking has been focussed on the subject of artificial tooth-making. They are trying porcelain teeth now. The climate of England is far better than most parts of

India. It is cool and bracing. It is neither so cold in the winter nor so hot in the summer as the Continent. The vast expanse of water which surrounds Great Britain on all sides throws upon it a large quantity of vapour, which hangs over it like a curtain intercepting the heat radiated by the earth in autumn and winter, and at the same time preventing the sun from shedding his full glory in summer. These vapours very frequently fall upon earth in the shape of drizzling rain, which keeps the rivers full, and makes the meadows beautifully green, on which fatten the mutton and beef. Once I asked a gentleman what the English people would do if by some chance they suffered one or two naval defeats and the whole coast blockaded, say for a couple of months by the enemy. "Would you not be reduced to great straits for want of food?" I enquired. He proudly answered.—"As long as we produce such good beef and mutton, nobody would defeat us." This drizzling rain constantly keeps the atmosphere surcharged with a large amount of moisture, but the soil is not damp. For paucity of land they dig down and bury the lowest storey of their houses underneath the surface of the earth. They have their kitchens in these underground rooms, which are quite dry and habitable, and many poor people live in them. If instead of the usual drizzle, the rain assumes the form of a shower, the newspapers there at once describe the phenomenon by saying that "rain fell in tropical torrents." The greatest peculiarity of the English climate is its changing habits. Within the space of twenty-four hours all sorts of weather might be experienced, now bitterly cold with a keen wind blowing from the east, now rain, now sunshine, now so close and warm, that we Indians had even to gasp for breath. Sitting in England the English people are inured to all sorts of climatic variations, which specially fit them for conquest and colonisation in all quarters of the globe.

One of these days Lord Northbrook kindly introduced me to Mr. John Bright. He had one of his daughters with him at the time. After a short conversation I left him with Lord Northbrook, and joined another gentleman who was standing close by. I remarked to him that the educated classes in India adored John Bright, the tribune of the people. This gentleman felt pleased at what I said and wished me to tell the same to Mr. Bright. Turning to Mr. Bright's daughter I whispered—"We love peace, we hold war a sin, and our religion teaches us to love every living thing as one's own self. Do you then wonder that my people have a very great respect for your father? Very much indeed do they love John Bright." Subsequently, I told Mr. Bright himself that my countrymen fully appreciated his noble work for the good of humanity, "and, Sir, I hope you will continue to take the same interest in my people as you have hitherto done." Mr. Bright observed—"I am getting old, and must soon retire to private life, but I shall always take a deep interest in India, and shall always be glad to hear that the people of India are progressing under British rule."

Another friend of India I had the honour of knowing was Miss Manning. The people of India are the adopted children of this generous-hearted lady. She devotes every moment of her life for our good. She is the life and soul of the National Indian Association. The soirees she holds at her house give the Indians an opportunity of knowing the English people, which otherwise they would not have been able to do. I am sorry that my duties prevented my being as much useful as I could wish to Miss Manning in the noble work she is doing. I have heard that advantage is occasionally taken of her kindness by some of our foolish youths who go to England without providing themselves with sufficient means.

I cannot too strongly impress upon our impetuous lads the unwisdom of going there in such a state. England is not India. Here one can go to any part of the country, and find shelter, food, and even clothing and expenses to go to school. Charity and hospitality are commendable, and my countrymen, both Hindus and Muhammadans, have long been famous for these noble virtues. But abuse of charity and hospitality is not commendable. Such abuse has in this country destroyed self-respect and pride of manhood even among the better classes. For, creation of beggars, idlers and worthless members of society is a meritorious act in this country, a sure road to heaven. Begging is sanctified here because as a profession it is followed by men of religion. Only give up work and live on others' shoulders, and all the angels of heaven will work night and day with spade and axe to clear for you the path to heaven. Thus religion working both on the mind of the giver and the mind of the receiver has created feelings which have destroyed all consciousness of humiliation and selfishness one would think inseparable from the act of begging.

Another lady who highly honoured me by her kindness was the celebrated Miss Florence Nightingale. Sir Edward Buck introduced me to her. She too has unbounded sympathy for the people of this ancient country. When shall we have such accomplished women who would grasp questions involving the welfare of nations? Does anybody ever think that by allowing the faculties of our women to get blunt we retard the course of evolution? If it is true that a human being inherits the developed faculties of both father and mother, is it not then true that we inherit only one half of what otherwise we would have done? Invalided and practically imprisoned as she is in her room, Miss Florence Nightingale has made the welfare of mankind the constant care of her life. She has figures and facts regarding the sanitary condition of the world at her fingers' ends, and from that little house in Park Lane she sheds a moral influence before which ministers and administrators bow their head. Never did I meet with a lady more anxious for information. Her questions were critical and always to the point, which revealed a depth of mind we are not accustomed to see. It was a surprise for me. She seemed to know everything about the present state of India and its people, and of the obstacles that lie in the path of India's more rapid progress. We have good many friends among the British people, both here and in England.

But what can they do unless we choose to rise to a higher plane of life?

Another friend of India I saw was Mr. Pierre Duff, the son of our great Doctor Duff. One day he took us to his house at Denmark Hill, near London. He got up all sorts of entertainments for our amusement. Mr. Duff remarked to me that our princes and others who go to England never take the slightest interest in the "Home for Asiatics" the English have in London. At Denmark Hill I first saw the late Mr. Bullen Smith, who was very kind to me personally ever afterwards. By his death, we have lost another friend. I have mentioned only a few of the ladies and gentlemen whom I found interested in the welfare of India, because these names are not unknown to my countrymen.

CHAPTER. V.

THE EXCURSIONS.

His Royal Highness, the Prince of Wales, with his usual urbanity, wished that the representatives of the various Colonies assembled at the Exhibition should be kindly received by the British people, so that they might carry back affectionate remembrances of the mother country. The proposal was wise and kind; but apart from its merits, it was warmly received by the English public because of the quarter from which it emanated, for the Prince, our future Emperor, is highly popular among all classes for his generous, noble and open nature. The Princess of Wales is simply adored, and rightly too. Invitations poured in from all parts of the country, from high and low, from Her Majesty Herself, from the nobility and the gentry, private gentlemen, merchant guilds, clubs, public institutions and town corporations. So many came that a Reception Committee had to be appointed to regulate them. I have been informed that there was a regular scramble for these invitations, not among the pure Colonials and the Indians who are too democratic for that, but chiefly among British-born Colonials and men with the faintest possible connection with the Exhibition or the Colonies. They understood the value of these invitations better than we did. Like Prince Le Boo of the Pelew Islands, we simply wondered why there should be any excitement at all over such a small matter. We gradually came to know better.

We found the caste-system in England more rigid and exclusive than what we have in this country. The whole English people may be primarily divided into two classes, the "Upper Ten Thousand," what they call the "Society," and the masses below them or people not belonging to "Society," or in other words gentlemen and non-gentlemen, castemen and no castemen. But within these two primary divisions there are innumerable grades and circles, the one above always looking down upon the one below, and the one below always striving to get into the one above. As soon as a man has earned a little competence he turns his attention to "get into society," *i.e.*, to be invited into the houses of the "Upper Ten Thousand." If he is an humbler individual he strives to get into the circle immediately above him. With this view people conceal their real incomes, and always try to pass for more than what they are really worth. Many shopkeepers and poor people are conservatives in their politics in the hope that their acquaintances would take them for respectable substantial men. For are not most of the aristocracy and moneyed men conservatives, and the ragged, unwashed—liberals and radicals?

English castes may be roughly summarised as follows:—(1) Royal family and the upper circle of old nobility; (2) lower circle of old nobility; (3) untitled relations of nobility with independent means, recently created nobility, and merchant princes who have formed marriage connections with aristocratic families; (4) near relations of nobility without any independent means waiting for a bequest or on the look out for a good marriage. These form what is called the "upper ten thousand" or the "society," which patronise, tolerate or lionise individuals not born in the purple, who have acquired eminence in the race-course, theatres, fine arts, science, literature or in public service. Among the non-society men there are innumerable castes based chiefly on money, a slight deference being also paid to birth. Like the Hindus, the English people do not eat, drink, or form marriage connections with individuals of a lower caste, and like our pious Bráhmans the punctilious man among them would plunge into a bath immediately after his return from a meeting of low caste people which he had to attend for electioneering or other purposes. Sometimes he takes a perfumed bath to thoroughly cleanse himself of the defilement. Once I asked a gentleman the reason for this: he gave me the same reason as a Travancore Bráhman would give for not touching a Pulliah. In the matter of food and drink caste-rules are not so strict there as they are in India, for in that country religion has not made such rules sacred and solid. An English Bráhman is allowed to eat and drink with a low caste man in hotels, passenger ships and other public places, in short where he cannot help it. But it must be said to his credit that even on such occasions he does his best to keep his caste intact by holding himself as much aloof as he can from people of lower grades. In passenger ships he soon forms a separate circle composed of people of his own rank, among whom he sits and with whom he takes the afternoon tea, that being the only occasion when it is possible for him to shew his superiority. Although such occasional mixing with people in lower grades of life does not make the English Bráhman liable to lose his caste, he must not therefore too freely mix with them. His people would look down upon him if he did so. High caste women and clergymen are however allowed to go to poor people's houses on charitable purposes.

Intermarriage between high and low castes is not to be thought of, except in cases where a poor English Bráhman is obliged to marry for the sake of money into the family of a merchant who has recently acquired his wealth and wants to get into society. The bride and his people are taken into society not without much grumbling, and it is only in subsequent generations that the family can thoroughly establish itself in it. But woe to him who marries a low caste woman without money: down descends upon him the thunder of excommunication. Notwithstanding antagonistic religious ordinances, the feeling of affectionate fraternity that exists between high caste and low caste people in India is not to be seen in England. There the high caste man neither loves nor hates his poorer neighbour. He simply refuses to think, know or recognise the existence of such a man in the world, except perhaps when he wants to secure his vote at the election time. The English caste system is based on conquest and wealth, the Indian system is based on piety, learning and trade. People whose ancestors came with William the Conqueror and obtained grants of land taken from the original possessors occupy the first place in English society. Additions have from time to time been made to this original body of conquering families by incorporation into it of men from lower orders who acquired wealth, power and eminence in public service. With the spread of education among the masses, the wider diffusion of wealth among all classes, and the larger facilities afforded to the people to acquire wealth by the promulgation of liberal laws, the power of the old aristocracy gradually waned, their exclusiveness consequently broke down, and incorporation with them of new blood from the lower castes became more frequent in recent times, so much so that many commoner now consider it a doubtful honour to be invested with a peerage. The ancient caste system is breaking down both in England and in India, owing to the same cause, *viz.*, mass education. But still in both countries respect for the high caste is yet very strong. In India it is because caste system is religion; in England because there is such a vast difference in the social life of people belonging to the high and low castes, and owing to the distance at which the one always keeps the other. It was therefore considered a matter of great condescension on the part of the Royal Family and the aristocracy to have opened their houses to the Colonists and Indians, and every one was naturally anxious to be the recipient of this hospitality. As for ourselves, but for this hospitality we could not have seen so much of English life as we did, and we therefore felt grateful for the opportunity thus given to us.

Early in July 1886, the Colonials and Indians were commanded by Her Majesty to come to lunch at Windsor Castle. The invitation card was worded as follows :—" The Lord Steward has received Her Majesty's command to invite—to luncheon at Windsor Castle on Monday, the 5th of July, at 2 o'clock." On the reverse, directions about dress were given, *viz.*, ladies to wear morning dress; gentlemen, evening coat, morning trousers, with orders and decorations; and it also contained the remark that " the Court will be in mourning."

On the 5th of July at half-past two in the morning little Twilight rose from her bed, and opened the shutters of heaven close by the Docks and Arsenals of Woolwich. Putting on her pretty gray apron, she gently tripped into the London world, and began to sweep the muggy mist that hung heavy all around. She swept the Thames, from Greenwich of Observatory fame, where begin the lines that intersect the hemispheres from pole to pole, to verdant Kew where she peeped through the glass roof to greet the feathery palm, happy in its delusion, to have taken the reeking clime within for its native Africa. She brushed the fog off the tall Monument, off the tower at Westminster where Big Ben tells the time, off housetops under which lay asleep tired London, and with the aid of the morning breeze shook the summer foliage in the Parks and drove away the gloom that hid among them for refuge. Thus from half past two to half past three, Morning Twilight busied herself to sweep, brush and dust the world and to make everything neat and tidy. When behold there was glory in the East! A jet of gaseous gold was suddenly spurted from the heavens, and all the tall chimneys of the town anxiously raised their heads to catch the bright effulgence. It rested for a while like a golden cap on the heads of these high minarets of the western world, and then unfolded itself and slid down as a brocade mantle covering the slate roofs, the balcony rails and finally the deserted roads below. Heaven and earth smiled, as it only could smile where such joyous radiance is rare,—in northern climes, or in high altitudes where vapours have grazed their fill on pines and cedars, and have departed for a season. It is a soft subdued and mellowed shine with which the golden orb brightens the world in those regions, caressingly from a side; while here, he rides rough-shod over our head burning and parching everything with incessant darts of liquid fire. Meanwhile, the author of all this radiance slowly raised his bright face up and above the horizon, and bade with a nod all the clocks of the monster town strike the hour of four. Still London slept, London woke not, for it was yet night. He glanced upon gaunt, huge houses, rising from the caverns of earth storey after storey up towards the sky, blinds down, silent, sombre and smoky, looking dismally on the streets below. These were quite empty, except where the policeman walked on his beat, or where the homeless vagrant rising from a door step stretched up his arms, and yawned and shook his rheumatic body, or where a string of carts rumbled on to Covent Garden. The golden effulgence searched through every nook and corner, the railings cast their shade, the dews began to dry, the trees whispered, and the birds gaily sang in the Parks. Still London woke not, still London slept, for it was night yet. Half past four. A pair of thick boots thumped heavily on the stone-paved footpath, eliciting deep curses from a nervous man overhead, just feeling drowsy after a restless night. Presently came another, and another. Within a few minutes the streets were fairly sprinkled with hurrying pedestrians. It is time to go for honey. Up, you Busy Bees, for the day is bright, the flowers have opened, the air is laden with perfume, and it is happier to work than not to work.

That comparison with bees (if bees are really busy), which they use, is happy and appropriate in that country. Not here. Taken on the whole not a moment of human time is lost there. Nay, Necessity often compels Rest to give up to Labour a large number of the hours allotted for her portion. Every man and woman there is busy as a bee, and the idleness of a few drones is amply made up by the industry of the workers. They all work, except a few gentlemen and ladies, and work for long hours too, usually from 8 in the morning to 9 in the evening. Again, that work is something different from what we do here. We make work slowly roll on heavy cumbersome time, there fleet time is harnessed to work and whipped and cajoled to move it with all its force and speed. Forty millions of human hands thus plough, sew, hammer and spin from day to night, aided by many many millions of hands represented by machinery, the product of which is compressed into that little bit of ground they call Britain. Making every allowance for climatic and physical disadvantages, one hundred and sixty millions of working hours at the lowest computation are every day lost in India owing more to the want of knowledge of how to employ labour profitably than to the indolent habits of her adult population. At one pice an hour the loss is twenty-five lacs of rupees a day; or in other words, if these idle hands could be taught to move profitably, the result of eighty days' work would be a railway system like the East Indian. Where are the prophets of heaven and earth gone? Will not these days bring down a holy one amongst us to teach us how to acquire means to live like civilised man, to teach us that idleness is a sin and work an act of piety, a balm for worldly cares and a passport for heaven? Or why do taxing brains get giddy in search of new openings by which to tap cash out of a cashless people, and not take in kind—in labour, and thus use the waste product to make roads, railways, canals, wells and tanks? In a society like this where the masses do not think or cannot think rightly, one true man like Peter the Great, with dictatorial powers and unhampered by parliamentry obstructions and senseless newspaper denunciations, can do more in ten years than what a constitutional government can do in a hundred. Look at Japan!

A solitary engine now reluctantly came out from a shed in the Underground Railway Station which had just finished its three hours' nap, and commenced to move backwards and forwards shunting for the workmen's train. On the platform the Book Stall keepers gathered the pennies paid by the labouring men for their morning papers. Outside came a Coffee Stall on its wheels, in which two sister caldrons boiled and fumed. Numerous cups and saucers of the cheapest description rattled on a plank board. Men with anxious looks soon surrounded the stall, and as each man had hastily gulped down the warming liquid, he laid a penny on the board and went his way. Newspaper boys now hurried through the streets and the milkman sent up his shrill cry. Servants of all work cleaned the door panels, shined the brass hinges and soaped and scrubbed the steps. Shop-keepers opened their shops, dusted all round and laid out their goods. By seven labouring London was up and alive. But not genteel folks, fatigued with dinners and balls, for London season was at its height now. They seldom rose before ten. Nor did the Colonials, who had to attend the numerous invitations and go through their effects in the morning.

Her Majesty most graciously placed a special train at the disposal of the Colonials and Indians which left Paddington at 1 P.M. Royal carriages were also ready at Windsor to convey us to the Castle. Sir George Birdwood with his usual kindness got the India Office to place us in charge of a Political Officer, Mr. Fitzgerald, brother of Sir Seymour Fitzgerald. We cannot sufficiently express our thanks for the kind consideration which this gentleman shewed towards us and the care he took of us all through the day. The streets at Windsor were thronged with an eager but well-behaved crowd who waited to see their fellow-subjects from all parts of the globe, and of all shades of colour. Cheer after cheer was sent forth as each carriage rolled towards the Castle, we Indians as usual getting the most hearty reception. Besides those connected with the Exhibition there were present at this Royal invitation the Raja of Narsingarh, the Thakur Sahib of Gondal, Rao Bahadur Sampat Rao, the brother of the Gaikwar, and a Muhammadan prince from the Surat side. We drove through the High Street, entered the Castle by Henry VIII's Gate and were immediately conveyed to the State Apartments. The guests when assembled there were asked to sign in the "Birth Day Book." This is a nicely bound volume with dates printed on its pages, which is kept in many houses and has its origin in that hobby for signatures. Each guest signed under the date in which he was born. We had to affix our signatures in such books in many houses, not only in English but also in our own language. A magnificent repast was then served to the guests. After lunch, Her Majesty held a Levèe where the Colonials and Indians were presented to her by the Prince of Wales. Her Majesty stood with the Prince of Wales on her right, the Princess of Wales on the left and other members of the Royal Family behind. As the usher called out the name of each guest, he entered the room and stood before the royal presence. The Prince mentioned to Her Majesty who he was, whereupon he made a profound bow and as is usual in such cases passed on, and is succeeded by another. Here again I noticed the same specially kind look with which Her Majesty always viewed her Indian subjects, and here it was very noticeable as comparison was easy owing to the guests passing in rapid succession. Since that time many other instances occurred to shew her Majesty's affection for her Indian children. On the close of the Levèe we were taken through the Castle, all parts of it being thrown open to us except the private apartments.

The State Apartments where we assembled are open to the public for four days in the week during Her Majesty's absence from Windsor Castle. For the greater part of the year she lives at Balmoral in Scotland and at Osborne. These apartments consist of ten rooms known as the Queen's Audience Chamber, the Queen's Presence Chamber, the Guard Chamber, St. George's Hall, the Grand Reception Room, the Waterloo Chamber, the Grand Vestibule, the State Ante Room, the Zuccarelli Room and the Vandyck Room. The ceilings of these rooms are decorated with allegorical paintings done by master hands and the walls embellished with old tapestries and portraits of historical personages. In the Audience Chamber the paintings on the ceiling represent Catherine of Braganza, Queen of Charles II, as Britannia, sitting on a car drawn by swans towards the temple of Virtue, and accompanied by Ceres, Flora, Pomona and other deities of olden times. Three specimens of Gobelin Tapestry adorn the walls, representing the history of Esther from the Old Testament. Over the door hangs a full-length portrait of Mary, Queen of the Scots, with the scene of her execution painted on the background. The Latin inscription under this background scene says—"The Queen—the daughter, consort and mother of kings, is struck by the axe of the executioner; and after being cruelly wounded by a first and second blow, at the third her head is severed in the presence of the commissioners and officers of Queen Elizabeth." In the upper corner of the picture there is another inscription which says—"Mary, Queen of Scotland, true princess and legitimate heiress of England and Ireland, and mother of James, king of Great Britain, who, harassed by the heresy of her people and overpowered by rebellion; came to England in the year 1568 for the sake of sanctuary; and relying on the word of her kinswoman, Queen Elizabeth, is perfidiously detained captive for 19 years, and traduced by a thousand calumnies, is by the cruel sentence of the English Parliament, at the instigation of heresy, handed over to execution; and on the 18th of February 1587, is beheaded by the common executioner in the 45th year of her life and reign." Ah, my poor Mary! what pitiable toy a heartless selfish world made of thee! Thou wast one of those unfortunate step-children of nature whose sad fate we read in history with a shudder. And of how many there is no record whom this cruel inexorable world daily tramples upon and crushes to death? Our dear cousin of England, Mary, wast well fitted for this hard world. We have been too soft for it. So let us seek peace, if there is any, out of this world.

The ceiling of the Queen's Presence Chamber also contains an allegorical painting executed by Antonio Verrio, a Neapolitan artist, who was invited to England by Charles II. In this also Catherine is the principal figure. She sits under a canopy which Time has spread for her and which is supported by Zephyrs. Under it, Justice is represented as driving away Sedition, Envy and other evil spirits. The walls contain Gobelin Tapestry in which the history of Esther is continued. An interesting collection of arms, armoury and relics of battle is tastefully arranged in the Guard Chamber. Among these could be seen a portion of the foremast of the ship Victory, cut through by a cannon ball at the battle of Trafalgar. Another relic of the same naval battle was a barshot which killed eight men in the same ship. From India, there are in that room two cannons taken from the Sikhs. St. George's Hall is a large room, 200 feet long and 34 feet broad, the ceiling of which is decorated with the arms of England's chivalry from the first institution of the Order of Garter to the present time, the names of all the knights of this Order being written on the panels of the windows, beginning with Edward III and the Black Prince on one side and ending on the other side with the Earl of Beaconsfield and the Marquis of Salisbury. The walls contain portraits of kings from James I to George IV. The Grand Reception Room is a highly ornamented apartment. The walls contain Gobelin Tapestry representing the story of Jason and Medea. The Waterloo Chamber is so named from the large number of portraits it contains of sovereigns, warriors and statesmen who took part in the events which culminated in the battle of Waterloo. Napoleon's portrait is not there, nor of any of those French generals who obtained lasting fame as warriors under that great man. Military trophies and suits of armour also adorn the walls of that lofty apartment called the Grand Vestibule, at one end of which is a statue by Bœhm of the Queen-Empress with her favourite dog "Sharp." Our friend of Naples, Verrio afore-mentioned, has pictured the gods in high merriment on the ceiling of the State Ante-room. It is a State dinner of the gods with all its accompaniments. The coving of the room is decorated with representations of fish and fowl, and the tapestry in the room alludes to the same subject. Nine large paintings by Zuccarelli adorn the room called after his name. Of these "The Meeting of Isaac and Rebecca" and "The Finding of Moses" are the most important. Another master artist has given name to the last room of the State Apartments. This is Vandyck, who was born at Antwerp in 1598 and brought to England by Charles I. The Vandyck Room contains 22 portraits executed by this celebrated painter.

One of the most magnificent monuments, by the consecration of which to illustrious dead sorrowful bereaved ever found consolation, is the Albert Memorial Chapel in Windsor Castle which Her Majesty, the Queen-Empress, erected in memory of her beloved Consort. Its majestic beauty reminds the Indian of his Táj. Every part of the Chapel is tastefully decorated, and the ornamentations are so executed as to render them very little liable to decay from atmospheric influences. Venetian glass-mosaic with gold leaf patterns adorn the roof of the Chapel.

The windows are of stained glass in which a combination of the most beautiful colours is displayed. Marble panels are arranged on the walls, but not inlaid like the Táj. Such mosaic art is however amply illustrated in the figures and the canopy behind the altar in which Lapis Lazuli, Porphyry, Alabaster, Malachite and other stones of various shades of colour are deeply fixed with exquisite taste. The panels of the Reredos are of Sicilian marble on which the Resurrection scene is carved in relief. The Altar Table is of Levanto marble, at the front of which are placed three wreaths of carved boxwood, with a Phœnix on one side, a Lamb in the middle, and a Pelican feeding its young with its own blood on the other side. Innumerable pieces of marble, of the most valuable descriptions, are used in paving the floor of this gorgeous Memorial Chapel. Among these might be observed the Corsican Green, Levanto Rosso, Moderic, Verdun, Red Fossil, Antique, Grand Antique, &c. The Cenotaph before the Altar is supported by angels, on which is carved in white marble a life size figure of the Prince, with his favourite dog at his feet. At its foot the Queen is represented in a praying attitude, while at the head "Science" is weeping. All round it the following inscription is carved :—" Albert, the Prince Consort, born August XXVI, MDCCCXIX ; died December XIV, MDCCCLXI ; buried in the Royal Mausoleum at Frogmore. I have fought the good fight : I have finished my course."

As stated in the inscription the Prince is not buried here, but at Frogmore at the neighbourhood of

Windsor, where Her Majesty has a home-farm. It is under a magnificent mausoleum of white marble that the remains of this illustrious Prince lie buried. As a rule, permission is given to no one to visit this sacred edifice, but on this occasion Her Majesty graciously allowed us to pay obeisance to the grave of her beloved husband. So we went there, and with a heavy heart stood within that solemn monument. Our hearts are weak and soft, easily affected by the sight of pain and sorrow. I felt as the heart of a weak Bengali can feel when I saw the small space which the present Sovereign of one-fourth of the human race has reserved for herself beside the place already occupied. We poor people make the sorrows of the great our own, for we feel it strange and wrong that they should suffer. They seem to us as not born to them, not made by nature fit to bear such trials. Our sympathy for the great, on such circumstances, is the more keen and lasting the more they are virtuous and good. The goodness of the Queen-Empress will be appreciated to its fullest extent when she is gone. Little do people know what her example has done for English Society. She sits at the head of it as the great emblem of Purity, and to her the English people owe not a little their domestic peace and happiness.

We saw the road called the Long Walk, which is three miles long, and which is said to be one of the finest avenues in the world, containing 1,600 very fine elm trees. Thence we went to the Shaw Farm, one of the three model farms of the Prince Consort, where various species of cattle are bred. Here by

Her Majesty's command were placed strawberries and cream to refresh her wearied guests. The strawberries were the produce of the farm and were one of the finest kinds I ever saw in that country. Near Windsor is the Eton College, considered as the highest school in the country. Thus we went from one place to another, seeing the various sights which Windsor had to show, and in this way we passed one of the many happy days which the considerate kindness of our English brethren made for us during our sojourn in that great country.

On July 10th, we went to a Garden Party held at Marlborough House by their Royal Highnesses, the Prince and the Princess of Wales. It took place in the afternoon between 4-30 to 7. Her Royal Highness the Princess of Wales received the guests. No one who has once seen it will ever forget the smiling face of the Princess, brightened by a halo of virtue and innocence. I do not know how to describe an English dress, otherwise I would have gladly described her costume which is considered to be perfect. If I am fortunate enough to have a lady to read my book, she would surely look for this all important information and would be disappointed. "Did you see the Queen?" or "Did you see the Princess?" a lady would ask in the first instance with a face in which you could clearly see her impatience to put the next question.—"How did she dress?" Could anything more clearly prove the barbarism of our soul than the answer—"I did not observe it," or at the utmost: "She wore a black dress." The Princess in short is the goddess of the

English people. She is worshipped and she is beloved by all. High and low, all revere her, all honour her. She is the pride of the nation. Would you then blame me if I lingered before her joyous presence one moment more than the time usually taken in the ceremonial introduction and reception? After the ceremony of the reception was over, the guests scattered themselves on the grounds and freely enjoyed themselves as they pleased. On such occasions the host as a rule does no longer interfere with them. Unlike our custom, the host does not look after each guest, does not ask him whether he has taken any refreshments, and does not press him over and over again to eat more than is good for him. Huge quantities of refreshments, in the shape of cakes and other sweets, fruits, ices, tea and coffee, and costly wines, are kept ready in one place, where you go and ask of the attendants for anything you require. Perfect freedom is enjoyed by every one. You eat and drink what you require, and do not take any refreshment if you do not need it. No eye is upon you. What a relief for the timid and the bashful, and for those who have a little partiality for champagne cups! Friends meet there and one introduces to the other his own acquaintances. These "Parties" therefore serve as an opportunity for people to know each other. In the Garden a Russian band was playing, and there were several Russian songstresses of note among them. They were dressed in oriental fashion, in chogas and waistbands. Her Majesty came to the Prince's party and cheerfully went among the other guests. She sat for a long time listening to the Russian songs in which she seemed to take great delight. At the end she honoured the chief of the band by personally thanking him for the performance of his party.

Marlborough House, St. James, is a new building, constructed in the beginning of the last century for the first Duke of Marlborough. In 1817 it was purchased for Princess Charlotte and Prince Leopold, since which time it has belonged to the Crown, and is now the residence of the Prince of Wales. Many of the presents which His Royal Highness received in India are kept here.

Within the narrow compass I have intended to assign to this account, it is not possible to describe in detail the various places to which I went and the things I saw. Suffice it to say that no amount of novel-reading would give the Indian an adequate idea of the refined magnificence which surrounds an Englishman in high life. "I am going to the abode of the gods," said the old Daflá of Assam to his neighbours when he left his mountain home for Calcutta to be modelled for the Exhibition. If our books have faithfully described the gods, their manners and customs, their power and prowess, their living and luxuries, then gazing round, superficially, at the land of France, Belgium or Britain well might a Hindu exclaim—"Sure, heaven is here." The whole country, the fields and the moors, the wood and the dale, the river and the swamp, have all been carefully brushed and picked, cut and levelled, as far as human care and ingenuity can make it. The beauty of the country is further enhanced by the undulating nature of the land. Meadows of the loveliest green, through which meander, like silver threads, rills, rivulets and canals full to the brim; crops standing on the fields in the order of geometrical precision; orchards laden with fruit; evergreen woods at intervals where pheasants roost; palatial mansions with long avenues; parks where the curious deer graze in peace; lakes where the wild duck swim and dive; green houses and palm houses; small villages which would count as towns in this country; and towns with their broad clean streets, symmetrical houses, tall chimneys and manufactories, full of bustle and life, cover the wavy surface of the land, and rapidly pass out of your sight as you run through it in a railway carriage, travelling at the rate of 50 to 60 miles an hour. That is the usual speed at which the railway trains are run in that country. Flocks of sheep dot the green meadows, herds of cows graze and ruminate close by, while huge plough horses stand and watch the frolicsome lambs that gaily frisk about. An assemblage of crows and sparrows could be seen picking worms among the deep furrows in a land lately ploughed. It is very curious that crows do not frequent human habitations in that country. As I have said, what forcibly strikes an Indian as he passes through Britain, Belgium or France is the scrupulous neatness of the country. No rank weed, no rotting vegetation, no filthy ditch meets his eye. Every where the land bears testimony to careful industry and good taste.

As they have made their country, so they have made their dwelling houses. In large mansions the long avenue of trees, which have joined their leafy boughs above your head, is a sight worth seeing, the beauty of which is sometimes enhanced by a murmuring rill that runs in the neighbourhood. The roads and parterres are metalled with stones and gravels of different colours, on the side of which are laid out flower-beds of that diversified arrangement which only a scientific gardener knows how to do. Occasionally thick bushes have been allowed to run wild, which form a pleasing contrast to the surrounding order and regularity. A sloping ridge may also have been taken advantage of to allow large trees to grow in their mountainous wildness. Hiding themselves among these trees the cuckoo loves to coo and the thrush to sing. I have not seen a cuckoo in that country, but I have often heard its cooing. It is not like the voice of our cuckoo—the continuous cooo, cooo, cooo. The voice of the cuckoo in England is more grave and solid, and the cooing comes at longer intervals. It is so different from ours that when I first heard it, I had to ask a friend—"What bird is that there?" Of course all these singing birds come to England only in summer. The stones have all been removed from the ground under these trees and in their stead plaster-of-Paris heads of comical and uncouth shapes are promiscuously and thickly strewn. Moss has grown over them, so that from a distance you would take them for real stones, and would not notice their comical aspect without a closer inspection. Lakes also lie unkempt with thick rushes on their banks among which the wild ducks make their nest, and the broad round leaves of the lily peacefully lay on their bosom, in the midst of which a solitary flower may be seen here and there resting in a drooping attitude on its long peduncle. Near the house there are the tennis-ground and other green plots where the young folks sport, while the old people look on sitting on rustic benches placed on the sides, and listen to the soothing music of a fountain that spurts from a high pedestal among the flower-beds close by. The whole ground is studded with marble statues, new and old, Italian and Greek. I have spoken of hothouses, palm-houses and fern-houses where tropical plants are reared. In the hothouses, bunches of muscatel and other varieties of grapes can be seen almost all the year round in all stages towards ripening. Attached to the mansion may be a conservatory where sitting near the gurgling fountain among the green plants, with the transparent glass roof overhead, you can smoke and meditate. Or you may pass on to the adjoining billiard room where, before you go to bed, you can watch for a short while the sleek ivory balls rolling against each other and childishly clap your hands with delight at a smart hit. In the meantime the sound of a piano may be reaching your ears from the Drawing Room on the other side, where a young lady in her evening dress, looking like the presiding angel of all celestial flowers, is engaged in bringing down the sweet harmony of heaven into this mundane world. Nowhere is the love of beauty and art more profusely and lavishly displayed than in the embellishment of this sitting room. The cushioned chairs and sofas, the tables and other furniture are the very perfection of elegance and comfort. The mantelpiece, the niches and corners are all tastefully filled with beautiful curios from all parts of the world. And what marvel of beauty are those window curtains ? And would you not also look up and follow the golden lines, the flowers and the figures with which the ceiling is decorated ? Or would you rather look down and admire the soft thick carpet under your feet wondering what ingenuity could bring forth from the loom those delicate interwoven patterns ? Some say that good singers have generally an ill-favoured exterior. Ah ! you would not think so if you had seen the beauty and superior finish of that wood and ivory piano which all this time has been charming your ears with peals of sweet music, while a large bouquet of flowers of various colours quietly sitting on an exquisitely ornamental vase has been busy to shed the freshest and richest perfume all over the room. Means for enriching your mind are not wanting either, for the library is filled with thousands of volumes collected from generation to generation. But they seem to invite you only to look at their superb binding, done in styles borrowed from all the world, and appear to say—"Pray, for goodness' sake don't open me, for I am not so beautiful to look at inside." And the family pictures, representing the scions of the house for several centuries, what a mint of money they must have cost ! In the dining room cleanliness is more studied than art ; but yet in every trifling detail that love of beauty which has now become inherent in the nation comes out in all its conspicuousness. A cloth of the most snowy whiteness without the faintest trace of any spot covers the table, on which are arranged plants and cut flowers, silver dishes of dazzling beauty with chased patterns, cruet-stands, goblets, decanters and all sorts of necessaries. Compare it with our mode of taking meals. The contrast in our disfavour is so great that it would be madness to think of any comparison at all. We are at fault even in the minutest details. Take for instance the salt that is on the table. What a nice salt-cellar it is that holds it, the nice little silver spoon to take it with, and for comparison with the whiteness and purity of the substance itself one can only think of loose unsullied snow that covers the swampy lands of Netherlands Holland in the depth of winter. Think how you take salt in this country, where it is put, and with what it gets mixed. Then in Europe they do not touch or give anything with the hand. It is extremely bad manners to give even a cigar to any one with your hand. In the matter of food, this custom is followed to a certain extent in South India. But in Bengal, one gets sickened to see how food is handled in time of feasts, in native hotels and in confectionery shops. The different dishes from which you eat the different courses of the dinner are ornamented with various kinds of designs, which would sometimes teach you the geography of Britain, natural history, architecture and the style in which various old castles in England are built. The very food itself is shaped and arranged in artful designs. In this country a rude attempt is made in this direction in the make of our sweetmeats, but as in everything else, the art has been carried to perfection in Europe. I would not have dwelt on this subject so long if this anxiety to be neat and clean and to possess materials for comfort and ease, combined with refined magnificence and unostentatious beauty, were confined only to the wealthy classes. On the contrary this is observed among all classes, and all strive to make themselves and everything around them as much refined as their means would permit. In this matter the difference between the English and ourselves is that there they earnestly wish it and laboriously work for it, whereas we here do not seem to wish for it and certainly do not work for it. Here, if one has not the means to pay for his wash, he goes in dirty clothes; in England one similarly situated would do the washing at home. The standard of respectability is still low in this country. In my opinion the greatest achievement of European civilisation lies in the fact that it has placed the means of enjoying material comfort within the reach of every honest worker not only in Europe but in all parts of the globe.

What interested me therefore in English life is the higher standard of living as compared with that of the Indian people. Love of comfort combined with beauty rules the English heart. They know better than we how to live well, and how to secure the means to live well. Instead of shunning the good things as so many traps to ensnare poor humanity, they gratefully accept them and exercise their faculties to improve them for their benefit. They have not allowed the drowning property of the water, the burning property of the fire, or the thorn of the rose to scare them away from the rightful use of such substances. Long ago, they came to know that asceticism is fanaticism, and fanaticism is insanity. They all ask for comfort and beauty, and there is a keen competition to supply this universal demand. Comfort and beauty thus come to be cheap, and within the reach of the lowly and the poor. That demand in this country can only be dimly perceived in a hazy form in the distant future. To an oriental, however, the artistic surroundings of English life seem to have too much of method in them, and therefore look stiff and tiring. As if all things have received an impress of the strong character of the English constitution. Artistic beauty there glares upon you like a full blown rose, and does not know like a bashful bud how softly to peep through emerald leaves in all its maidenly sweetness. Such is our art. But, oh my countrymen! do not glory in it. It is rather our misfortune that we can yet produce such art. For it is all poetry, a fairy dream delineated in all its picturesque sweetness. Such poetry ill-fits this hard hungry world, which plucks the sweet lotus and would not allow it to play with the Zephyr on the blue bosom of the wide lake, fleeces and slaughters the sporting lamb that does no harm, shoots the soft-eyed gazelle, and enchains the mild elephant that browses like a cloud on our hillside jungles. Prosy wakefulness thrives in this world of ours, my countrymen! not the trance of poetry; so when prose in the shape of steam and mechanism is the master of millions, poetry in the shape of hatchised chisel hardly gets five rupees a month, a handful of millets or rice to stay the pangs of hunger, and a two-penny date-leaf mat to lie down upon on a cold night. Our art is doomed to die and it ought to die, if it cannot earn more than ten shillings a month. The destruction of Indian art-manufactures will be coeval with the increase in the value of labour. At any rate Indian art-manufactures as an industry can no longer be of material advantage to this country to any appreciable extent. Modern mechanism would also help in its destruction. Lancashire has destroyed fine muslins, Paisley Kashmir shawls of the finest patterns, and Birmingham now threatens metal manufactures. Eventually it involves both the original and the imitation in common ruin.

As an illustration of the way in which the artistic instinct of the English people finds vent in every detail of life, I would mention the card which invited us to a Ball given by the Lord Mayor in honour of the Colonials and Indians, and which was held in the Guildhall on Friday, the 25th June 1886. This card is a regular picture by itself, so I have got it mounted and intend to preserve it as a memento of the occasion. The character of the design is oriental. On all sides it is bounded with a fringe that might have been copied from a cornice in the palace of Harun-al-Rashid. Next come the border, ground-worked with fifty-two species of Indian and Colonial flowers all shining in their natural colours. Among these may be noticed the *Acmena elliptica* or the Lilly Pilly of Sydney, *Swainsona greyana* or the Poison Pea of the Darling River, *Coptis trifolia* or the Gold

Thread of Canada, *Cissampelos Pareira* or the Velvet Leaf of the West Indies, *Citrus limonum* or the Lemon tree of West Africa, *Vitis vinifera* or the Black Grape of Cape Town and *Viola odorata*, the Banafshá of Upper India. These flowers have formed a framework for the Arms and Names of the various Colonies. Cyprus heads the list on the left, then comes under it Canada, Malta, Cape of Good Hope and Natal. Further down, a harbour with a large sailing vessel and fishing boats, a rocky shore with an outline of clouds in the far distance, all arranged in an uncoloured circle, represent Cape Town. Under it successively come West Indies, British Guiana, West Africa, New Foundland, Falkland Islands and New Guinea, which closes the list on the left. On the right, arranged in a style which in Saracenic architecture is called the "Reply" or the *Jawáb*, come Mauritius in "answer" to Cyprus. Then come New Zealand having in its Arms figures of two men, one holding a pair of scales and the other a staff. Then Hong-Kong, New South Wales and Queensland. For the *Jawáb* to Cape Town we have on the right the harbour of Sydney with a large steam vessel, and a domed palace, and churches and buildings on a well-wooded shore. Straits Settlements, North Borneo, Ceylon, Victoria, Australia and Fiji come under Sydney and finish the right side of the card. At the top, a picture of London is given on the right and that of the Guildhall on the left. Between these two stand the Arms of the city of London supported on the one side by a London Rifle Volunteer and an Australian Volunteer, while on the other an English Guardsman and a Native Indian Soldier mount guard. The National and Royal Standards appear at the back, and at the base of the group is a portion of the Canadian Arms, *viz.*, the Rose, the Shamrock and the Thistle, with the words *Domine Dirige Nos.* printed under it. In the lower border a picture of the town of Ottawa occupies the left side, and on the right is that of Calcutta with the Government House, the Maidan and the Ochterlony Monument. Between these two are the Arms of the Lord Mayor and the Sheriffs. The ground in the centre of the card has an Indian arch on the top supported by two ribbed columns. On one side of it is an aboriginal Red Indian from America, alongside a Negro with a basket of pine-apples. Further back, under a tree-fern, stand two Kangaroos on their hind feet near two lambs and a pair of Emu. On the other side, an Indian Syce stands near an Australian rider with his horse. Further back, a tiger-hunting scene, an elephant and two tigers. In the middle of the card are the words of the Invitation. The card is chromo-printed.

As mentioned before, the Ball took place on the 25th of June 1886. It was a grand affair, in which about six thousand people took part, the elite of London society, besides the Colonials and Indians. The guests were presented in due form to the Lord Mayor, the Right Honourable John Staples, F.S.A. The dancing commenced at nine. I cannot say anything about the dancing, because I do not know it and do not understand it. I looked on, and occasionally introduced myself to those who, like me, did not take part in the dance. The dancing lasted the whole night.

We were invited to the Tallow Chandlers' Hall to see an amateur dramatic performance. I saw many such performances in my own country, but these cannot be compared with what I witnessed in London. It is impossible to conceive how without a professional training the ladies and gentlemen, who acted in the performance, could play their parts so admirably. Even the London audience, accustomed to see the best of such things, were enraptured at the superior skill displayed by the amateurs in representing the various parts of the plot. We also went to the various London theatres—The Lyceum, the Savoy, the Drury Lane, the Adelphi, the Globe, the Gaiety, the Princess,' the Comedy, the Hay-market, the Strand, the Covent Garden, the Avenue, and various others to which free tickets were kindly given to us. I have not the power to describe these theatres. I can only say that, compared to them, those we have got in Beadon Street, are mere child's play. Not only those in Beadon Street, but even English theatres in Calcutta, Madras and Bombay.

Nothing more is necessary to shew the length of distance that separates the Indian from the European than the theatres in the two countries. The distance is very great. But, alas! I cannot convince a certain section of my countrymen of this. Ignorance is nothing if it is not a firm notion of illimitable infallible wisdom. The pity is that only one hundred years ago the Europeans and Indians were almost in the same stage of social advancement, and it is only within this time, or I may say only within the last fifty years, that they have made such rapid strides as to leave us far behind. We are advancing no doubt, but at a snail's pace, while they are going at railway speed. Of course all this magnificence is possible in England where wealth flows from all parts of the world. But in broken, fallen, impoverished France, how is it possible to maintain such a splendid place of amusement as the Eden Theatre in Paris? Austria does not get any foreign tribute, but how can she have such a place as the Bungtheatre in Vienna? Even poor Italy, how can she have those opera houses at Venice, Florence and Rome? Our land is more fruitful than these, thought I, as I looked on the vine-yards of France, the rye-fields of Germany, the pine-forests of Bohemia and the olive-gardens of South Italy, and yet we are so poor. The Australian aborigines lived from time immemorial in sheds got up in half an hour from fresh-cut branches, had no other covering to protect them from cold except a Kangaroo skin, and the pangs of hunger were so gnawing as to compel them to eat worms and other loathsome things. Most of them yet live in that state of poverty and starvation. Yet in the hands of the Europeans the same land has been made so fruitful! I wonder whether among these Polynesians, economists have not by this time sprung up to lay down, with the utmost gravity and lucidity, the principle that the poverty and hunger of these aboriginal races are solely due to the amount of wealth taken away by the English from their country. We here are all economists of that description.

I know, I am treading what is for me a very dangerous ground, little as I know of this most intricate subject. But it is my misfortune not to be satisfied with a hasty look on one side of the shield. I must go round and see what the other side is like. With all humility, therefore, I will state here what I see on the other side. I have no book of reference with me, but I call from memory the fact that instead of gold and silver being drained from the country, we receive annually about ten crores of rupees worth of these precious metals, which are not re-exported but hoarded in the country. In that part of the country from which I come gold was very scarce thirty years ago, and the women had to be content with shell, lac, glass, brass or at best silver ornaments, but now even the low classes wear golden jewellery. We buy these ten millions (sterling pounds) worth of gold and silver out of the 85 millions worth of raw produce annually sent out of the country. Out of the remaining 75 millions, we buy 34 millions of things which in the ordinary course of trade we must get in exchange from foreign countries. Again, out of the remaining 41 millions we purchase cotton goods to the value of 24 millions, and pay from the ordinary revenue 17 millions for home charges. The average for the last six years was 19 crores, difference being made up by borrowing. The loss to the country is in these two items. We send to foreign countries about 17 millions worth of raw cotton, yarn, &c., and get back 24 millions of manufactured cotton, difference 7 millions, from which has to be deducted the interest on capital laid out on the manufactory and machinery. Or say 5 millions we pay to England as value of labour to make our clothing, which, if we could make them ourselves, might have remained in this country. Then the other item of 17 millions which England takes from us for home charges includes,—besides the cost of civil and military administrations, furlough allowances and pensions, and the savings of officials living in India—the interest on money lent to this country for construction of railways and other works of public utility. Such interest is paid to England by almost all foreign countries except America, and I wish England had lent us more money at 4 per cent. interest and this money been spent on railways in the interior of the country. Taking all this into consideration, I hardly think that the sum which England takes out of India and which could have been kept within India had India been a self-governed country, exceeds more than 15 millions a year. But against this sum must be set (1) about eight millions which England earned by compelling China to take our opium, which we could not have done ; (2) the increased production of raw materials by bringing large areas of land under cultivation due to the establishment of peace, the railways, and the impetus to trade which England has given ; (3) the value of the great power of the British Empire at our back to protect us from foreign aggression. If we give their due weight to all these calculations, I think it will be possible to see that our connection with England has not resulted in such a loss to us in a pecuniary point of view as many suppose both in England and India. I state this as my opinion with considerable diffidence, for I have not sufficiently studied the subject and possess a very imperfect knowledge of its details. I however mention this because I am not aware of such a credit having ever been given to England.

In former times all the money was collected in capital towns, like Delhi and Lucknow, and spent there, and in the pompous pageantry displayed in the courts, people saw the manifestation of wealth. It was a splendid sight, the Great Mogul on his Peacock Throne bedecked with gems of inestimable value, with the Grand Vizier prostrate before him, courtiers with clasped hands all around, and the executioner ready with his axe standing on his left side. Those glories have been described. But what has history to do with the millions that tilled, and sowed and reaped and starved for ever and ever? History has not said whether these millions had, before the English came into the country, more clothing on their back, more chattels in their hovels, and more gold on their person. We can only infer that they had more grain in their barn-houses, but yet Muhammadan historians constantly speak of famines as devastating as the last Madras famine, when human beings ate the putrid flesh of human beings. I have seen the beautiful picture of Indian peasant-life in the last century drawn by Holwell, Verlest and the authorities on which Burke founded his famous panegyric on human happiness in Bengal. But, apart from the sentimental influences that guided not a little the hand of these painters to give the picture a hue somewhat of the rosy kind, and apart from the justly favourable impression that rude plenty made in their minds by contrast with the squalid misery they witnessed on all sides in their own country, it seems to me that their knowledge of India was superficial, at least limited only to the outlying Districts on the seacoast, where there was more land than men to cultivate and keep its exuberant fertility under control, and where therefore the vampires that sucked them dry higher up were more at the mercy of the peasants than they of them. Yet, notwithstanding this sufficiency of land, this fertility of the soil, and the rude plenty as a natural consequence, we find the loss of a single crop result in 1770 in a catastrophe of a most heart-rending description, destroying, as if by one fell stroke, one-third of the whole population of Bengal. It has yet to be proved that the people were better off in former days than they are now, and that they had more grain at the time than the purchasing power of grain which they now possess, but unfortunately we have no reliable record of their condition in those days. Unfortunately too we have not yet learnt that the few upper classes do not form the nation, and that high and low, all individuals are so many units of the nation. National wealth is more evenly distributed now, hence we do not see it. But yet we are very poor compared with most of the European nations, and the cause of that poverty is not to be found in the drain of gold and silver said to be carried on by the English Government, but in the demoralised, stagnate condition of our national character. If the incidence of trade-value per head is an index to the material prosperity of a people, then that of India is surprisingly small compared with other nations. The average trade-value of India is only 12 shillings per head, while that of Great Britain and Ireland is 350 shillings. France has 168s, Germany 145s, and United States 105s. I forget the figures for Holland and Belgium, but I think they are greater even than that of Great Britain.

We now require to be taught how to increase the quantity, quality and value of individual produce. Practically, at present, we have in this country only the product of unskilled unintelligent labour to represent our national income. What was formerly skilled labour has now come to be reduced to the level of unskilled labour. The changes that have been wrought by science, education and fostering laws in the position of skilled labour in civilised countries have not yet found their way to India. Here, little difference is perceptible between the material condition of a village blacksmith or carpenter and that of an agricultural labourer, the training and requirements in both cases demanding only practice and experience, no great intelligence or expenditure of money, and the remuneration in each case representing almost only the value of manual labour. What we require are remuneration and prospects for intelligent and expensive training with, if absolutely necessary, a moderate amount of capital to begin with. We now require to be shewn remunerative ways for the exercise of body and mind and capital combined, instead of for body only. Many of the artificial obstructions that stood in the way of intelligence and education employing themselves in productive labour have now been practically removed. Caste-system has come to disregard old notions of respectability or disrespectability attached to trades, and in defiance of all its traditional instincts has learnt to recognise respectability only in education and wealth, no matter the kind of trade they are brought to bear upon. Unchanging and immutable as we seem to be, love of comfort, wealth and power has always been with us, as with other nations in the world, a great dissolvent of social and religious ordinances, whenever they dared raise their adamantine wall against the natural aspirations of the human mind. Such ordinances break like crockery whenever they come in collision with the iron laws of nature. The dawn of our history first shed its dim light on such seemingly adamantine ordinances looming in the misty horizon, but, behold, not far off the great dissolvent hard at work corroding its way through all bars and barriers. Nothing has made the world more false to itself and more false to its creed than religious doctrines teaching to despise wealth and power. The human world acts not as a free agent in its mad struggles for wealth and power, nor in its cringing servility to wealth and power. A transcendental mind may smile at my remark; but I am speaking of the world, not of transcendental minds, which are above the world. We saw hard rules carefully reared against a Bráhman's bearing arms, yet a Parasu-Rám thrice-seven times destroys with his axe the arrogant warrior-caste, men, women and children, which dared raise its voice against the encroachments of the priestly race, and latterly a reverend Bráhman like Drona fights on the side of injustice in return for luxurious food and raiment. The earlier one you have deified and the latter one you have placed among the greatest heroes of Hindu history. Another dishonourable trade for a Bráhman is the profession of a clerk. Yet what do we see thousands of Bráhmans doing to-day? I will not name other trades the high castes now follow in defiance of all rules and regulations to the contrary. Thus Respectability has now come down from her lofty pedestal, and the way has been cleared for the employment of intelligence, education and capital on productive labour. The question now is how to employ intelligence, education and capital profitably. Unfortunately, very little attention has been directed towards the solution of this most difficult problem. Most of the agitation that is now going on in the country is of an extremely chaotic character. Its foundation is unstable, its purposes vague, its plans often unmatured, unwise and incoherent. The Indian mind delights to revel in its search for the unattainable. Those are not far wrong who say that under the superficial western gloss you perceive the eastern condition of mind in all its intensity. One of the principal traits of that condition is its inability to look beyond the immediate. Organisms in this condition stand but a poor chance in their competition with those who, in addition to their mastery over the immediate, can also grasp and mould to their will the mediate and the exmediate. They who take the vast deep ocean at the sweep of a glance can but smile at the over-busy ripples which the Shallow cunningly raises on her breast to hide the loose sand just beneath. Oh, my poor little Shallow! in vain are those playful ripplets! They can no more make you the deep ocean, than the power of elegant diction can make me an ancient Greek or a Roman. A good deal of dredging is necessary both for you and me, and it is to this dredging-business we should both pay our first attention. A faint power of discernment of the rightful sources from which authority and position are naturally to flow is now perceptible amongst us. Fostering hands are required to tenderly nourish this embryo, and sober minds to guide it into its rightful cause when it grows up to vigorous working condition. In the meantime we constantly keep before our mind the great aphorism:—" It is madness, and downright contradiction, to think that those things which never have been done as yet, can be done except by means never as yet tried." O Francis Bacon! what a mighty truth hast thou confined in these simple words!

We went to the Lyceum Theatre where "Faust" was being played at the time. Mr. Henry Irving, the celebrated actor, played the part of Mephistopheles and Miss Ellen Terry, the famous actress that of Margaret. The Lyceum Theatre is a fine building, with a corinthian portico surmounted by a dome and a balustrade. The interior is elegantly decorated and painted by able hands. It can accommodate about five thousand persons, and every night it was more than full. The theatre opened at 8 P.M., but every evening the door-way leading to the pit was crammed to suffocation, and thus jammed to each other a large number of people patiently waited from 6 till the time when the door was opened. The names of Mr. Henry Irving and Miss Ellen Terry and the wonderful scenes displayed on the stage, that every night brought to the Lyceum such a large multitude of people. The scenes were really wonderful, a triumph of science and human ingenuity. They shewed how far man succeeded to usurp the power hitherto attributed to supernatural beings. There sat Mephistopheles, in the midst of a thousand-tongued flame, caressing it as his most friendly element! Then there were the Devil's Kitchen where fallen, woe-begone skeleton spirits cooked, boiled and roasted fiery, loathsome things every moment of their existence; the duel in which the Devil's sword flashed liquid lightning; the burning volcano with its lava and hot cinder; the devil's dance; and lastly the angels from heaven, with hands outstretched for the dead Margaret. At the Drury Lane Theatre we saw "Human Nature." Morning with the rising sun, night with the full moon, a cloudy heaven with thunder and lightning, the mountains of Soudan, Trafalgar Square and other scenes were so vividly shewn here that they seemed quite natural. It is said that Mr. Henry Irving spent £20,000 to make the necessary alterations in the stage to bring in "Faust." At the Alhambra a large number of girls could be seen dancing all at once. There must have been more than a hundred, but I forget the exact number. It was quite a fairy scene, weird and dazzling, the like of which I never saw in my own country. At the Savoy Theatre the Mikado was being played at the time.

CHAP. V. AN AGRICULTURAL EXCURSION.

I think many of my countrymen must have seen this piece in the Indian theatres, but here they have hardly seen the best of it. I saw the same piece played at Oxford, but nothing like that in London.

An agricultural excursion into the country was arranged for the Colonials and Indians, through the kindness of the Duke of Bedford. They were invited to see the Crawley Farm and the Experimental Field at Woburn, where trials of various kinds are conducted under the management of the Royal Agricultural Society of England. The Abbey, the Duke's home farm and his parks and gardens at Woburn were also included in the programme. On Wednesday, the 23rd June, 1886, a special train with the guests of the Duke steamed out of Euston Station for Ridgmont. It ran through a very fine country, fresh and green with summer vegetation, among which quietly slept the golden sunshine, dreaming of wheat and barley, of strawberries and raspberries and of apples and pears, which it had yet to ripen. Oh, how innocent it looked! It was full of smiles, and seemed to know not what sunstroke is, the deceitful thing! Or the simoom that madly careers among moving mountains of sand from Morocco to Arabia, and sends caravan camels down on their knees to escape the pestilential breath. Or the burning blasts that roar over the plains of India, devouring the grass on the fields, withering the leaves on the trees and starving the mother cow that gives us milk. Or the long drought that brings famine, kills millions, and reduces the country to a howling desert. It seemed to know no such wicked things. It seemed to know only to sport among the ripples in the lake, to kiss the laughing lily, to redden the cheek of the plump peach turned towards it, to suffuse with a crimson glow the face of the artless maiden on the fields, to make the birds sing among the thick wood, and to gladden the heart of the world. Or to invite those fat rosy boys to come out and put off their hats and coats, and heartily go at cricket on the village green, and thoroughly enjoy the holiday given to them in honour of the Colonials and Indians. Or to tempt the farmer's sorrowful daughter, left at home to look after the baby, to take her stand behind the curtain, above the trellis entwined with rose, and have a peep into the rushing train that whistled past the snug little cottage, while papa and mamma, Charlie and Ann, had gone in their Sunday clothes to wait at the railway gate, and when the time came to hurrah and hurrah and wave and wave their hats and handkerchiefs, at their white and red, brown and sable brethren from many lands. For it was a holiday the Duke gave to his people in honour of his guests. Ardent and vociferous were the out-bursts of welcome that greeted us on our way, and the nearer we approached our destination, the thicker was the crowd and the warmer the welcome. Carriages were kept ready to meet the arrival of the train at Ridgmont which took us to the Crawley Farm and thence to the Experimental Field. The Secretary to the Royal Agricultural Society and a gentleman of great celebrity as an agricultural chemist explained to us the method and object of the various trials there going on for some years. We then drove through the Park to the Park Farm where we saw very fine cattle of many breeds. The guests of the Duke were hungry by this time, and they were therefore made to alight at the West Front of Woburn Abbey where a magnificent repast was served to them. The Duke himself presided at the luncheon and the customary speeches were made. After lunch the visitors under the guidance of the Marquis of Tavistock (the Duke's son) were shewn over the Abbey, where the family pictures are kept. Among these pictures were several by eminent artists. After the Abbey was seen, the guests enjoyed themselves wandering about the gardens until six in the evening, when the posthorn summoned them to their carriages. They took the special train at Flitwick which left for St. Pancras Station, London, at 6-30.

I was rather disappointed at the way experiments were conducted at Woburn. Where could one expect to see a perfect system if not in England? All that man has known up to date is present there in its best condition, and the brightest of human intellect is always busy to use, guide, control and improve the inheritance of man. In agriculture, as in other things the most expert and enthusiastic hobbyists are at work. Yet, to my mind, there appeared to be serious flaws at the very basis of the work I silently heard explained at Woburn. It is the misfortune of agricultural experiments to want in most cases intelligence, experience, persistence and patience. By a judicious exercise of these qualities alone can the foundation be laid on which trials are to have a firm basis to produce trustworthy results.

But experimenters are always in a hurry to prove a preconceived theory. They often forget to lay down a reliable basis on which to rest their executive operations. Curious results follow, and for all blame the scapegoat weather is made answerable. Comparative agricultural experiments, instead of being jumbled up into one chaotic mass, should in my opinion be divided into two distinct series of operations. The preliminary operation, which I have spoken of as the fundamental basis, should aim at bringing about a continued sameness of circumstances in lands to be subjected to different modes of treatment, to find out their respective values. If two acres of land are manured, one with cowdung and the other with oil-cake in order to ascertain their respective manurial values, from the produce of wheat sown upon them, the utmost care should first of all be taken to preclude the possibility of the difference in outturn being accountable to any other circumstance than the superiority or inferiority of any of the two manures. The soil and the surrounding circumstances of the two plots of land should be made exactly the same. All agricultural experimenters see to that in a rough way, but they have not the patience to prove it.

To our ordinary judgment the soil and other circumstances may appear to be the same, but we can little know of other things that lie beyond the power of our calculation, and which can only be proved, found out and provided for or guarded against by a course of preliminary experiments. I am almost sure that if a crop is grown on two plots of unmanured land, of which the soil and attendant circumstances are identical to the best of our judgment, there will be still some difference in the outturn. That difference must be destroyed before the actual experiments to ascertain the value of the two manures are undertaken. Then as the trial must have to be continued for some years, the fields must be made quite independent of all variations in the weather. A shower a week before or after the crop has attained a certain stage of growth makes all the difference in the outturn. In England where they have all the aid which science can give, where they have got the means and the will, where they grow areca-palm under a glass roof, it is not impossible to maintain year after year the same temperature, humidity and moisture in the fields operated upon. I know, it is very bold of me to criticise the work of men who are far superior to me in knowledge of such matters. But that sufficient care was not taken in the Woburn experiments to lay down the preliminary basis, I have indicated above, is shewn by the result of a continued experiment to prove the comparative value of decorticated cotton-cake and maize-meal manures, in their natural state, and also of their chemical equivalents. It is a fact proved long ago by that surest of all proofs, *viz.*, the judgment of the ignorant cultivators, that decorticated cotton-cake has a very high manurial value compared with maize-meal. The estimated money value of the one is £5-13-0 per ton, while that of the other is £1-5-1. More valuable results from land treated with decorticated cotton-cake were therefore expected than from land treated with maize-meal manure. The experiments were

continued for nine years, *i.e.*, from 1877 to 1885, with the object of obtaining a further and more scientific confirmation of the superiority of the cotton-cake manure. But year after year, in crop after crop in the rotation followed in the experiment, the outturn per acre did by no means bring out the superiority of cotton-cake manure. The experimenters were astonished. *Then* they sought for an explanation. They say—
" In searching for an explanation of this unexpected result it has been suggested, and indeed there is strong evidence in the experiments themselves for believing, that this is due to the large amount of unexhausted manure in the soil, and that owing to this, and the consequent accumulation of nitrogen, the maximum crop the land is capable of producing has been obtained by the use of the additional maize-meal, or its artificial equivalent, the richer cotton-cake being thus unable to show its superiority." Now, if the comparative value of the two manures, whether natural or artificial, were not previously known, what conclusion could be drawn from the results of the Woburn experiments? The unnatural and mischievous conclusion from the nine years' careful experiments conducted under the Royal Agricultural Society of England would be that maize-meal manure was in no way inferior to the cotton-cake manure. Again, it can be proved from the outturn yielded by a plot of unmanured land, on which wheat was sown year after year, that results of scientific precision cannot be secured unless variations in the weather are guarded against. Thus the produce of dressed corn on an acre of unmanured land was as follows from 1877 to

CHAP. V.   RESULTS OF EXPERIMENTS.   243

1885 :—1877—22·5 Bushels ; 1878—15·8 B. ; 1879—10·1 B. ; 1880—9·6 B. ; 1881—25·7 B. ; 1882—12 B. ; 1883—16 B. ; 1884—23 B. ; 1885—21·2 B. The figures from 1877 to 1880 seemed quite natural, for they shewed gradual exhaustion of land by continual cropping. Then all at a jump the outturn came up to the unprecedented figure of 25·7 bushels, and after that the irregularity continued in a more or less marked degree. There was a slight deterioration in the fulness of the grain : the weight per bushel was 61·8 lbs. in the first year, which though varied greatly in subsequent years never again attained that figure. It was 55·2 lbs. in 1885. Was the increase and decrease in produce due to seasonable and unseasonable weather ? Then all that I can say is that absolute reliance cannot be placed on the result of an experiment undertaken to prove the value of one thing while another very powerful agency is at work to cause all sorts of anomalies. It pains me to speak lightly of a series of experiments conducted under the auspices of such eminent men, especially when I visited the place as a guest. But experiments are made in this country, and I hope they will be made on a more extensive scale as education advances and their value appreciated. I feel it therefore my duty to point out the misleading circumstances which, as far as possible, should be provided against, otherwise the value of such trials will be greatly diminished. Notwithstanding these defects, the Woburn experiments have yielded very valuable results. Among other things they have proved in a most unmistakable way the great importance of artificial manures with a topdressing of ammonia salts. All these experiments are mainly due to the liberality of the Duke of Bedford, who has placed about 127 acres of land at the disposal of the Royal Agricultural Society for the purpose. I have stated the defects that occurred to me in the Woburn experiments. But in such operations they have in England the advantage of continuity which succeeding generations can maintain there in the work of their fathers. Otherwise, a single life will be too short for the exploration of those secrets which nature carefully keeps hidden in her bosom, as priceless gems to bestow only on her most deserving sons. In this sphere, such a son is Sir John Bennet Lawes, the father of agricultural experiments. I have not seen his operations carried on at Rothamstead. Mr. Ford, of the "Mark Lane Express," I think, once wanted to take me there, but I could not make time for the trip.

With many scientific men improvement in agriculture is a hobby. Ordinary men may laugh at it, but a hobby is not for ordinary men. They have *likings*. Europe and America have derived inestimable benefits from *hobbies*, or call it speciality if you like. But a hobby is more than a speciality. It is the earnest unwearied devotion to, and the power to enjoy insatiable pleasure in, a certain subject, a feeling often bordering on insanity, that has led to those wonderful discoveries to which the world owes not a little of its modern progress. We have no such hobbies here, and to that is chiefly due our present mediocrity. No discoveries, no inventions, no world-wide reputation. Our hobby is religion; sometimes it is more than a hobby, it is insanity. Happily, society worships insanity in religion. Is religion our hobby because we are a weak race? For we find that in every country the weaker sex, the sick and the infirm are always highly religious. Following this course of nature, the strong in all ages and in all countries in order to be more religious made themselves artificially weak by starvation and penances. As with the weak in body, so with the weak in spirit. It is the solacing shelter for the bereaved, the disappointed, the oppressed and the persecuted. It is no doubt the soothing remedy for sore heart like that of Monte Cristo in prison, or of that pining wretch whose story was narrated to me by the guide who led me through the subterranean cells under the Doges' Palace at Venice. A large section of my countrymen has the hobby to bring about at their own pleasure the mortification of mind and body which prepares one fully to enjoy the benefits of that remedy. Any other hobby my people have not. It is impossible for them to have any other hobby, considering how early they are heavily burdened with family cares. To turn our heart to our God is good; but religion becomes insanity both in its morbid form of sombre mysticism and in its raving state of violent fanaticism. Of the two forms of insanity, I would prefer the latter.

The Countess of Rosebery invited us to her London residence near the Foreign Office, the Duchess of Westminster to her town mansion near the Hyde Park, the Marquis of Salisbury to Hatfield, and the Duke of Northumberland to a Garden Party at Sion House. Up to 1874, the Duke's London residence was the Northumberland House in the Strand. This edifice was demolished in that year for the sake of street improvements, and the Duke then made Sion House his town residence. It is in the Suburbs, near the Kew Gardens, a few miles to the west of London. There was a stone lion at the top of the Northumberland House, which has now been removed to Sion House. A curious story is related about this lion, which shews how people are credulous all over the world. Once, a man gave out that he saw the lion wag its tail. Immediately a large crowd formed around the place to see the lion do it again. People flocked from a distance to witness this strange phenomenon, and all day long the street was so fully blocked that the police could scarcely keep it clear for traffic. But the proud animal disappointed the eager multitude. Even all the opera glasses and telescopes that were brought to bear upon it could not persuade it to move its tail again. Sion House has a history. It was formerly a monastery, founded by Henry V and dedicated to St. Saviour and St. Bridget of Sion. Henry VIII disestablished the "Daughters of Sion," and gave the estate to Protector Somerset who built the palace. It subsequently came into the possession of the Duke of Northumberland. From this place Lady Jane Grey went to the Tower of London to lay claim to the throne of England on the death of Edward VI, and hence also were taken the children of Charles I to St. James Palace to see their father before the execution.

At the special request of a friend, I went to Cambridge to see a University ceremony, that of conferring the LL.D. Degree to Sir George Birdwood, Sir Edward Buck and the Mahárájá of Narsingarh. A special train was provided for the journey. On our arrival we were taken charge of by a reception committee, formed jointly by the authorities of the town corporation and the University. They conducted us to the various places of interest, and when we were tired they took us to the Guildhall, where a magnificent banquet was held in honour of the guests. The University ceremony took place in the afternoon at the Senate House. This is a handsome building, Corinthian in style, of which the capitals of the columns and pilasters are said to have been made in imitation of those at the temple of Jupiter Stator at Rome. The ceiling is richly decorated and the floor is of black and white marble. We took our seat on the side of the dais which was occupied by the Vice Chancellor and other members of the University. The undergraduates, numbering many hundreds, sat in the galleries overhead, and from that place of vantage they directed against the University Authorities as well as against their Professors occupying the dais an incessant fire of chaffing and mirthful remarks indicating good humour and exuberant spirits. The Professors and the Doctors took the chaffing of the students with equal good humour, and of all the incidents of the ceremony we enjoyed this the most. The ceremony was opened by a speech from the Vice Chancellor. One by one, the gentlemen on whom the degree was conferred, were then brought to the dais and a Professor delivered a long oration in Latin, detailing the manifold qualities which earned for him the honor. The students frequently interrupted by their remarks, and the Professor smiling adroitly turned his discourse to answer the queries raised. Of course we could not understand all that he said, but could only gather a little of the substance of his speech. When the discourse was finished, the robe of honour was put upon the newly made Doctor. His place was then taken by another and the same ceremony gone through. The students were not yet satisfied: they wanted more speeches, but they did not get their wish.

We went to see the University Library, which contains upwards of 460,000 books besides many manuscripts. Thence we went to King's College, which was founded by Henry VI in 1441. Here we were taken over a beautiful Chapel, the many objects of interest in which our distinguished guides pointed out to us—the proportions of the building, the windows, the buttresses, the turrets and the well-designed parapets. But what I most admired were the coloured glass windows, on which biblical scenes were painted in artful designs. Among these might be seen the Birth of the Virgin, the Marriage of Joseph and Mary, the Annunciation, the Nativity, the Circumcision, the Adoration of the Magi, the Massacre of the Innocents, &c., &c. The paintings were executed between the years 1515 to 1531. After King's College, I visited two more colleges, in the compound of one of which a tree was shewn to me, said to have been planted by Milton. I plucked a leaf from it.

Messrs. Ransomes, Sims and Jeffries invited us to see the Orwell Works at Ipswich, where large quantities of agricultural machinery are every year made and despatched to all parts of the world. A special train, placed at our disposal by the Great Eastern Railway, took us to a place on the bank of the River Gipping opposite the town of Ipswich. We crossed the river by a steamer belonging to the Orwell Works. Standing on deck of this steamer, we could see the wide expanse of the German Ocean which is only twelve miles from Ipswich. On our arrival, we were first taken to the various places of interest of which the people of this town are justly proud. In Great Britain wherever I went I met with this "local" pride. "How do you like our little town?" they would always ask. They are justified to put such a question, for they set aside all private quarrels, and combine to work for the good of their towns and villages. They make large bequests for the construction of town halls and the establishment of libraries, museums and other institutions of permanent utility. Even such a small place as Ipswich can boast of a handsome Town Hall, built in the Renaissance style, of a Museum, a School of Science and Art, a Corn Hall, a Public Hall, an Art Gallery, an Arboretum, a Mechanics' Institute and Working Men's College. Among places of interest were shewn to us the "Sparrowe's House," a bit of old architecture where Charles II lay concealed after the battle of Worcester, and the Public House made famous by Charles Dickens by his making it the scene of one of the most important of Mr. Pickwick's nocturnal adventures. We were next taken to see the Orwell Works, which take their name from the River Orwell "of which the good people of Ipswich are so proud." They have got here a Foundry said to be one of the "largest, best lighted, and ventilated foundries in the country," where molten metal may be constantly seen pouring into ladles which are carried on trucks to the moulds. Here hundreds of thousands of ploughshares are turned out every year. While trucks were going on tramways both longitudinally and transversely from one part of the building to the other, overhead might be seen heavy cumbrous things noiselessly moving on travelling cranes. From the Foundry we passed on to the Smith's Shop, where a large number of furnaces are laid, on which bars and plates of iron are heated and then by one heavy blow shaped into any particular piece of an implement of which repetitions are required. Among various other things which are too numerous to relate, we were shown the working of a Steam Threshing Machine, specially adapted for use in hot countries. The representatives of the Firm provided a magnificent lunch for their guests. It is needless for me to say that they shewed us the utmost attention, for wherever we went they all tried to surpass each other in kindness and hospitality. Mr. Jeffries, Mrs. Jeffries and children were specially kind to us, for they had with them Mr. R. B. Mukharji, a high officer of the Kashmir State, specially sent there by His Highness the Mahárájá of Kashmir to learn agricultural engineering. They were enthusiastic in his praise. Mr. Jeffries,

Mrs. Jeffries and the children, they all requested me to convey to him their kindest regards. I asked the youngest child, a little girl of about four years, whether *she* had anything to say for that gentleman. She said—"Dive my love to Mr. Mukharji."

All the large towns in Great Britain invited the Colonials and Indians, and vied with each other to shew them the greatest amount of hospitality and kindness. Among these the reception given to them by the people of Manchester was one of the grandest and most magnificent. Nothing could exceed the liberality of this cosmopolitan city, where one hundred thousand men and women work day and night to produce those fabrics which now cover the tatooed body of the cannibals in the south, protect from cold the shivering Talmucks in the north, bedeck the fashionable lady of Yokohama in the east, and make the hood to cover the face of the Sioux warrior in the west. Could the persecuted barber Richard Arkwright, the watchmaker John Kay or the weaver James Hargreaves, ever dream that the water-frame and spinning jenny would be the means to revolutionise the weaving industry in the world, to bring untold wealth to England, and to be the remote cause of wars, conquests and taxes in many parts of the globe? Or could they think that their little inventions, at first misunderstood and spurned at, would in time produce numerous collateral industries, would bring to existence gigantic engineering and machinery works, extensive bleaching establishments, and various kindred manufacturing agencies? Yet all this has happened. I never saw a likeness of

Richard Arkwright, or of John Kay or James Hargreaves; nor of their equally persecuted predecessors in the same line, John Wyatt, Louis Paul, and Thomas Highs; nor of their successors, Crompton, the inventor of the mule spinning machine, Dyer, the inventor of the carding machine, Cartwright, Sharp, Roberts and Horrocks, the inventors and improvers of power looms, Johnson and Radcliffe, the inventors of the dressing machine, and Joshua Heilman, the inventor of the combing machine. Yet, I thought, I could bring to my mind both the sad desponding faces of the early pioneers and the triumphant bearing of later inventors and millowners, as I stood, down upon earth, a tiny little object, among lofty chimneys overlooking huge massive buildings, rising storey upon storey with countless windows, letting in light for numerous eyes that watched and guided the ever-moving spindle. Not only did our kind hosts of Manchester give us plenty of food and drink, put us up in the best of hotels and get up parties and conversaziones for our entertainment (which by the way they know how to do in right royal style), but what is more they placed intellectual enjoyment before our mind by allowing us the opportunity to see the weaving mills, the dyeing and printing industries, and the various engineering establishments which create a source of labour more cheap than that of the village weaver in India, who would be content with four pence a day as the joint earnings of himself, his wife and a couple of children.

Thus the seeds which half a dozen men sowed on British soil one hundred and twenty years ago speedily took root, flourished and fructified. They have produced wonderful results for Manchester, for Lancashire, for Great Britain, and, if you would forbear for a moment to look with a jaundiced eye, for the world at large. The same people have brought the same seeds here on the Indian soil, but among us they have fared as badly as straw-berry seedlings would fare among the burning sands of Sahara. Why? Because there is a difference between the national character of the two peoples. Almost the same difference that exists between a ten-thousand-spindle mill and the village-loom in India, between a railway train and a bamboo-made bullock cart, between a five-thousand-horse-power steamer and a country cargo boat. This may be exaggeration, but still it gives an idea of the difference that exists between the European national character and the Indian national character taken as a whole. It is very stupid of me no doubt, but I must confess that I have grave doubts that a representative governing body, if elected by the people of India to-day, would achieve that wonderful progress which European nations have achieved for themselves. I wonder what kind of men the people would elect, if they were entirely left to themselves. Anyhow, I fancy from what is going on in the country, a parliament distilled out of the people as they are to-day, would first of all take up the cow-killing question.

The prevention of cowslaughtering may be a very good thing and I have nothing to say against that. On the other hand as a Hindu and a Bráhman, and specially in deference to the feelings of a large section of my countrymen, I shall feel glad if the slaughter of cows can be prevented. I shall be gladder still if the slaughter of *all* animals either by man or other animals can be prevented, and if the whole universe be full of peace, amity and good-will, with no envy, war, pain, disease or death. But this is wishing to reconstruct the world according to my own fashion. I have, however, no plan, cut and dried, sufficiently perfect to reconcile all odds and ends into an unquestionable, uncriticisable harmony. I am therefore submissive, and look upon the cow-saving agitation as can only be attended with partial success in a simple insignificant community like that of the Todás, who are restrained by the Collector of the Nilgiris from sending a too large number of buffaloes with the departing soul of every patriarch of the race; or even among a more complex people possessing ample pasture lands to admit of an indefinite multiplication of its herds. It is amusing to see old Hinduism in her dotage crying for the moon, asking for little play-things which she cried for and got in her infancy three thousand years ago. But for the young Indian nationality it would be wise to ask for things suitable to the age. It would be wiser to ask only that which it was possible to get. It would be wiser still, under the present circumstances, to base all demands on such a clear open ground as to make it possible for suspicious eyes to see that no duplicity or dishonesty lay hidden underneath. The economical garb in which the cow-saving agitation has been clothed seems to be woven of a long yarn, but very flimsy in texture. On the very threshold of the question is the impossibility to imagine an endless supply of food for an endless number of cows, even paying no thought to the present state of cattle-fodder in the country, the rate of increase in the population, the progressive decrease in the uncultivated-cultivable area, and the increasingly rigorous conservation of forest tracts. It is impossible to conceive such an unlimited supply of cattle-food even if every human being and all other animals are turned out of India and the whole continent allowed to be filled with cows. Perhaps this difficulty has been provided for by the conclusion that the cows, by a process of slow starvation will, in a few generations, like trees in a Japanese toy garden, get reduced to the size of goats and learn to graze on gravel as the diminutive cattle of the Chota Nagpur plateau seem to do. Is there in the law of adaptation an unlimited scope for this dwarfing process to adjust the size of the cow to the ever-decreasing supply of grass and gravel? This little difficulty may have been satisfactorily disposed of by some such smashing argument, but the existing state of things suggests some other commonplace considerations which cannot be entirely removed out of sight. For instance, it is not quite understood who is the person to be restrained by repressive legislation from forcing the people to sell their cows for slaughter when, as proved by the agitators from their own facts and figures, it is more profitable for cow-keepers in an economical point of view to keep cows for milk. For, if it is so very profitable to them to keep the cows for milk, it must be under some kind of compulsion that they send them for slaughter. There is not the slightest ground for supposing that the people find it more profitable to sell dry, barren and old cows than to keep them; that the number of cows must always be limited to the amount of food-supply; that milk is dear where it is most wanted, *viz.*, in towns and densely-populated districts, not because cows are slaughtered but because it is expensive to maintain cows in those places; that it is cheaper where it is least wanted, *viz.*, in forest tracts and sparsely populated districts, not because cows are not sold there for slaughter but because it is less expensive there to keep cows; that in such tracts the Banjárás and other tribes formerly kept a large number of cows not for milk but for breeding purposes to supply the demand for draught animals, which demand has now considerably diminished owing to the opening of the railways, and hence fewer cows are now kept; that in such tracts a buffalo is a more valuable animal than a cow for its less fastidious taste in the matter of grazing, larger quantity of milk, four times richer in butter, &c, &c. But the cow-saving agitation is essentially a religious one, and as such it should be treated. It would be admirable first to expunge, explain away, or give a false meaning to all those passages in our old books where the killing and eating of beef and veal by our forefathers are mentioned, and then to convert to our beef-eschewing religion, the thirteen hundred millions of human beings who consider it a legitimate article of food. It is dangerous to seek the aid of the legislature, backed by eighty thousand British bayonets, to prohibit a practice distasteful to you in a religious point of view, but not distasteful to millions following a religion different from yours. For other religionists have strong opinions too on certain subjects. Idol-worship is held a heinous sin by those who are in power over us. Then according to one religion, tobacco-smoking is as good an introduction to the over-tropical regions of the spiritual universe, as according to another a good rupee put on the palm of a sleek Bráhman is to heaven. If you establish the principle of prohibiting by force a practice in others considered sinful by you, would you object to *their* using force to prohibit certain practices of yours held sinful by them? This cow-saving agitation is highly mischievous at the present time considering that only in the last century, even when the Delhi empire was tottering to its very foundations, this subject formed one of the causes of the war declared by Emperor Bahádur Sháh against Ráná Ajit Sinha of Udaipur.

I have used this subject as a straw to shew the direction in which the national mind still blows. I would not be surprised if my people, left to themselves, did what China has done with her railway. "Were not our forefathers happy without telegraphs and railways?"—is a question sometimes put to me by educated patriots. The fact is we are ignorant or oblivious of the past, careless of the present, and blind to the future. I wish somebody would analyse for me the earth we tread upon, the food we eat, the water we drink and the air we breathe, to tell me what proportion of morphine each contains. For have we not made this world a dream-land where we move like phantoms? It is needless to say that to be up to date in the book of human progress, we ought first of all to improve our national character. Without that all efforts to educate and reform a government, which is at least a century ahead of the nation, will be so much labour spent in vain. I have therefore formed great expectations of the National Congress, and entertain the strong hope that it will prove a powerful aid to Government in its noble endeavours to raise the degraded masses from the slough of ignorance, superstition and pernicious customs. It is a providential chance given to us, this connection of ours with the British race with its liberal traditions, high position in the world, elevating habits of life, hereditary aptitudes for mighty performances, a brilliant history and untold wealth. We hitherto saw only caste-rule in its worst form. If a more clear light could be thrown upon the past history of India, it would reveal only a continuous debasement of race after race by successive waves of conquerors. The government of unincorporateable millions by a handful of a superior race by means of elevation not debasement, by equity not force, has, perhaps for the first time in the history of the world, been successfully achieved by the British in India. The Congress is a natural product of this noble policy; and now that the time has come for it, it will live either under the name of "National Congress," or some other name. That small section of the British nation which sighs to make England what Spain was, which apprehends unnameable disasters from the exercise of perfect justice and liberality, which considers it an imperative necessity to defend a wrong and thus fails to be in sympathy with the noblest of human heritage, which by its distrustful habits creates a reciprocation of distrust, which believes it to be its interest to keep the races of India in a perpetual state of social, moral and intellectual degradation, which appeals to racial and sectarian jealousies to perpetuate this degradation, and which wants subjects not fellow-citizens, will have no lasting voice in the policy of noble-hearted Britain, the land of freedom and liberty. She who has shewed us our birthright, taught us our birthright, given us our birthright will disdain to hold out a mess of pottage to the hungering nose of the Esaus of our land. She will always consider it a self-degradation to keep the people of India in a state of degradation, and to deny to them the opportunity for self-development, the full rights of British citizenship and the full rewards of virtue and intelligence. To deserve the goodwill of Britain great foresight, circumspection, tact and the power of discerning substance from shadow are necessary in our public leaders. A hankering for things sublime should not be allowed to get morbid, and thus to exclude from their mind things lowly but more vital to the welfare of the nation. By constantly recurring to this subject, I am laying myself open to the charge of bestowing fulsome adulation on the British Government; but those who possess an insight into the working of this Government know pretty well that no selfish ends can be gained by the praise of a body in its abstraction. And it is in its pure abstraction that I have always viewed it, and have refused to go down to concrete details in search of defects and shortcomings. Patriotism is in danger of being made a toy for ardent youths to play with, and I feel it my duty to draw the attention of our leaders to this looming danger. Let not the patriotic mind lose its balance.

Besides cotton mills and other manufacturing establishments, we visited many places of interest in Manchester. Of these the Royal Exchange deserves the foremost mention. It is a colossal classic edifice, resounding with the hum of a busy multitude, that conveys to the visitor's mind the sense of the enormous mercantile transactions conducted in this fitting centre of Manchester commerce. How these people can combine, and subscribe large sums of money for a public object, without thirsting for a title or coveting a smile from those in power, is amply shewn by the Town Hall at Manchester. It is a palatial building costing more than a crore of rupees, which has under its roof a large public hall, a Mayor's parlour, a council chamber, a banqueting saloon and reception rooms, all gorgeously decorated and elegantly furnished. The front of this noble edifice is embellished with statuary, and is surmounted by a tower which has four clock dials. Manchester possesses a Cathedral built in the fifteenth century, of which the chief features are the well-ornamented roof, the carved wood-work and the stained windows. It also possesses a free library, with many branches in different parts of the town. The chief resort of the Manchester literary world is the Athenæum, with its theatre, library, lecture and news-rooms. Among other educational institutions may be mentioned the Grammar School, founded in 1515, which provides mental and physical instruction to upwards of nine hundred boys. It has a lecture-room, a chemical laboratory, a library and a magnificent gymnasium. But the chief educational centre in the present day is Owen's College, built and entirely organised through a bequest by a Manchester merchant. It is the head-quarters of the Victoria University. There is also a School of Art in Manchester, with a large gallery of pictures and spacious studios. Manchester is 188 miles from London, and is four and a quarter of an hour's journey from that place.

From Manchester we went to Liverpool, which in a commercial point of view is the most important town in Great Britain. In the latter part of the seventeenth century, when Auranzeb was carrying on his disastrous war with the Marhattas in the South of India, Liverpool was only a small fishing village. Now twenty-thousand ships annually leave this port for all parts of the globe. Of these the most important are the Atlantic steam-vessels which go to America. These vessels chiefly belong to the "Cunard," "Inman," "White Star," "National," "Guion," "Anchor" and "Allan" Lines. Among many places of interest we visited, may be mentioned the St. George's Hall, a building of Corinthian architecture, with magnificent rooms superbly decorated with polished granite, porphyry and other valuable stones. Its Grand Hall, which can accommodate 2500 persons, has a large organ with 8000 pipes. We also went to the Town Hall and the Exchange Buildings. Liverpool also possesses a free library and a museum largely endowed by private munificence. The library contains upwards of 100,000 volumes.

From Liverpool we went to Birkenhead on the other side of the Mersey. Although at the commencement of the present century it was a little hamlet containing a population of about 100 souls, Birkenhead is now a large town, with extensive dockyards, where large ships are built. It has now a population of 70,000, and possesses a Market Hall, a Music Hall, a Free Library, a School of Art, and a large park. Ferry steamers continually ply between Liverpool and Birkenhead. We however went by the railway, lately laid in a tunnel, excavated under the bed of the Mersey, which is here more an arm of the sea than the estuary of a small river. Many of my countrymen asked me whether I saw the Thames Tunnel, which was certainly one of the sights of London in former times. But it is no longer so, for since then much larger tunnels, requiring far greater engineering skill, have been excavated in England and in other parts of Europe. The tunnels across Mount Cenis and St. Gothard in the Alps are instances, and that under the Mersey through which we passed from Liverpool to Birkenhead is another. The Thames Tunnel is now used by the East London Railway, through which it has carried its lines from north to the south side of the Thames. Compared to modern tunnels it is very small, having two arched ways, and is only 1200 feet long, 14 feet wide, $16\frac{1}{2}$ feet high, and 16 feet below the river. I cannot say exactly how long the Mersey tunnel is, but considering the time we took to cross it, it must be between three and four miles in length. Mersey must be very deep here, for we had to go down in a lift many hundreds of feet underground before we reached the level of the tunnel where the railway line is laid. If the tunnel under the English Channel joining England with France had been allowed, then it would have eclipsed all works of similar nature now in existence. From Birkenhead the Colonists and Indians came back to Liverpool, and thence they went to Chester, where the Duke of Westminster invited them to his country residence.

The last excursion of the Colonials and Indians was to Bristol, Bath and Wells. Bristol is 118 miles from London and is only three hours' journey by rail. We came to Bristol on 6th September 1886, and were very kindly received by the Mayor and other local dignitaries. At three o'clock on that day, the Society of Merchant Venturers received the visitors at luncheon in the Merchants' Hall. This Society is one of the many Mediæval Guilds which Bristol once possessed. It is not known when it was founded, but records exist to shew that it was in a fully organized state in 1467, and that in 1500 an elaborate code was framed for its regulation. Such Societies laid the foundation of English prosperity, for these "Venturers" "put themselves, their factors, servants, goods and merchandize in peril upon the sea" for exploration and trade "in Muscovy and other foreign countries." My countrymen know very well the achievements of another body of Merchant Adventurers who sent their "factors and servants" to trade to the East.

The Society of Bristol Merchant Venturers was not less active, for its annals record one continued series of patriotic and commercial enterprises. It established plantations in Virginia and New England, it sent expeditions for the discovery of a northwest passage to India, and made various contributions for the suppression of pirates whether "Spaniards and Dunkirkes" or the "Turks of Algier." The wharves and quays of Bristol owe their origin to this society, and it also established almshouses, hospitals, trade schools, technical schools, girl schools and other public institutions. The Merchant Venturers' school now affords instruction to upwards of one thousand pupils. The Bristol Incorporated Chamber of Commerce and Shipping also joined in the reception given to the Colonials and Indians. The Mayor held a banquet in honor of the visitors at the Mansion House, and the Mayoress of Bristol had a Ball at the Victoria Rooms, Clifton. But the greatest enjoyment which the visitors received was in the madrigal concert given by the Bristol Madrigal Society in the latter place. This Society has a reputation all over England, and Sir John Rogers, President of the London Madrigal Society in 1843, once said—" If you want to know what a madrigal is, go to Bristol."

We were also taken to see the various manufacturing industries of Bristol. Among these I went to see the tobacco manufactory of Messrs. Willis & Co. Everything is done here by machinery, from tobacco cutting to the making of cigarettes. This firm get their tobacco from all parts of the world which they manipulate according to their own method. I was sorry to find they get no tobacco from India. I also went to see the Cathedral, which was built in the thirteenth century. The bold arch-way of the Great Gate House, the rectangular Chapter-Room with arcaded walls, the roof covered with sculptured moulding and diaper ornament, and the rich stained glass are the chief features of this interesting edifice. At Bristol we were quartered near Clifton Down, a lovely undulated plain, which is the favourite resort of all classes of the people. The suspension bridge here thrown across a *Khud*, which is the bed of a river, is one of the wonders of England. It is a large chain bridge with a span of 702 feet from saddle to saddle and weighing about 1500 tons, which has been placed 245 feet above the river, and as if firmly tied to the rock on each side.

It is a religious duty for every Indian to pay his homage to the tomb of his illustrious countryman, Rájá Rám Mohan Roy. The sky was cloudy, and it was drizzling, when on that afternoon of the 7th September 1886, I knelt down at the foot of the grave and prayed to Heaven to shew us what is truth, and what is more, to give us the courage to act truly throughout our lives, as this man whose ashes lay under the earth before me did in his life. "That I may not be a coward," I earnestly asked of Heaven. What thoughts came to my mind at the time, I leave it to my countrymen to imagine. When I was thus meditating a gentleman came to me, and said that he was specially deputed by the authorities to shew us all the records about Rám Mohan Roy's death, and the removal of his body to the present cemetery.

I saw the papers, but I need not give an account of them here, as these I believe have been incorporated in various books, both English and vernacular. With a heavy heart I left the place, sad to think what little progress we had made to remove the abuses in our society since Rájá Rám Mohan Roy died.

At Bristol I saw two Bengali gentlemen, Mr. R. C. Dutt and Mr. B. L. Gupta. They had been travelling in Norway and had lately arrived in England. It was midsummer when they were in Norway, and so they witnessed the phenomenon of the sun shining continuously for days and days without once thinking of going to set. Both the gentlemen spoke very highly of the kind and hospitable nature of the Scandinavian peasantry.

The Bristol reception was the only one in which I saw any Bengali gentlemen taking part. They seemed to keep themselves aloof from all things savouring of officialism and conservatism. They did not muster strong at the Northbrook Indian Club, which "has been established for the use of Indian gentlemen residing in England, and of others who have resided in India, or who take an active interest in Indian affairs; and with the object of promoting social intercourse between persons of these classes." The Bengalis in England frequent the liberal clubs, and associate with the liberals of Great Britain. It is interesting to watch the circumstances that are driving the Bengali to the liberal fold. He has largely assimilated western ideas; he is therefore impatient of class exclusiveness, and he tries to keep himself distant from those that possess and defend the continuance of class privileges. As a result of western education, he has dethroned the high castes of Hindu society, whom he worshipped and venerated from time out of memory, and he is now in no hurry to set other idols in their place. He makes no allowance for the defects of human nature, but wonders why the British should not always do what is right and just. He has boldly put the question—"Are the Indians free-born British subjects, with the full rights of a British citizen?" For this he is not liked, and he is held up to ridicule. He is blamed for not giving up freedom and an income of Rs. 8 per month at home to turn a soldier on Rs. 7 a month abroad. He is blamed for many other things, sometimes rightly, often wrongly, and occasionally untruthfully, to the great detriment to English good name in India. He has many faults no doubt, faults inherent in the Indian character, which the circumstances and the surroundings of his life have made it difficult to eradicate. Nevertheless the Bengali has been called "the Scotsman of India." It is complimentry; he does not deserve that comparison, for a Scotsman always does what he thinks of doing. Neither is the Bengali so calm, sedate and persevering in all his actions. A Scotsman always thinks gravely and acts gravely. A Bengali very often thinks gravity but acts frivolity. The Bengali is the infant French-man of India. He is emotional and impulsive, not discreet and politic. But with all his faults, liberalism in India and Bengaliism are getting to be synonymous. In England therefore he goes where he thinks he finds sympathy for his aspirations. He throws himself headlong into that side, and does not try to keep the other side pleased with him as well.

From Bristol we came to Bath, a lovely little town lying in a dale formed by a cordon of low hills. Bath claims great antiquity, its early history being lost among the misty darkness of legendary times. Its foundation is, however, not ascribed to the gods, or to the skilful architect who built the houses in heaven and sometimes in earth as a mark of special favour. That credit is given to Bladud, a king's son, who was afflicted with leprosy, and who therefore in the sore grief of his heart wandered about as a vagabond, until he came to the neighbourhood of where Bath now is, and engaged himself as a swineherd to a farmer of the place. The herd caught the fell disease from the hapless prince who, dreading the displeasure of his employer, removed his charge to a picturesque valley where numerous hot springs made a wide morass. At the sight of the springs the pigs at once plunged into the tepid water, and to the astonishment of the royal swineherd got cured of the eruptions in a short time. The prince was of a logical turn of mind for he had studied philosophy at Athens, and so after deep cogitation he came to the conclusion that if the spring water was good for the pigs, it ought to be good for him. He was not wrong, as the results proved, for cured and rejoiced he soon went back to his home. In time he succeeded to the throne of his father, the king of Britain, and in gratitude for his cure he built a large city on the spot where he received so much benefit. One of the numerous ancient baths discovered in the place, called the King's Bath, is still pointed out to the visitor as the one specially erected for the use of King Bladud. An effigy of the king is there, with an inscription recording among other things the fact of his being the founder of these baths 863 years before Christ. Bath was a place of great note under the Romans, who highly appreciated the curative properties of its water, and built here reservoirs and magnificent suites of baths. These are being discovered from time to time for the last three centuries. Just before we went there, a large hall, measuring 36 feet by 55 feet with a bath in the centre, was dug out. Bath was a great fashionable resort in the last century, but the wealthy now chiefly patronise the mineral waters in the Continent. Bath springs are now the property of the town corporation, who have built a "Grand Pump Room" at a cost of £10,000. The mineral springs at Bath yield 385,000 gallons of water daily at temperatures of 117° and 120° Fah. These waters are said to be beneficial in cases of gout, rheumatism, sciatica, neuralgia, paralysis, nervous debility and skin affections. The constituent parts in 100,000 are:—Calcium, 377; Magnesium, 47·4; Potassium, 39·5; Sodium, 129; Lithium, traces; Iron, 6·1; Sulphuric Acid, 869; Carbonic Acid (combined,) 86; Chlorine, 280; Silicia, 30; Strontium, traces; Alkaline Sulphides, traces; Carbonic Acid Gas at normal temperature and pressure (cubic centimetres per litre,) 65·3. Total Solid Contents in 100,000,—1864·0; Specific Gravity, 1·0015. I have gone into such particulars with the object that, if any of my countrymen wish to utilise the hot springs in this country, as a place of fashionable resort, he may find some help in these details. For each bath a charge of 6d., 1s., 1s. 6d., 2s., 2s. 6d., or 3s. is levied according to the nature of the bath taken. For drinking water the rate is 1s. 6d. per head per week.

In August 1886 I went to Scotland. I went by sea and came back by rail. Edinburgh is 397 miles from London, nine hours journey by rail; the sea voyage takes 36 hours. On 25th August, the steamer "Penguin" left her moorings in St. Katherine's Wharf, and sailed down the Thames until its muddy waters hid themselves under the broad blue bosom of the North Sea, when she made straight for Leith. For a long while we did not lose sight of the land, with the gaunt white cliffs broken or smoothed by the ceaseless dashing of the surf, the green fields that came a long way down to meet the blue sea, the picturesque villages and towns with Church steeples that took a wide view of the ocean by looking over the tops of houses and trees, and the undulating eminences with scattered specks of white formed by grazing flocks and herds of sheep and cattle. All these could be distinguished, for the sun shone bright, while his rays sported among the waves and made rainbow after rainbow among the spray thrown up by the revolving paddles of the steamer. In the night the moon rose with a radiant face, for out there no endless chimneys wove for her a thick sooty veil, except the funnels of numerous steamers that continually ply in these seas, but the gossamer fabric they made was in no time wafted away on the back of the breeze that blew for France. Next day afternoon we entered the Firth of Forth and passed several rocky islands close to North Berwick. One of these was pointed out as the place selected by a monk for his residence in those days when there were monks in Scotland. It is a little piece of rock, where it was not possible to grow anything for food. So I enquired on what the monk lived. An idle question no doubt, for there is no knowing what religious enthusiasts cannot do. In India they thrive on leaves, dress themselves with ashes, and sleep comfortably on sharp iron spikes. Perhaps this holy man here brought a couple of goats with him. It was dark when we arrived at Leith, which is two miles from Edinburgh, and of which it is the port and now an intregal part.

The people of Scotland may well be proud of Edinburgh. Beginning with an assemblage of rocky hills—

> " Whose ridgy back heaves to the sky
> Piled deep and massy, close and high,"—

sloping down gentler eminences, and spreading over a wide and luxuriant plain bordered by the blue fringe of the Firth of Forth, Edinburgh certainly is one of the most picturesque towns ever built by man on the face of the earth. Looking down from the Castle Hill or from the Salisbury Crags, or Carlton Hill or from the Nelson Monument, the eye grasps a glorious prospect of enchanting beauty never to be forgotten in life. A grand panorama is opened before it of swelling hills, deep ravines, slopes ornamented with trained vegetation, piles of ancient houses contrasted by graceful modern edifices, quaint narrow lanes with wide and magnificent thoroughfares of later times and verdant plains dotted with many a noble building. On one side stretches the wide expanse of the Firth of Forth with the grey hills of Fifeshire on the background, while on the other side rise the distant Highland mountains of Ben Lodi, Ben Lomond and others of less note. I visited most of the interesting places in Edinburgh. I walked up and down the Prince's Street, considered as the finest road-site in Europe, and took a ramble round the ornamental grounds adjoining, known as the Prince's Street Gardens. On my way to the Castle I saw the Gothic Cathedral of St. Giles, the centre of religious upheavals in Scotland, from which honest John Knox hurled his stirring sermons. Close at hand was the County Square where into the pavement, stones have been let in the form of a heart, and which is known as the "Heart of Midlothian." In the Castle the visitor is shewn "Queen Mary's Room" where James VI was born, and from which the little infant was let down the precipice in a basket to be conveyed to Stirling. In another room called the "Crown Room" are kept the Scotch Regalia. A huge piece of old-fashioned ordnance, christened Mons Meg, cast in 1486, is kept in the Castle. From the Castle Hill I came to Holyrood through High Street and Canongate, leaving behind me the house of John Knox and those of the proud Morays, Montroses, Argylls and other noble families connected with the most stirring episodes of Scottish history.

Holyrood was founded in the early part of the twelfth century by King David I, who built it as an

Abbey for the reception of canons regular of the order of St. Augustine. Apart from its antiquity and architectural and other attractions, it is the events connected with the beautiful and unfortunate Mary, Queen of the Scots, that have made Holyrood an object of thrilling interest. Here she came and lived after her return from France in 1561; here she was married to Lord Darnley; here Rizzio, the Italian, was murdered as he clutched her gown for protection; here the nuptial festivals were held after her marriage with the infamous Bothwell; and here she was kept a prisoner by her own subjects before she was removed to the castle of Lochleven. The halls are shewn to the visitor where royal entertainments were held, in the midst of which the unfortunate Queen shone the brightest among the bright beauties of Scotland, enchanting all who beheld her by the loveliness of her person and the graces of her manner; also, alas! the apartments, where Darnley made her young heart weep, where the brutal Ruthven stabbed the unfortunate Rizzio, and where the guide asks you to look closely for traces of blood said to be still perceptible on the floor. My eye-sight was not however sufficiently strong to detect them.

One feels sick at the recollection of the various tragic scenes enacted in those bloody days. My countrymen accuse the Europeans of brutality and blood-thirstiness. There is no doubt that the sense of justice, mercy and charity is more developed in the Indian mind than in the European. But it must be remembered that as heat is inseparable from fire, brutality is inseparable from an aggressive and a conquering race. In fact, this defect of character, in a moral point of view, is the very cause that leads to conquest. We might have taken credit for this superiority of our mind had it not been the result of a calamitous inferiority in another respect. Our sense of justice, mercy and charity is the result of our physical weakness, and not our physical weakness the result of these higher attributes of mind. In a perfect man all the senses, both of body and mind, are fully developed, but always under control. He need not be aggressive, but he must be able to defend himself. He should possess the power to protect himself and others, for all are not good in this world. A Great Teacher taught the world to present its left cheek to one who had just slapped the right. Our books have also taught us to consider forgiveness as the greatest of virtues. With all humility, with the most profound respect for the great teachers who taught the cultivation of the noblest acts of human life—Charity and Forgiveness—I would nevertheless most reluctantly and most sorrowfully tell my countrymen, specially the low castes from whose mind the high castes have crushed out all independence, all manliness, all self-respect, always to return blow for blow, be the return-blow ever so feeble and be the consequence ever so serious. For the doctrine of absolute forgiveness is unworkable in the world as it is, and it is a sin inasmuch as it encourages the wrong-doer in his evil course to the great harm of the human family as a whole. So what you call brutality in the European is merely a frenzied outburst of a virtue necessary for the good government of the world and necessary for the progress of humanity. This frenzied outburst whenever and wherever it happens is to be deplored, but not the virtue itself that lies at the root of it.

Among the apartments in Holyrood shewn to the visitor may be mentioned Lord Darnley's Rooms. These consist of his Audience Chamber, his Sitting Room, Bed Room and Dressing Room. All these apartments contain many old pieces of tapestry and numerous pictures. The apartments of Mary, Queen of the Scots, consist of an Audience Chamber, her Bed-room and Supping Room. It was in the last place that Rizzio was murdered. In the Bed Room there is a bed said to be the identical one which Mary used. Among other places I visited in Edinburgh, I must mention the monument erected in honour of Sir Walter Scott. It stands near the Waverly Bridge, and was designed by a local architect. The fine Gothic outlines of the monument are considered unequalled both in design and execution.

From Edinburgh I went to Perth. At the railway station there, I met Dr. Watt and two residents of the place—Mr. Honey and Mr. Dunsmore. These gentlemen arranged that I should stay at Perth as the guest of Mr. Dunsmore. He took me home where good Mrs. Dunsmore gave me a very hearty welcome. John and Buchanan their little boys, and Caroline their little girl of about three years, were all so very affectionate towards me that in less than an hour's time I felt quite at home. I also saw Mr. Dunsmore's mother, who gave me a reception equally kind and warm. She lives in a separate house, and the old lady was very glad to see me, for she never saw an Indian before. She is just like ourselves, for she would not allow me to come away until I had taken something at her house. The Scotch at home are free and easy, so that in a short while you can feel at one with them, and may pour out your simple heart without making them look *what-care-I-for-you.*

Next day the three gentlemen I named above took me with them to Lochleven, some miles distant from Perth, to fish for trouts. On the way Mr. Dunsmore related various anecdotes. He pointed to a Highland peak and said that when he was a boy of eight or ten years of age, there lived perched upon the summit of that hill a big stalwart man, with a huge turban on his head, a retired officer of the Panjáb campaigns. He built his nest high up there, a commodious bungalow, and claimed the neighbouring hills and rills as his domain. One day Mr. Dunsmore and a friend, a boy of the same age as he, went to fish for salmon in one of those very rills which the mighty lord from the Panjáb claimed for his own. Little Robert Dunsmore was fully intent on the sport, when to his horror what would he hear but a thundering voice behind saying,—" You rascally imps, I have caught you at length ; I will now hand you over to the police," and on turning back what would he see but the huge monster of the turban coming upon him down the hill with the impetuosity of a sweeping avalanche of the Alpine regions ! He was frightened and panic-stricken, and did not know what to do. His friend, who sat a little way off, saw what was passing and in a moment grasped the whole situation. He at once left his rod, and came up running, crying all the while—"What is it Bob, what is it Bob, what is the man doing to you?" When he drew near he threw off his coat, stuck up his sleeves and defiantly challenged the man-mountain to fight him on the spot. The old gentleman was highly amused, he burst out into a hearty laugh, and let both the Lilliputians off, duly praising them for their courage and pluck. We in this country do not do such naughty things, for we are good boys. Peary Churn Sircar in one of his books for little folks (Second Book of Reading?) has said—"A good boy never fights"—to which may I be permitted to add?—" but sneaks away when a bad boy beats him."

Thus, happy as school-boys, we went our way along the wide even road over the Ochill Hills to Kinross on the bank of the lake. Here we took a boat and rowed up and down the lake in search of trouts. It was no easy matter to hold the rod, to throw the long line on the water, and dexterously and slowly so to drag it as to keep the bait of an artificial fly or a minnow just afloat to entice the trout to *rise*. I did not know how to do all this. I therefore sat quietly on the boat and watched the sport. Sometimes I looked at the sparkling ripples that played with a gentle breeze on the bosom of the deep blue lake, and every one of which shewed a little sun within, like a mirror, all its own. Often the eye would take a sweep over the ripples to the sloping pebbled bank, and on to the green grass above, and thence to the high mountains, covered with verdure, that solemnly looked down upon the lake from almost all sides.

Or, when the boat would turn round, it would sadly look upon the little island where lay the ruins of the castle in which Mary, Queen of the Scots, was kept in confinement. Was that the spot where the loyal abbot made his garden to favour Mary's escape from her confinement? It would seem to question the bank opposite the island. In the meantime we had got a number of trouts. After the fishing was over, we went to the island to see the ruins of the castle, and then came back to Kinross and thence to Perth.

Next day was Sunday. The Scotch people keep the Sabbath more punctually than their neighbours of the South. Instead of leaving me at home all alone, Mr. Dunsmore took me to the Church, and on the way he shewed me a little old house which tradition says was the one in which the "Fair Maid of Perth" lived. After church we went to the Kinnoul Hills, gathering blackberries on the way. From a place called the "Wicks of Baiglie," we had a magnificent view of Perth and its beautiful surroundings. There is a popular saying that Perth lies between two inches. The meaning of it is that adjoining the River Tay, on each side of Perth, are two favourite resorts of the people called the North Inch and the South Inch. It was in the North Inch that the celebrated conflict described by Sir Walter Scott in his "Fair Maid of Perth" took place. The "Wicks of Baiglie" commanded an unparalleled prospect all round, including the picturesque town, the North and Sotuh Inches, the neighbouring hills, and the winding shaded course of the Tay far away to where it gradually widens into a Firth.

From Perth I went to Pitlorchry, a little station on the Highland Railway, beautifully situated among the hills. From Pitlochry, I walked to Blair Athole across the famous Killie-crankie Pass, and through a succession of woods, glens, ravines and rivers that diversified a mountain-scenery perhaps unequalled in the world.

At Blair Athole three gentlemen kindly offered to take me with them on a pedestrian excursion across Glen Tilt to Braemar, which offer I thankfully accepted. For a few miles at the commencement and at the end of our journey, a carriage road was available which we took advantage of. In the middle, were two chains of high mountains enclosing between them the narrow valley of the River Tilt, called a glen in that country. A footpath followed the course of the river. This part of the road, some 16 miles, we went on foot. The weather favoured us: while all the time I was in Scotland it was bright and sunny, this day alone was cloudy, but not rainy. So we merrily walked our way, cheered by the sweet perfume of the heather that covered the mountain sides like a thick Indian carpet of subdued colours, and refreshed by the murmuring sound of the Tilt, which flew swift when the rocks on each side encroached upon her bed, ran calm and placid when the rocks receded, and grew angry and furious when unmannerly boulders disturbed her peaceful course. When tired we all sat upon a rock, and took the food we brought with us, and drank the cool clear water which Tilt supplied us in abundance. The country through which we passed was almost uninhabited. The noble race of men, which the Highlands of Scotland formerly reared, have sought its home elsewhere. The wild deer now nibble at the heather, where formerly passionate strains of music from the bag-pipe of the piper cheered the clansmen in their festive board, or recalled to the mind of the valiant youths the heroism of their ancestors. The broad bosoms of the men are now of no use to the Chiefs to stand as a shield against the destructive blows of their relentless enemies. The heart of the antler, to offer as a mark to wealthy sportsmen of the South, now pays more than the brawny hands of the peasant that delved and toiled for a scanty crop among the rocky land. So they have gone, and the world has lost a brave race of men which, by singular good fortune, found one of the sweetest writers to make its romantic achievements resound through every clime.

It was late in the afternoon when the rumbling sound of the Linn of Dee reached our ears. The soft twilight was slowly creeping on the evening air when we stood on the bridge over the Dee. We looked down, and saw with wonder how the rocks on either side squeezed the waters of the river into so narrow a compass that a child might easily leap across it. Chafing at the restraint put upon her, the Dee impatiently bounds from the rock, like the tigress when she has broken asunder the noose laid on her track by the watchful hunter. At length freed from her toilings amongst the rocks, the smart little river in a pretty pouty way leaps down on the stony shelf below and in revenge makes there a deep pool as dark as Erebus. Here Byron nearly lost his life. Moore in his life of the poet says—"As he (Byron) was scrambling along a declivity that overhung the fall, a heather caught his lame foot and he fell. Already he was rolling downwards, when the attendant quickly caught hold of him, and was but just in time to save him from being killed." Here we found a carriage waiting for us, in which we drove to Bræmar, passing on the way Mar Lodge, a princely mansion belonging to the Earl of Fife. At Bræmar all of us could not get accommodation in the hotels, they were so full, and two of us had to seek for shelter in a Highland shieling. Next morning while I was sitting on the hillside outside the cottage, a little boy came jumping there and asked me who I was. I told him that I came from India. He said, "My father is in India too." "What is your father's name?" I asked. "Smeaton," he replied. "Is his name Mr. D. Smeaton, and is he now in Burmah?" I asked again. He ran home, and came back in a moment and said that his father's name was Mr. D. Smeaton and that he was in Burmah. So, little Arthur was an Indian after all, for while we were in Europe we looked upon all Anglo-Indians as our countrymen. He played around me as long as I sat there, and took an affectionate leave when we parted. At Bræmar, the local chiefs, the Earl of Fife and Colonel Farquharson, hold every year a gathering of their tenants in the right old Highland style. The clans march under their chiefs, clad in full Highland costume, armed with claymore or Lochaber axe, with banners waving and bagpipes screaming. The Queen and the Prince of

Wales often honour this "Gathering of the Clans" with their presence. But both the Gælic language and the Highland kilt are fast disappearing.

I left my friends at Bræmar and pursued my journey alone to Ballater. But scarcely had the coach travelled a couple of miles, when a fellow passenger entered into conversation with me. He pointed out to me Balmoral, the Queen's Highland residence; Invercauld, the family seat of the Farquharsons; Abergeldie, the estate belonging to the Prince of Wales; and the snow-clad summit of Lochnagar made famous by Byron. Mr. Newland, my new friend, would not allow me to leave Ballater until he had taken me round the neighbouring hills. He was deputed by a Society, formed with the object of preventing the landlords from enclosing the footpaths on which pedestrians love to ramble among the Highlands in summer, to collect evidence about the existence of such roads. This Society has already compelled the landlords to reopen many such footpaths closed by them. It will be seen from it that the proverb—" What is every body's business is nobody's business," has now no significance in that country. If a village common or a road is encroached upon, they all combine, subscribe large sums of money, and have the matter fought out, however powerful and wealthy the encroacher may be.

In our villages within the last few years, the zamindars (permanent farmers of land revenue) have swallowed up the lands set aside from time immemorial as "common pasture" (*Gochar*) and, as far as I am aware, not a voice has been raised against it either by the villagemen, or by the public orators, or Government. And yet a fitter subject for agitation by a cow-loving people could hardly be imagined. "Your memorialists would humbly pray that the slaughter of cows be prohibited by law, that the English officers in charge of the Agricultural Departments be reprimanded for their meddlesome habit of endeavouring to increase the supply of cattle-food in the country, and that your memorialists be allowed to freely enjoy their newly-acquired right of killing the cows by slow starvation," that is the form of petition one can suggest on seeing the weak emaciated condition of cattle in this country compared with their plump sleek state in Europe. I am sad and surprised to find that this fact, palpable to all eyes, is denied. Let us learn to boldly avow what is wrong in us, if we want to be respected even by our enemies.

Mr. Newland and I drove across the Balmoral Estate, and we also went to many farm-houses in the neighbourhood, asking the old people there about the footpaths. Wherever we went they offered us whiskey and tea, just as you offer sweetmeats, betel-leaves and smoke to respectable strangers in your house. In one place we met a number of tramps, both men and women. Tramps have no fixed abode or occupation, but go about the country begging or stealing. Tramp-life is equivalent to *Fakir*-life in India, *minus* the religious paraphernalia. Religion has become so tough and flinty in Europe that it is practically getting out of fashion. Accustomed as we are to the religious vagrancy in India, I could hardly realise the sweets of tramp-life in England, where food is not abundant, where the air is cold, where it rains all the year round and snows in the winter, where they keep their front doors locked, where the heart of the people has become tramp-proof by evolution, where bull-dogs and man-traps guard the orchards at night, where no *chhatrams* exist in which one can lay down his head without paying, where most lands are enclosed, and where prosecution for trespass is more than common. For the same reason gypsies have practically disappeared from England. The few that are there have taken to the trade of mending broken pots. We came across a little gypsy encampment near the Killiecrankie Pass.

At Ballater I saw Sir William Muir. He expressed great anxiety at the growing misunderstanding between Englishmen and natives of India. I also greatly deplored the circumstance and said that " I would always feel it my duty to do all that I could to bridge the gulf that unhappily at present divides the two races. But all our efforts will be fruitless if some of the influential newspapers conducted by Englishmen in India do not adopt a kinder tone towards the natives of the country. Papers conducted in party spirit is unsuitable for India, and what is more, they teach a dangerous lesson to periodicals published by the Indians in English or vernacular." That this misunderstanding is largely due to mutual ignorance, there can be no doubt. The same cause produced the same results during the Muhammadan time. Abul Fazl in his preface to *Razm Námah* states that "the Emperor Akbar convinced that the fanatical hatred prevailing between Hindus and Muhammadans mainly arose from mutual ignorance, sought to render the books of the former accessible to the latter. He therefore selected the Mahábhárata to be translated by competent authorities of both races." I think the rulers and the ruled of the time knew much more of each other three hundred years ago than they do now. Speaking of newspapers conducted by Englishmen in India, I must go a little on the other side and regret the necessity that forces periodicals, friendly to the children of the soil, to adopt a language, in their criticisms of Government measures, which is likely to teach my countrymen to doubt the sincerity and honesty of the Government and to despise the moral susceptibilities of its officers. Alas, the circumstance! that forces our friends to lower themselves down to the mental level where we now stand, and prevents them from pulling us up to their own mental height, from which we can take a wider survey of things around. The strong and one-sided language of partisanship is not here taken at its proper value; but the sentiments, of which it is the vehicle, are accepted as revealed truths, specially when they come from a friendly quarter. The extreme sentiments poured forth on each side by friendly and unfriendly English papers, gushing madly up through a bold hard language, which presents no restraint but intensifies their impetuosity, form the perennial source of that mud-laden stream which goes down to the newly-created soil of journalism in India, to sow, nourish and invigorate the weeds, at the sight of which, eventually, their very authors are the first to wring their hands in despair, are the loudest in their lamentations, and the most inconsolable in their sorrow. "Right and truth, in their subtlest abstract conception, will be my only friends left in this world," I thought, after my imprudent criticisms of both friends and foes, as they are commonly called, I pretend not to know on what grounds and with what justice. But the world has been much more charitable to me than I expected, and its leniency to me has ever been indeed a pleasurable surprise. I hope I shall continue to be judged in the same kindly spirit.

From Ballater I went by rail to Aberdeen. It will be impossible to describe all the places to which I went. I may mention here that Aberdeen is a seaport town with a population of about 110,000. It is also the seat of a university. It possesses a handsome Art Gallery, an Industrial Museum, a Mechanic's Institute and an Art School founded by a gift of £6000 made by a private individual. Two Daily, with their evening editions, and two Weekly Newspapers are published in the town, which will show what progress education has made in Great Britain.

Nothing is more absolutely necessary for the regeneration of India than education, universal education, compulsory education and if possible free education. The National Congress and all the public associations in the country, Hindus and Musalmans, Englishmen and Indians, should combine to bring about universal education in India. Where is the money to come from? We already levy a tax on marriages for the benefit of the village schools; let it be legalised.

Then tax gold and silver imported into this country; nobody would feel the worse for it. Tax anything you like, but give us education; for it is better to die of starvation than to live like beasts.

At Aberdeen I went to the seaside, on the further end of the town, where large boats laden with fresh-caught herrings are brought in. They also catch fish in the open sea by steamers. Herrings are very much like our *Hilsa* fish, equally bony and oily, but not so sweet. The best fish in England is the Salmon (*Salmo salar, Linn;* Salmonidæ,) which is found in abundance in all the Arctic seas, and which enters the rivers in spring to spawn. In going up the rivers the salmon often takes tremendous leaps to surmount rapids and cascades. Another fish they like in that country is the sole, a flat salt-water fish with both the eyes on one side, which goes to sleep after nicely covering itself with sand. Other kinds of fish I saw on the table there were sturgeon, pike, roach, haddock, cod, tench, turbot, plaice, eel, mackerel, lamprey, lock, whitebait, &c. Whitebait is a small fish which they eat fried. Of shell-fish, they are extremely fond of turtle-soup, real or mock. They have great preference for the green turtle *(Chelonia Midas)*, brought from the West India Islands. But to them the greatest delicacy is of course the oysters, of which they chiefly use only one species, the *Ostrea edulis*. Outside many London shops you will see signboards with "Natives" upon them. They do not mean that any of us are kept for sale there but that the people can get there the most delicate of all oysters which grow off the English coast, named "natives" in contradistinction to those brought from France and other places. They have got huge lobsters, cray fish and crabs in that country. They boil the lobster, mince it into small pieces, and eat it with green salad, the whole forming what they call the "lobster salad." Mussels, cockles, whelks, limpets and scallops are commonly eaten by the poorer people.

From Aberdeen I came back to Perth by way of Dundee, and immediately started for Aberfeldy in the Highlands. Thence I went to Killin Pier across the Loch Tay by a fine little steamer. The country around here is simply indescribably beautiful. The music that played on board the steamer, while we were on the bosom of the pretty lake with its deep blue waters; the slopy bank carpetted with grass, before which the brightest emerald would fade in shame; higher up a thickly wooded forest, through which only the most audacious sunshine could with difficulty pierce its way down to the ground, strewn with yellow autumnal leaves shed by deciduous undergrowths; and above all the many-headed mountains guarding like giants the charms of the lovely little loch, all contributed to make the scene fairy-like, dreamy and enchanting in the highest degree. I have not seen Kashmir, and cannot therefore say if that place can be compared with Scotland. But I have seen many other places in India, both hills and plains, and I can confidently say that Scotland is the most beautiful country I ever saw. The Himalayas are too wild and too grand; they raise a feeling of awe in the mind, but do not soothe and charm. Nil-girls, had they such fine lakes, might have stood a chance of being compared with the mountain scenery of Scotland. Scotland is an epitome of all the charms of the world. It has the sea on almost all sides, it has huge precipitous mountains, undulating hills, flat plains, forests, lakes, rivers, everything that the eye of the artist loves to dwell upon.

A little island sits upon the waters of Loch Tay, that fondly nestles in its bosom the dilapidated skeleton of an old castle. It reproachfully looks upon the waters around, which fell asleep at their post on a wintry morning long ago, when the Macgregors, protected from their arrows by the fascines they pushed before them across the frozen lake, attacked and overpowered the protectors of the castle. What vicissitudes the lands around have passed through, or for the matter of that, most inhabited lands on the face of earth! Only, they wanted the wand of a magician like Sir Walter Scott to cast upon them a halo of romance. Benmore yonder, with its head raised 3,843 feet above the level of the sea, witnessed the sanguinary struggle which deprived the Clan Mac-Nab of their lands in Glen-Dochart, leaving to them only the little weed-covered graveyard in Killin, by the side of which I pensively sat for a long while. Where the locomotive engine of the Killin Railway shrieked and snorted before its departure for Oban, the war-horse neighed and claymores clanged in bygone days. The little village of Dalree, to which we shortly came, remembers the bloody morning in 1306, when Bruce desperately fought with the followers of Macdougall of Lorn, ending in one of the many narrow escapes of his eventful life. Did not Tyndrum, our next halting place, send her quota of armed band to murder neighbour Glencoe in her sleep? Next came we to Dalmally, in the heart of the Breadalbane-Campbell territory, with Ben Cruachan and other Bens of note and Glen-Orchy, Glen Strae and other valleys of beautiful appearance by her side, all of which oft heard afar the plaintive wail of the hunted race of Macgregors—

"Glen-Orchy's proud mountains, Kilchurn and her towers,
Glen-Strae and Glen Lyon no longer are ours;
We're landless, landless, landless, Grigalach!
Landless, landless, landless!

Thus through hills and glens, made ever-memorable by stories of love and war, of noble heroism and rapine of the most heartless description, I wended my way to Oban, a seaport on the west coast of Scotland. From Dalmally I came to Kilchurn. The railway now ran alongside Loch Awe for a certain distance. Just as we left Loch Awe behind, we got the first glimpse of Loch Etive, and in a short time arrived at Ach-na-cloich. A little steamer plies between Ach-na-cloich and Lochetivehead, at which place travellers take the coach for Glencoe and Ballachulish. We then came to Connel Ferry Station, and thence to Loch-Nell, the view across which towards Fort William and Ben Nevis is grand and magnificent. My next halting place was Oban, and from Oban I came to Glasgow by steamer through the canal and by way of Loch Fyne.

Glasgow, which in the last century was only a little fishing town hardly containing a population of more than 12,000 souls, is now one of the largest ports in the world, while the number of its inhabitants at the present time cannot be counted at less than half a million. It is entirely a product of the indomitable spirit, the remarkable energy and the thorough business application of the people of Scotland. They have at an enormous expense converted a small river, the Clyde, into a wide navigable channel with a noble harbour of docks and quays, which afford accommodation to thousands of shipping. These ships go to all parts of the world, specially to India and America, and carry on an enormous trade in tobacco, cotton, sugar and other products. The shoe-less urchins of the Glasgow streets are not therefore unfamiliar with the dark faces of sunburnt sailors who come to their port from the southern climes, or with the cigarettes which they surreptitiously bring with them from dutiless countries, or with the cocoanut which evidently they carry in their pockets to cultivate a friendly feeling with the young hopefuls of sea-faring Scotland. For, my turban attracted a crowd of these clamouring boys, who followed me with loud cries of "Johny, give us a cigarette; Johny give us a cocoanut." The river at Glasgow is spanned by several well-built bridges, and the town is intersected by many fine streets, with numerous handsome buildings rising many storeys high on each side. Argyll street, the main artery of the town, is constantly full of a busy crowd, with trams and coaches running towards all directions. From one point of it bifurcates the High Street, that leads you up to the historical "Bell O'Brae," where the Scottish hero,

William Wallace, defeated the English forces. Buchanan Street with its handsome environments is the favourite resort of the rich and the fashionable, where they promenade and do the shopping. It has the George Square in the neighbourhood, surrounded by numerous public buildings, and containing statues of many eminent men, among which may be noticed a colossal figure of Sir Walter Scott, supported by a lofty Doric column. Nor is Glasgow deficient in parks and public gardens, where the British people seek health and recreation as a change from the hard toil of everyday life. The High Green and the Low Green, the King's Park and the Queen's Park, the Kelvin Grove and the Botanic Gardens, all exquisitely laid out, not only delight the eye, but instruct the mind in the nature of our green friends around, and create in the heart of the rough and the rustic a chastening taste for all that is charming to behold. Glasgow is not only a prominent centre of British enterprise, but it is noted also as an important seat of British intellectuality. Within that magnificent pile of Gothic structure, known as the New University, built at a cost of over half a crore of rupees, many of my countrymen have already received their well-earned degrees, and in the International Exhibition to be opened near it in a few days (1888), Indian handicrafts will no doubt form one of, if not the most, interesting section. Within the University buildings are also the Library and the Museum containing the celebrated Hunterian collection. Probably the only old building in Glasgow is the cruciform Cathedral with its noble tower, its lofty spire and the usual complement of stained glass windows. The Cathedral was founded in the twelfth and the University in the fifteenth century. Near Glasgow are two important places, Paisley and Greenock. Kashmir shawls were formerly imitated at Paisley, which, as might have been expected, resulted in the destruction of the trade both in the original and the imitation. From the vast ship-building yards of Greenock have been launched some of the finest ocean steamers, while its spacious harbour affords a safe refuge to numberless vessels of the mercantile marine. From Greenock excursionists go down the Clyde to enjoy the magnificent scenery of the lochs and the rocky islands on the west coast of Scotland. The "Lord of the Isles," the "Columbia" and other fine steamers carry the excursionists to Loch Lomond and Loch Fyne, to Rothesay in the Isle of Bute, to Ardrishaig, Inverary and other places of beautiful scenery. While I was at Glasgow "The Great Eastern," the largest steamer in the world, was lying off Greenock, and I went to see it. This steamer has been found useless either to carry passengers or goods and it has become a white elephant in the hands of the proprietors. It is going to be broken up.

The space at my command would not allow me to give a detailed description of the various other places to which I went, but I cannot resist the temptation of describing an excursion to—

"Where the rude Trosachs' dread defile
Opens on Katrine's lake and isle." (Scott.)

Mr. John Muir of Deanston House, Doune, kindly took me to the Trosachs. From Doune we travelled by rail up to where the bold crags of Callander, supported by a mighty army of mountain peaks, jealously guard the haunted regions, where Roderic Dhu performed his valorous deeds and where the heart of the heroic Ellen throbbed with sweet pangs of love. But it would be sheer presumption on my part to attempt a scenic description of those mountains, valleys and lakes consecrated to all time by the honeyed strains of the mighty ministrel of Scotland. In all humility therefore I must refrain. At Callander we took the coach and travelled on towards the Trosachs. The road lay for a certain distance along the margin of Loch Vennachar, the shores of which are more or less clothed with a thick wood and cut by streams which pour their waters into the lake. We passed the Coilantogle Ford, the scene of the fight between Roderic Dhu and the Knight of Snowdon, and next we came to the "Wood of wailing," where according to tradition a water-kelpie or lake demon ate up a number of children. The story goes that one day the children were playing on the bank of the lake, when a beautiful horse issued forth from the water. He looked so handsome and so gentle that one of the boys ventured to get upon his back. His example was followed by another, and then another and yet another, the horse, in the meantime lengthening his back to make room for all. When all had mounted he suddenly plunged himself into the lake, where in a dark little subaqueous cave he devoured all the boys except one who, by a singular good fortune, escaped to tell the tale. This kelpie is of the same genus as the "Matted Old

Woman" of the Bengal tanks, the "Stone-ghost" of the Birbhum rivers and the "Pándubá" of the Gandak. Like the crocodiles of the Nile he possesses an extraordinary amount of patience, for he has often to wait and watch a long while for his prey. There is but one other instance on record of his having obtained a hearty meal. That was when he got hold of a funeral party who, according to Sir Walter Scott, were passing along the shore of the haunted lake. Next we came near Loch Achray and then to the Brig of Turk, which is a bridge thrown across a little stream where, like the incident related in many of our nursery tales of the hunting king having outstripped all his followers in the heat of the chase, the Knight of Snowdon suddenly found himself alone—

> "Few were the stragglers, following far,
> That reached the lake of Vennachar;
> And when the Brig of Turk was won,
> The headmost horseman rode alone."

Leaving Loch Achray behind we shortly after entered the Pass of the Trosachs, formed by two steep mountains, the Ben Alan on the right and Ben Venue on the left. The rugged sides of the hills are densely covered with rowan, birch, hawthorn, oak and other trees, and the whole appearance of the Pass is something like the gorges one often meets with in the Himalayas. On the other end of the Trosachs is the Lake Katrine. Formerly Loch Katrine could not be reached from the Trosachs except by a very difficult and dangerous path, called the "Ladders." This path consisted merely of rude steps, cut on the side of the steep hills over which hung ropes suspended from the boughs of trees, which the adventurous traveller held for support as he descended the dangerous precipice. A broad and easy road has now been made, along which the coach travelled up to the very brink of the lake. A little steamer with the appropriate name of "Rob Roy" takes the excursionists across the lake. We passed the Ellen Isle where Ellen Douglas conveyed the Knight of Snowdon. Shortly after a boat met the steamer, which took us to the Queen's Cottage near the mouth of the tunnel by which the water of the Lake Katrine is taken to Glasgow, a distance of forty-eight miles. One of the magistrates of Glasgow received us as his guests in the Queen's Cottage. He then took us in a boat to the other extremity of the lake, which is very bleak and desolate, the mountains being full of broken rocks and boulders. The country formerly belonged to the Macgregors, and it was the scene of many of the daring exploits of Rob Roy. We also went to see the burial place of the Macgregor Clan. It is nothing but a small enclosure on the side of the lake where a large number of stones lay scattered. We heard that to this place the body of General Macgregor, of the Indian army who had lately died in Egypt, was being brought. The present Macgregors ought to look after the burial place of their ancestors. For a full description of the Trosachs and Loch Katrine, I must refer my readers to the "Lady of the Lake."

In October 1886 I went to Oxford, where I worked for a month under Sir Monier Williams in the Indian Institute he has formed in connection with the University. It is needless to say that Sir Monier Williams has great sympathy for the Indian people, as all oriental scholars have. He has contributed not a little to teach the higher classes of English gentlemen the lesson that, in dealing with the Indian people, they have to deal with a race of men who, from very ancient times, have shewed a depth of mind and profundity of wisdom not surpassed by even modern Europeans. This lesson is all the more important because the close connection of the British with the American, African and Australian races has engendered in the English mind ideas about the non-European peoples of the world not at all complimentary or beneficial to the Indians. The more the Europeans are progressing in knowledge and civilisation, the more is the gulf widening between them and the comparatively slow-moving people of India. Knowledge and power are as much distancing man from the brute creation, as they are distancing civilised man from savage man. There is difference; but the difference is in degree. This sense of power is producing a sense of security in the European bosom. So in their scrambles for the property of non-European races they throw overboard all sense of justice and morality, and in absolute reliance on the annihilating power of their breechloaders and machine guns, they are as ready to dart upon the land of the Negus in Africa as on the land of the Annamites in Eastern Asia. This, often in forgetfulness of the fact that the age which sentimentalists fondly look back upon as the golden age, but which we call as the stone age or bronze age of

1 K

cruel treacheries and brutal massacres, has long since past, let us hope for ever, from this world. This again, in forgetfulness of the fact that among these non-European races are races who have souls in which the light of divinity shines brighter than in that of the European, and who, dark and half-naked as they are, can in all sincerity raise their weak hands in horror against all acts contrary to the dictates of mercy, charity, justice and forgiveness, that more differentiate man from the brute creation than all the railways, telegraphs and gattling guns. Alas, Alas! Why are the sheep that quietly graze on the green meadows of England so innocent and meek? Day and night they teach a dangerous lesson that innocence is made for butchery. They also suggest the policy of reducing nations to the state of sheepish innocence. At any rate it is not good for India, nor is it good for England, nor is it good for the world that English lads should come out among a sensitive people, inordinately vain of their past achievements, with the notion that the dark complexion and the semi-nude condition of the Indians entitle them to be classified with the Bushmen of the Cape or the Papuans of Australasia.

The present European connection with non-European races has a wider significance than its relation to India. The human family is now passing through a different phase of development to what it knew in bygone ages. When man was a brute, self-assertion caused the elimination of inferior races by brutality. Self-abnegation had no place then in the human mind. In course of time, man was differentiated from the brute, the human mind rose higher, and the human heart began to beat fast in sympathy for fellow-man. Self-abnegation now found an honoured place in the human constitution. But yet it was a little infant, only little larger than that in the mind of a lower being which prompted self-sacrifice for the safety of its offspring. Time rolled on, the infant grew, gradually causing more and more displacement of self-assertion from the human mind. But self-assertion was yet strong. By compromises, with exceptions and under restrictions, it secured the sanction of religion for its work of extermination and absorption, the very same religion from which self-abnegation drew all its strength. Time rolled on, self-abnegation grew in size and strength, and with or without the support of religion promised to bring under its influence not only families and clans, but races and nations all over the globe, under every condition and under every circumstance. It now sighted its goal in the remote distance by the beacon-fire which, here in India at least, Lord Krishna set kindling in the Bhágvata-Gìtá—the goal where self-assertion and self-abnegation are both destroyed, for self itself is effaced there, lost in the immensity it acquires by identifying itself with the whole world, with anything and everything; but let us say for present purposes that the narrow self gets itself lost in its wide sympathy for all human beings of every colour, creed and nationality. That goal is far yet, and quite beyond the range of practical discussion at the present moment. Self-abnegation is yet far too weak, and self-assertion far too strong. Though Religion has now withdrawn her support from its work of spoliation, self-assertion has still found a valuable co-adjutor in science, which draws all its inspiration from the laws that regulate the unceasing displacement of matter. Science yet knows nothing beyond the motion of matter from one place to another, and in the pride of the power which such a knowledge has placed in its hands, it has expressed a readiness to jeer at the common belief in things behind the motion of matter, and at sentiments by the exercise of which the human soul feels itself refreshed, refined and ennobled. But as religion has improved and reformed, so will science; and science will put self-assertion out of the way of temptation by devising for it means to maintain the existence of self without destruction of its immediate kith and kin. In the meantime another complication has arisen in the world to interfere with self-assertion in its work of extermination and absorption. The world had time enough to produce races of inferior men of such a peculiar structure as will not be exterminated by fire, sword, strychnine, smallpox-clothing, rum, gin or heavy loads of ivory, but have shewn such an obstinate determination to live as to stagger all calculation of self-assertion and science. With such a tenacity for life, stranger still is the low capacity of their mind which prevents their assimilating the power which other sections of humanity have gained. They are thus too strong to die out and too low to be absorbed. What were formerly varieties, have now developed into species. What does it mean? In my opinion, a new phase of development humanity is passing through at the present moment. I may be wrong; it may be these races will improve their mental capacity in time. But a watchful observation of appearances around has suggested to my mind the fear that the evolution of a low order of humanity is in course of being accomplished, which will occupy among higher human beings a position somewhat above that of the cattle. This evolution of a new order of human beings is the natural consequence of progress on the one side and the want of capacity to assimilate that progress on the other side.

Has Providence brought about our connection with England to rescue this ancient and highly intellectual people of India from such a fate? Our seacoasts tasted the bitter fruits of Portuguese domination, which did not materially differ from those of Spanish domination in America. We have not disappointed the Metcalfes and the Macaulays among British administrators in their noble efforts to elevate the Indian races. These efforts have proved to our mind the position which, in their relation to each other, the British nation in its administration of India attaches to the two great questions—The Elevation of the People and the Safety of the Empire. The claims of the first to priority have been recognised. It has been acknowledged on all hands as the end whereof the Empire is the means. Yet there is danger of the Indian people degenerating into the lower order as a natural consequence of an act of the British themselves. It is the persistent refusal to educate the Indian people to defend their hearth and home if occasion for such an exertion ever arises. Should the Indian people ever find itself in the position of the domestic, harmless, sheep,—the same sheep that once possessed the power to brave the king of the forests with its hard round horns,—to be handed over to one by the other, to the brigand by the shepherd, to the butcher by the brigand, and to the consumer by the butcher, would the British then look back with self-complacency on their work in India? The loss of India will not make such a great difference to England as my countrymen generally suppose. But it will reduce us to the lower order of human beings. Will not the British take measures to save us from such a contingency? I am sure there will be no risk to the British Indian Empire if they give us military education. I feel sure it will add to the strength of the Empire. That which makes us feel at one with the Empire is an accession of strength to the Empire. As for ourselves, the Bengalis, we have a special claim to the consideration of our Government on this question. Government makes special arrangements to make up deficiencies in other races. Why not one for us to remedy a particular deficiency of ours? Oh, Sir George Campbell! How little did my people understand you! Those few who could speak amongst us saw you threaten their interests for the benefit of the millions. Those millions, alas! were not only dumb but blind. Come once again to us, Sir George, and let us see if our speakers have now magnanimity, our dumb their voice, and our blind their sight!

Sir Monier Williams is doing much to instil into the youthful mind of the British students the true circumstances relating to India and her people, and for his doing so he must be looked upon as a great benefactor by both the races. We are now in the midst of a collision between the dominating influence of power and the levelling influence of western education, that has brought out from the inmost Indian man his sense of sacred manhood. He who breaks the force of this collision and throws oil into our swelling surging waters deserves the gratitude of both England and India. Nor is Lady Monier Williams behindhand in the noble work of her husband. She takes an active interest in the movement and often works hard for its success. Her kindness for the Indians often takes a practical form. The first time I went to Sir Monier Williams, he said "you are my *Abhyágata*" *i.e.*, guest in the oriental sense of the word. No doubt, in Europe, a guest is a honoured being in the house of his host, but in the East he is a sacred being as long as he is under the roof of the latter. Sir Monier Williams is a Sanskrit scholar and he knew our feelings on the subject, so he and his lady treated me accordingly all the time I was in Oxford.

I visited the various Colleges at Oxford, which year after year let loose the mighty intellectual forces that have placed England in the vanguard of modern civilisation. I saw the Christ Church, with its Diocesan Cathedral and the Shrine of St. Frideswood, where Pitt and Gladstone knelt and prayed in their boyhood. I saw the Oriel, the Balliol, the Queen's and the glorious pile of the Magdalen College with its tower, its picturesque cloisters and its shady walks, trodden in bygone days by Wolsey, Addison and John Hampden. I saw also numerous other colleges, with their kitchens where food is cooked in a scientific way for the large number of students. I went to the Examination Hall, beautifully inlaid with marble of various colours brought from the countries and islands in South Europe. Nor did I neglect the Bodleian and Radcliffe Libraries, with their incalculable stores of books, nor the University Museum and Observatory with their valuable collections. The objects to be seen in this ancient city are too numerous to relate here.

At Oxford I saw Broughton—Broughton Sheridan Hunter, the eldest son of Sir William Hunter. Broughton and I were very good friends when he was a child of six or seven years' age. Since I set my foot in England I had been asking every body about him. Some one informed me that he was in Germany, and I was thinking of going there to see him. All of a sudden I heard from Lady Monier Williams that he was at Oxford. So one evening I went to see him, and in order to take him by surprise I did not send up my name. And it *was* a surprise for him to see an oriental with his dark face, turban and loose dress, suddenly enter his room instead of some European friend belonging to the University. He stammered out something about my having made a mistake, and he was more confused when I positively assured him that I made no such thing. Meanwhile, pretty little Mrs. Broughton, who sat by and watched the whole scene, enjoyed the fun in the naughtiest way imaginable. Had not that mischievous twinkle in her eye been one of the sweetest things one can lay his sight upon, I would have at once taken pity on Broughton and explained the whole matter there and then. The end however soon came, and Broughton was so glad, and Mrs. Broughton Hunter was so glad and everyone was so glad to see me. Since that day we passed many happy evenings together during my stay at Oxford.*

The hotel at Oxford where I put up was entirely managed by a young woman. It was a large old first-class establishment with ancient associations. Not only at Oxford but in all places where I went, I found women doing the most responsible work in hotels, shops, public-houses, post-offices, manufactories, everywhere. My countrymen will hardly credit the amount of work they have to do. At Glasgow I saw a girl-clerk in one of the large hotels, who had to work from nine in the morning till one o'clock the next morning. In the various restaurants of London, the girls work from 7-30 in the morning till 12 in the night. And such hard work too they have to perform! Accustomed as we are to see women relieved of as much heavy work as possible, and perhaps our sympathies being more easily awakened by the prettiness, neat tidy habits, and sweet trades-man-like manners of girls found in such establishments, we could not but feel for the hard work they had to do. Of course necessity has no law, but we could hardly believe in the selfish necessity

---

* Poor Broughton! Since the above appeared in the *Indian Nation* I have received the sorrowful news of Broughton's untimely death. In him, I have lost a brother.

of remaining bachelors, for men who had means to support a family. In this the women have something to blame for. Men love a little liberty, but the women of that country will not allow it. Are the women in this country more dependent on the whims of their husbands than the men in that country on the caprices of their wives? I will not hazard an answer. The high standard of living, the difficulty of supporting a family, the large number of men who lead a bachelors's life, and the excess of female over male population are the causes why so many women go unmarried. If the standard of civilisation were higher in this country, and if colour and race prejudice in the European in India were less rancorous, I would have recommended European wives to men who sell their ancestral lands to raise money to pay for a wife. When Bráhmans have taken to selling boots, spirits, tinned beef and ham, Indian caste-rules are not worth a moment's consideration. Anyhow intermarriage between the two races is out of question now. For who can seriously think of mating civilised Europeans with veritable savages who, like the barbarous Mishmis of the Eastern Himalayas, haggle and higgle for the price to be paid for their little boys and girls? I would as soon ask a European barber at Calcutta to hug in friendship his swarthy brother who goes about the streets with the little bundle containing his apparatus under his arm. The Ràjput who killed his new-born daughter had firmness and principle in him. But he has none who pays or takes the price of a child. Call it dowry, or explain it away any way you like, both you and I know what it means. One thing I very carefully observed in England is the honesty of these shop-girls. All day long pennies are pouring into their hands, but pilfering is practically unknown. Not only girls, but boys and shop-assistants are generally very honest. Put them in charge of independent establishments or send them as agents to distant countries, among the hills of Assam or to the diamond fields of South Africa, they will always do their work with the greatest honesty. This is why British trade flourishes, and this was how the East India Company acquired the empire of India.

A few pages back, I hoped that the age of cruel treacheries, brutal massacres, and wholesale extermination or helotisation of nations had passed away from this world. Not so, if newspaper reports are true about what is going on in the far West, in Brazil. There, it is said, the Christians, the civilised Europeans, are exterminating the poor Indians with strychnine and mercury in order to take possession of their lands. Our friends, the Christian Spaniards, poison their drinking wells, their granaries, and their preserved meat, and when they go back to see the result of their operations they behold with satisfaction men, women and children, by hundreds and thousands, stiff and cold after their violent convulsions. Good God! how the whole European world is silent about this horrible affair! Has the fountain-head of their tears run dry after crying so much over Muhammadan misdeeds in Bulgaria? Or is it that both religion and science still authorise the extermination of those Indian vermin in Brazil? I am very much surprised indeed that England should remain so silent over this cruel work. If England would only trust us, she could go on doing her knightly mission in defiance of the whole world. They seem to feel indignant only when a non-European does anything wrong. Two benevolent gentlemen lately witnessed in Haidarabad a barbarous sacrifice of goats and buffaloes offered by some low castes to the Goddess of Smallpox, and so in great indignation they at once wrote—"And these (low castes) are the brethren of the men whom a slight veneer of English education presumptuously leads to National Congresses and demands for Native Parliaments." These two gentlemen are very merciful, and the two hundred and fifty millions of the Indian people, including Bráhmans and Rájputs, Sikhs and Jainas, Shaikhs and Sayyids, are all cannibals. *There is* humour in the two gentlemen. If the money which Christian missions annually spend in this country is placed at our disposal, we can use it more profitably for the world at large in preaching, by precept and example, the Christian charity that is inherent in us among the nations of Europe.

In November 1886, my friend Mr. Thomas Wardle, invited me to his house at Leek in Staffordshire. The members of the Nicholson Institute at that place requested me to deliver a lecture on India. I did not know how to deliver a lecture, but I said something about the interests of England and India being identical. I suggested that the English people should pay some attention to teaching us how to earn more money than we do now. For shall we not return a portion of this money to England to buy her manufactures? England can take from India many raw materials which she now takes from foreign countries. Why does she buy £420,000 worth of opium from Turkey? What are the vegetable dying extracts of which she annually receives £348,000 worth from foreign countries? The fact is there is no one to look after the commercial interests of India either in Great Britain or in foreign countries, while even little Belgium has her consuls all over the world. I asked Englishmen to aid us in teaching our countrymen to look a little way beyond their village precincts and their mango *topes*, and to carry their mind a little higher than petty squabbles about castes and almanacks. Then, England can teach us how to convert into gold the numerous raw materials which now rot in the jungles, but which modern science has now brought within the reach of utilisation. Again, England can teach us to manufacture many little things which she now gets from foreign countries. Can we not make for her the lace which she now annually buys from Holland, Belgium, and France, to the value of more than one million sterling pounds? As I stepped down the platform, a pretty little girl came up to me and spoke Hindustáni. The words flowed so sweet from her lips that I was delighted to hear the language after such a long time and in such an out-of-the-way place. She was the daughter of Mr Longley, Secretary to the Great Eastern Hotel at Calcutta.

CHAPTER VI.

LAST DAYS IN ENGLAND.

I spent the last days of my stay in England seeing the various sights of London and the neighbourhood. Twice I went to Parliament and heard the debates then going on on the everlasting Irish question. The solemn feeling which the name of Parliament inspires in one at a distance was not heightened in my mind as I sat listening in the Visitors' Gallery. I could hardly realise in my mind the fact that the words that fell there decided the destiny of nations. It looked so like a debating club of old boys! Nor are the Houses of Parliament as a building very impressive. They looked like a vast shed, built in a Gothic style, with numerous courts, apartments and dark corridors. The edifice is new having been constructed between the years 1840-57, upon the site of the old Palace of Westminster and of St. Stephen's Chapel. The most notable feature outside is the *Clock Tower*, 320 feet high, with a large clock which is considered one of the best in the world, having never varied in its life more than four seconds in a day. It is wound up twice a week, and it takes five hours to wind up the striking part. A large bell strikes the hours, which is known by the name of "*Big Ben.*" "*Great Tom of Westminster*" formerly did that duty; it was removed in 1699 to the

Cathedral of St. Paul by permission of William III. *Great Tom* once made a funny mistake in the reign of William and Mary. One midnight it struck thirteen instead of twelve. This irregularity on its part owed its detection mainly to the vigilance of a sentinel at the Royal Palace at Windsor several miles off. He fell asleep whilst on duty upon a terrace at Windsor Castle, and was tried and condemned by a court martial. He pleaded not guilty on the plea that *Great Tom of Westminster* struck thirteen at midnight. He was however disbelieved by his judges, but everything became clear as noonday when several other persons came forward and swore that he spoke the truth. He was pardoned. The Houses of Parliament are entered through the Palace Yard and Westminster Hall up a broad flight of steps into St. Stephen's Hall, where Statues of Hampden, Selden, Fox, Chatham, Clarendon, Grattan, Falkland, Walpole and Mansfield are arranged on either side. Thence the visitor goes to the Octagonal Hall, the right hand passage from which leads to the House of Lords and the left to the House of Commons. The House of Lords, 97 feet long, 45 feet high and 45 feet wide, is well decorated with gilding and colour, wrought metal, carved work, frescoes, and arms of the sovereigns and chancellors of England. On one end of the chamber is the Throne, with two seats on either side on a less elevated dais, one for the Prince of Wales and the other for any distinguished personage next in honour. Before the Throne is the *Woolsack*, on which sits the Lord Chancellor. The Peers sit on seats ranged on either side of the chamber or on cross benches. There is practically nothing to speak of about the House of Commons. It is a large Hall, 70 feet long, 45 feet high and 45 feet wide, surrounded by galleries on all sides below and above. The Speaker's chair is on the further end in the same place occupied by the Throne in the House of Lords. Members sit in the galleries below, while over them are the galleries for visitors, reporters and the public. Since the dynamite explosion of 1885, strangers are not allowed to see the Houses, unless introduced into the Lords by a written order from a Peer and into the Commons by that from a Member.

Near the Parliament Houses is the celebrated Westminster Abbey, where the sovereigns of England are crowned and where rest the ashes of the greatest men in the annals of England. It stands upon the site of a temple dedicated to Apollo. Its conversion to a Christian Church is attributed by some to king Lucius (A.D. 184) and by others to king Sebert (A.D. 610 or 616). Commanded by St. Peter in a dream, Edward the Confessor rebuilt the sacred edifice in the shape of a cross and plentifully endowed it with precious relics. He gave to it "part of the place and manger where Christ was born, and also of the frankincense offered to him by the Eastern Magi; of the table of the Lord; of the bread which he blessed; of the seat where he was presented in the Temple; of the wilderness where he fasted; of the gaol where he was imprisoned; of his undivided garment; of the sponge, lance, and scourge, with which he was tortured; of the sepulchre, and cloth that bound his head; and of the mountains of Golgotha and Calvary;

great part of the Holy Cross inclosed in a certain one particularly beautified, and distinguished with many other pieces of the same, and great part of one of the nails belonging to it; and likewise the cross that floated against wind and wave over sea from Normandy, hither with that King. Many pieces of the vestments of the Virgin Mary; of the linen which she wore; of the window in which the angel stood when he saluted her; of her milk; of her hair; of her shoes, and of her bed; also of the girdle which she worked with her own hands, always wore, and dropped to St. Thomas, the apostle, at her assumption; of the hairs of St. Peter's beard, and part of his cross." Edward the Confessor was buried here, but the present building is not the one built by him. It was constructed during the reign of Edward I and II, and considerable additions were made to it from time to time by subsequent sovereigns and abbots. For instance, the Jerusalem Chamber was built by Abbot Litlington in the reign of Edward III. In it died Henry IV, whose last moments have been so touchingly described by Shakespeare—

>KING HENRY.—Doth any name particular belong
>   Unto the lodging where I first did swoon?
>WARWICK.—'Tis called Jerusalem, my noble lord.
>KING HENRY.—Laud be to God! Even there my life
>   must end.
> It hath been prophesied to me many years,
> I should not die but in Jerusalem;
> Which vainly I suppos'd, the Holy Land:—
> But bear me to that chamber; there I'll lie;
> In that *Jerusalem* shall Harry die.

Westminster Abbey passed through many vicissitudes during its life of twelve hundred years. In its early days kings, nobles and pious votaries vied with each other to endow it with lands and perquisites, and to embellish the sacred edifice with capitals, mouldings, statues and all sorts of sculptured decorations, the beauty of which was enhanced by a skilful inlay of precious stones, by embossed gold and by fretwork of silver. Master-painters executed the frescoes, experts painted on the glass-windows scenes of biblical life, and the walls were covered with rich tapestry, wrought by soft snowy hands that were plighted long ago to bold warriors who fought and died far away in Palestine. Solemn monks performed the various rites, incense burnt in the censers filling the whole place with a sweet perfume, and all knelt there and prayed, all believed, all reverentially spoke in hushed voices, *all* were ready to lay down their lives for the sake of the Father, Mother, the Son and the Saints, and all were as ready to take *your* life if you differed from them in the most trifling article of faith. Ah, those days! when devils were as plentiful and fond of mixing with human affairs, as the means possessed by man to thwart their evil machinations, and to ruthlessly cast them out of human society. For did not the very sight of the Confessor's coffin, when carried in 1269 to Westminster Abbey on the shoulders of Henry the Third and his brother Richard, King of the Romans, at once dispossess an Irishman and an Englishman of the devils that were in them? What a great fascination past days have on the human mind, and how we clothe the world of that time with a soft dim light, quietly sleeping on the everlasting spring, among fragrant flowers of variegated hues, sloping hills, green forests with overhanging boughs laden with fruit, musical rills and whispering zephyrs, where human life, bereft of all its struggles and turmoils that *we* know of, sweetly glided on to eternity in company with dancing fairies and sporting sylvan spirits! We are all poets and prophets by nature, only a fanatical poet makes a successful prophet. However reverentially we may recall to our mind the days that are gone, it is necessary that a disenchantment should take place, and that in wishing to be child again we should not forget that there were big boys to beat us, and mysterious apprehensions to torture us, and that there existed such things as marbles and sweets, the want of which caused us a world of unhappiness. But yet, what would we not give if knowledge and reason would but confirm the various creations of imagination, past and present, and satisfy the deep yearnings of our heart for gods and goddesses, genii and fairies, Rosicrucians and Mahátmás, and all sorts of subtle beings with powers greater than our own? Or, at least, let the whole working of the Universe be made clear to man and brought within the reach of his comprehension. Revelation after revelation has been vouchsafed to the world, but yet after all that deadly war they waged against each other from time immemorial the answers to the questions—Whence? Whither? and Why?—are as far from solution as ever.

In a later age, Westminster Abbey saw things totally dissimilar to those described above. Abuses in the Christian Church were indeed ripening the Reformation, when holy men like Peachum and Lockit quarrelled with each other and carved on the very walls of the sacred place gross caricatures, like those representing a monk being carried off by the Evil One, a woman wringing her hands in despair and an assistant sprite laughing for joy. Then came Henry the Eighth, with his spendthrift courtiers and hungry sycophants, to plunder all the ecclesiastical valuables, to wrench off the head of massive silver from the monument of Henry V, and to send to the melting pot the metal chasings of the shrine and the lead of the roof. But it received its crowning humiliation from the hands of Cromwell's Ironsides, who turned it into a barrack, mutilated the statues, stripped it of its ornaments, pawned the organ pipes and enjoyed the proceeds in a carousal over the ashes of Edward the Confessor. Westminster Abbey is such a confused heap of monuments and chapels that it is impossible to put an account of it, in an intelligible form, within the short space I have at my command. It contains not only the tombs and monuments of kings, queens and great men, but also of many obscure personages. This made Goldsmith to put into the mouth of his Chinese Philosopher the question—"*That* I take to be the tomb of some very great man. By the peculiar excellence of the workmanship and the magnificence of the design, this must be a trophy raised to the memory of some king who has saved his country from ruin, or lawgiver who has reduced his fellow citizens from anarchy into just subjection." But his surprise knew no bounds when he was informed that no such great deeds were necessary to get a final resting place within the precincts of the Abbey. The section where the bones of great men are interred or their memorials kept is called the "Poet's Corner." Here could be seen the graves, medallions, busts, tablets or monuments consecrated to the memories of men well known even in India, such as Ben Jonson, Samuel Butler, John Milton, Thomas Gray, Matthew Prior, &c., &c. In the Chapel dedicated to Edward the Confessor are kept the two *Coronation Chairs*, still used by the sovereigns of Great Britain for that purpose. One of them contains the famous Stone of Scone, a piece of greyish red sandstone, on which the Scottish kings were crowned, and which Edward I brought away to England. The Scots had very great reverence for this piece of stone, and believed that wherever it was carried the supreme power would go with it. Addison has saved me and all future dabblers in ink the trouble of making any serious reflections over the ashes that lie in Westminster Abbey. "When I see kings," wrote he in the *Spectator*, "lying by those who deposed them; when I consider rival wits placed side by side, or the holy men that divided the world with their contests and disputes, I reflect with sorrow and disappointment on the little competitions, factions and debates of mankind." To which may be added the terse saying of a great poet of the East—

Bas námwar bazer dafn kardah ánd;
Kaz hastesh ba-rue zamín ek nishán namánd.
O án pír láshú rá kih sipardand zer khák;
Khákash chunán bakhurd kazo istkhuán namánd.

"Many famous men have been buried, but not a single sign of them remains upon earth. That old man's corpse which was put under earth, has been so eaten by the soil that not a single bone remains."

I went to see the Tower of London, with which the history of England is so intimately connected. It was built by William the Conqueror in 1078, and to the original building subsequent sovereigns made many important additions. Royalty sometimes used the Tower as a place of refuge, as was done by Richard the Second during the insurrection of Wat Tyler. The different sections of the Tower are known as the White Tower, the Middle Tower, the Byward Tower, the Traitor's Gate on St. Thomas's Tower, the Beauchamp Tower, the Devereux Tower, &c. It was in the White Tower that Richard II abdicated the throne in favour of his cousin, Henry of Bolingbroke. A very interesting collection of arms and armoury of different ages has been preserved in the Tower, which among other things include a chain armour used in the Battle of Hastings, and the arms and accoutrements of the time of Agincourt and the Wars of the Roses. In the Tower are also kept the Regalia or the Crown Jewels of England, with the famous *Kohinúr* among them. But the Tower of London is interesting to the general public for the large number of noble heads that were cut off here by order of the former monarchs of England, and on account of the historical personages that were imprisoned here from time to time. It was here that Balliol, Bruce, Wallace, and John, King of France, were kept in confinement by Edward III. A place is shewn in the Tower as the "Site of the ancient Scaffold," where Queen Anne Boleyn and many others were beheaded. The Executioners were most busy in the time of Henry VIII. For an account of these executions, I must refer my readers to the history of England. The last man that was beheaded in the Tower was Simon, Lord Lovat, in 1747, for his share in the rebellion on behalf of Prince Charles Edward.

I went up the Monument erected to commemorate the Great Fire in London in 1666. It is 202 feet high. The top is reached by a winding staircase inside, consisting of 345 steps. That awful fire destroyed 460 streets and 13,200 houses. I also went to see St. Paul's Cathedral, where one day they invited us to be present at a service. Of course I saw the Zoological Gardens. Among other places to which I went I may mention the Bank of England, the National Gallery, the Hampton Court, and the Exchange. I also visited some of the hospitals, specially St. Bartholomew's, some of the cemeteries, notably that at Kensal Green where our renowned countryman, Dwarka Nath Tagore, is buried, some of the Clubs, like the Athenæum, and some of the co-operative stores, like the Army and Navy. Often I rambled among the fields in the neighbourhood of London near Chiswick and other places the names of which I forget, and in the Parks at Battersea, Finsbury, Regent's, Greenwich, Richmond, &c. How delightful it was to have a rowing on the Thames at Richmond! A visitor in London should not forget to go to *Madame Tussaud's*, where a large collection of life-size wax figures of kings, notable persons, celebrated thieves and murderers are kept for show. These figures are instinct with life and expression, and in some the eyes are so contrived to move as to make one mistake them for living beings. A section of the establishment is called the Chamber of Horrors, where figures of noted criminals and relics of historical as well as private atrocities are carefully preserved. Among these may be seen the image of Charles Peace, the notorious murderer and burglar, who apart from the ordinary disguises assumed by criminals of his class, possessed the wonderful power of so contorting his face in different ways as to appear on each occasion altogether a different man even to his most intimate acquaintances. He made a mistake by taking his birth in England. Such a wonderful power could easily raise him to the rank of godhead in this country. There are also in this Chamber of Horrors heads and likenesses of Marat, Robespierre and other notorieties of the French Revolution. The original knife and lunette, which decapitated 21,000 persons during the French Revolution, amongst whom were Louis XVI and Marie Antoinette, are shewn here. I went to see the Albert Hall and the Crystal Palace. Like the Thames Tunnel, the Crystal Palace has a traditionary hold in the minds of my countrymen, as one of the wonders of England. Its fame no doubt is largely due to its name. But there is no novelty now in a small tunnel under a narrow river, when mountains and seabeds are pierced by railways; or in a glass roof, when a portion of almost every office and hotel is imperceptibly separated from the sky above by this transparent material, and when by its aid tropical gardens are reared amidst the inclement weather of northern Europe. Nevertheless Crystal Palace is a vast edifice with a magnificent nave and two aisles and transepts. It is said that it cost a million and a half of sterling pounds. It is now used as a place of amusement where large numbers of people go, specially on Thursdays, when they have splendid fire-works to entertain the visitors.

We were invited by many of the Literary Societies in London. The vast establishment of the *Times'* Office also threw its doors open to us. Most of my countrymen have read an account of this wonderful establishment, and I need not therefore give a description of it here. Visitors in England should not fail to see the British Museum, the South Kensington Museum and the Botanical Gardens at Kew. The British Museum is well-worthy of the great nation to which it belongs. It had its origin with a private man, named Sir Robert Cotton, who formed a large collection of manuscripts and state papers. His son further augmented the collection, and his grandson presented it to the nation in the year 1700. The building where this collection was first kept was burnt by fire in 1731, which event led the Government of the time to consider the scheme to provide a suitable repository for such collections. An Act was passed in 1753, which gave the national sanction to the foundation of the British Museum. Perhaps nowhere in the world is the early history of man so vividly represented as in this institution. It would take a life-time to study the various objects that are so carefully preserved in this great repository of human knowledge. To an old and ancient race like ourselves the departments of antiquities must be the most interesting. So often and often did I linger among the Assyrian and Egyptian galleries, curiously looking at terracota tablets with inscriptions in the wedge or cuneiform characters, which served as deeds and documents 2500 years ago. Here was a petition to the king of Assyria from poor Nabu-balat-su-ikbi, denying the charge of treason brought against him; there a tablet recorded the sale of a slave, named Arbail-sarrat, about 648 B.C. Another tablet shewed the sale of a female slave, Hambusu, and her daughter, to Luku for one *mana* and eight *shekels* of silver. This transaction took place about the year 659 B.C. There was also a letter from Sennacherib, whilst still crown prince, to his father concerning the affairs of the kingdom. In that age, men cheated their brothers' widows as they do now, for I found among these tablets one with a detailed account of a law-suit brought by Bumanitu against her brother-in-law. These tablets record various other transactions in ordinary household affairs. Houses were let, gardens sold, agreements made about the dowries of Babylonian ladies, and similar transactions are all recorded there. The Egyptian collections are still more ancient, the earliest relics being at least 3800 years old. There is a very fine collection of hieroglyphic, demotic and the comparatively modern hieratic paphyri. Among the last may be seen treatises on medicine, geometry, arithmetic and other sciences. The collection of mummies is a splendid one. One I noticed was that of Tochenemum, daughter of

Petchonsu, door-keeper of the temple of Amen-Ra, who lived at least 1000 years before Christ. The antiquities of Greece and Rome are also well represented. The Asiatic collection is however not so good. It is said that if the racks in the library of the British Museum were spread out in one single line they would cover a space forty miles long. But what struck me most was the interest which people took in the objects displayed there. Acquirement of knowledge is a pleasure to them, and the most advanced among them feel the greatest satisfaction by practising the virtue of placing within the reach of the nation the means of acquiring knowledge. The collections at the British Museum mostly consist of objects contributed by private individuals. *Our* virtues have a different tendency. Men and gods so act and react upon each other that it is time for our gods to make a modification in their tastes. In this age of self-help, they must get rid of their penurious and exacting habits. However we may sympathise with them for the etherial nature of their constitution, we cannot really expend money to provide them with bodies of gold or silver, even of clay. Nor should they depend upon us for shelter, food, wearing apparel and ornaments for personal adornment. For the money they absorb is required for schools, museums, scientific institutions and other means of throwing light into the mind of this benighted people. If they in mercy allowed us, their humble servants, to recast our national budget, we in gratitude would twist and turn the meanings of Sanskrit verses and give them such a scientific status as would make them secure for a long time to come against all arguments of missionaries, theists, agnostics and atheists.

The Museums in Europe, where ethnographical specimens from all parts of the world have been collected, bring to the mind of an Indian a feeling of humiliation and sorrow. There he finds himself ranked among barbarous tribes with their cannibalism, human-sacrifice, tattooing and all sorts of cruel and curious customs that denote a savage life. The races of Europe, who have long discarded these practices, now look upon such acts with horror. It is a pity that, while we here are trying our best to revive old Hinduism, as existed say a hundred years ago—with of course human-sacrifice, *Aghori*-cannibalism, burning of widows, and all kinds of pious rites and ceremonies,—the people of Europe should look upon such modes of securing earthly and heavenly bliss with disfavour. It seems these Europeans are deaf to all sound argument, and will not listen to the profound esoteric explanations we tender for these practical outpourings of our religious fervour. We therefore cannot do better than, armed with all our unintelligible sacred books, take our stand on the lofty platform which a handful of European savants have built for us, look down with scorn on the wilful obstinacy of the European people, and patriotically despise their railways, telegraphs, their sciences and all their teachings. For have we not all these things written thousands of years ago in the books here under our arm? And many things besides, which our wisdom will show to us as soon as they are rediscovered or reinvented in Europe or

America? We have of late made an important addition to our already overflowing national glory by satisfactorily establishing our relationship with the priests of ancient Mexico, who artistically carved out with their sacrificial knives, and reverentially laid before the altar, the bleeding throbbing hearts of most beautiful youths who, but a day before, were dallying with the sweetest maidens of the empire, but whose bodies now lay below, still quivering with life, to be shortly dressed, cooked and eaten by the pious worshippers. Such acts were no doubt the most beautiful points of ancient religions: my countrymen are enamoured of them, and they are mad after reviving them in an esoteric shape. But, alas! we live in a vicious age. There is no toleration now-a-days. Who say the British tolerate the free exercise of our religion? Will they tolerate the brave *Aghori* to feed on putrid human flesh?—the *Aghori* whose all acts are sanctified, for in the very depth of his devotion he has buried all sense of sweet and sour, joy and sorrow, good and bad. Or will they allow us to moisten the parched tongue of our goddess with the blood of a tender youth free from all blemishes? Or, will they allow us to burn our widowed sisters to give a happy release to their souls longing for an immediate flight to heaven? Have they not trampled with a strong foot on the religious observances of our friends, the *Thugs*, the anointed of the gods, to carry out principles so ably generalised by Malthus, and as heavenly emissaries protected and cherished by kings and nobles? Did they not prohibit on pain of death or transportation for life the sacred rite of *Meriá* practised from time immemorial by our neighbours the Kandhs? O, they are now thinking of doing something to free our widows from an ascetic life to which we force them for their eternal good! Verily, this land has become the land of infidels—a regular *Dár-ul-harb*, to borrow with many grateful acknowledgments an appropriate term from our friends the Musalmans—and not fit for a good Hindu to live in. When they discouraged human sacrifice, they denuded the tree of Hinduism of its leaves, and as a result brought famines to the country as the peasantry in the Central Provinces will assure you, for there was no poverty, no famine before the English came to India [*Vide* History, specially the writings of Muhammadan historians as embodied in the eight volumes published under the authority of Sir Henry Elliot]. When they abolished the *Sati* they lopped off its branches. But the greatest act of tyranny the English committed against our religion has yet to be told : when they made the waterworks of Calcutta, they laid their inexorable axe at the root and felled the tree of Hinduism ! We did all we could to stop their sacrilegious proceedings. We nationalised each question as it came up. We held meetings and passed resolutions against the abolition of *Sati*, the establishment of schools and the introduction of waterworks. But for the few renegades, like Ram Mohan Roy, Mahendra Lál Sarkár, Malabari, and those men of Bombay who make cotton mills, our name would have remained as pure as ever, for nobody could then blame us if there was no *Sati* to-day, if there were

English schools and colleges in India, and if carcases of animals did not rot in our streets as it is said they do in Constantinople.

To speak seriously, it is time for us to realise our true position among the nations of the world, and not to revel in imagination and labour under hallucinations. It matters little now what we were many thousands years ago, even if we were all that was good and all that was great. It matters little now whether the *Mahànimba* of our books was the same as the *Cinchona officinalis* of to-day, whether Kurubarsha was the present Russia and whether Egypt and Mexico were colonised from India. It matters much to be able to see what we are to-day, for by that the world will judge us, not by that which we were. An antiquarian or a scholar may take a respectful interest in us, but every man and woman in Europe are not antiquarians or Sanskrit scholars. The truth is that the songs, which a nomadic race sang in the plains of the Panjáb many thousands of years ago, have not struck the world dumb or paralysed its mind with amazement. The world at a distance cannot make a distinction between a Kandh and a Bráhman, between a Jaina and a Muhammadan. It avails nothing if the Jaina condemns animal-sacrifice or the Muhammadan disavows *Sati*. There we are, all in a lump, to be judged by the most striking acts committed in our country. Our ancient civilisation is now out of date, and could only have been effective if Europe were to-day, what it was three hundred years ago. Or even I may say the distance between the two races was not very great fifty years ago. The discoveries and inventions that took place during the last fifty years have brought us within the sphere of those religious and philosophical principles, which men in all ages formulate from time to time for application on inferior races in order to satisfy their conscience and reconcile the general maxims of morality. Human beings are led by self-interest, and a leader is he who puts this self-interest on an intelligent and practical basis. He is either a man of strength, a man of religion, or a man of learning. Nowhere will you find mercy or respect for your age and past achievements except from the man of emotion, who is led more by the instincts which God has planted in his bosom than by the teachings of conquerors, patriots, prophets and philosophers. The most devout Christian can in all conscience tyrannise over a dark-skinned man, aye, work him to death, if he can only prove to his mind that he has got the blood of Ham in his veins. The most ardent votary of Reason can satisfy himself on the morality of carrying fire and sword to all parts of the world, to burn, pillage and murder the defenceless for the benefit of the powerful and, as he will call it, to help nature in its path of progress by destruction which brings about reconstruction. And as for the strong and the patriot, he goes about in quest of gain and glory in defiance of religion and reason. This is world, and it has been so as far back as man can remember. It behoves us therefore to see wherein we are deficient, and to try to make up that deficiency, if we are to gain the respect of our friendly rulers and the respect of the world. Otherwise let us quietly submit to be classed with savages.

The South Kensington Museum contains specimens of art. The place is full of plaster-casts of monuments, triumphal columns, architectural designs and statues. Among these may be mentioned Trajan's Column from the original in Rome. Pottery, ivory, bronze, gold and silver, wood and all sorts of handicrafts from all parts of the world, both antique and modern, are represented there. Among these collections may be seen the four Chinese Villas, which the Emperor of China sent as a present to the Empress Josephine, first wife of Napoleon. The vessel conveying these presents was captured on the way by a British man-of-war. After the Treaty of Amiens in 1802, the restitution of these presents was offered, but was declined. One villa represents a fine building, with a thatched roof ornamented with rows of pearls, on all sides surrounded by trees with golden stems and emerald leaves. The effect is extremely pretty. An extensive collection of pictures has also been presented to this Museum by a gentleman named John Sheepshanks. A section of the Museum is devoted to an extensive collection of Indian artware, which was the property of the East India Company and afterwards of the India office. The Botanical Gardens at Kew are a monument of British genius and perseverance. The vegetable kingdom of the British Empire, which includes one-sixth of the dry surface of the globe, is represented here. The Gardens contain also a Museum of Economic Botany.

It was now December. There was snow on the ground and the days were short. It was time for me to leave England. In eight months we saw things which no Indian remaining in his own country can hope to see in all his life. There is something in the atmosphere of England which opens the eyes and widens the mind. We were favoured with special opportunities, which can scarcely fall to the lot of the student or the tourist. The kindness with which we were everywhere received, by high and low, from our august sovereign the Queen Empress, down to the poorest peasant in the Midland, will be ever remembered with love and gratitude.

On the 13th of December, I left England for Rotterdam in Holland.

CHAPTER VII.

IN THE CONTINENT.

My journey through the Continent of Europe was a rapid one. I will not therefore be able to say much of the places to which I went. I am not a gifted traveller, like the European tourist who comes out to India. A hurried railway journey from Bombay to Calcutta, a day's halt here, a day's halt there in a railway hotel or a Collector's bungalow, and a tiger-hunting in the Tarái, lay open before his knowing mind the mysteries of this fabled land. He comes to know everything—about the formation of our country down to the Azoic period, about our soil with the plants that grow upon it, about our mountains, forests, seas and rivers with their Mammalia, Birds, Reptiles and Fishes, and all the masses of Invertebrata that live in them, about our air with the germs flying in all directions, about everything. But above all if you want to have reliable information about your religion, your manners, customs and superstitions, how you live, how you eat and drink, what you think, and so forth, you must read that nice little book which he publishes immediately after his return home. I say I am not a genius of that species, so my readers must content themselves with a bare outline of my rapid tour across the Continent.

Early on the morning of the 14th December 1886, I found myself on the River Maas, up which the little vessel "Princess of Wales" steamed her way to Rotterdam. The country on both sides the river was a green flat which, as every one knows, Dutch ingenuity has wrested from the roaring billows. Like a good politician, they have set the wind to neutralise the water. The country was full of windmills. Moved by the impulse given by the morning breeze, the vanes revolved on all sides, pumping water from the marshes, grinding corn or sawing wood. I have long wondered why wind-mills have not been used in India. It is such an old thing that it could not have escaped the notice of the early Hindus. There must be some insuperable difficulty in the way, at least insuperable in former times. Is it the great variation in the wind that prevails in this country, from a dead calm to a mighty hurricane that carries everything before it ? But surely modern mechanical knowledge can devise means for equalising in all sorts of weather the pressure of the wind on the sails. I saw an American windmill set up at Cawnpore, but do not know how it worked. Another little windmill was brought to the Bulandshahr fair some years ago, and the carpenter who made it was mightily proud of his achievement. The people looked upon it as a wonderful thing. We arrived at Rotterdam at 9-30 A. M. Rotterdam is a place of great importance, indeed the second place in the Kingdom of Holland. It is intersected by many canals which serve as streets. The shady walk near the river, called Boompjes, was built on wooden piles. The earth here is too soft to afford a secure foundation ; so they drive down it piles of wood, and upon this woody structure they construct streets and huge many-storeyed buildings. The whole town of Amsterdam with its thousands of houses has been built in this way, as also Venice in Italy. Rotterdam has its Botanical Gardens and Zoological Gardens. It also possesses a Society of Experimental Philosophy.

From Rotterdam I went to Haarlem, another important town in Holland. Here I was the guest of my friend, Mr. Van Eeden, the Director of the Colonial Museum. He took me to see the sights of Haarlem, among which his own Museum was a highly interesting one. Here he has got together, on behalf of his Government, a splendid collection of objects from the Dutch East Indies. The Dutch call their possessions in the East by the name of "India." Java, Sumatra, Borneo and the Phillipine Islands are "India" to them. In the Dutch Colonial Museum, I saw things made of snake-skin. The French use it as an ornamental covering for boxes, and they will be glad to buy from us the raw article, for the supply is anything but abundant. So here is a hint to those who have made it their profession to kill snakes for Government reward. A variety of ornamental things is made from feathers of birds in Sumatra and Java. A bright plumage is attractive, but it attracts both the welcome and the unwelcome. Enormous quantities of birds' feathers are used in Europe for the decoration of ladies' hats, and a brisk trade goes on in it in South Europe. In the Phillipine Islands they make very fine cloth from pine-apple fibre. Our pine-apple leaves are put to no use whatever, for it is not easy to extract fibre from them in this country.

We went to the Town Hall, where there is a picture gallery. The good citizens of Haarlem point with pride to the picture representing the "Siege of Haarlem." On that occasion, men and women bravely fought against the attacking Spaniards. The instinct of resisting oppression is strong all over Europe, and it works with equal force both individually and collectively. Another thing Haarlem has to be proud of. L. Coster, to whom the Dutch attribute the invention of type-printing in Europe, was a native of Haarlem. He has his statue facing the house he lived in. Another monument has also been erected to Coster near the place where he formed his first notions of block-printing. Linnæus wrote his "Systema" at Haarlem. Haarlem also possesses a Scientific Museum and a Botanical Library. In the last place, I saw a lady engaged in painting botanical illustrations. She was a good botanist. In Europe scientific knowledge is not confined to men alone. A strong current of development runs through the atmosphere there, which carries onwards even the most lumbering oriental mind. Such a current has set in in this country, but there is a marked want of sensibility in those that are moving on. Or do they admit it not for the consolation which inferiority gets by refusing to believe in superiority, which envy receives by calumniating the envied? Patriotism is no such thing: it is truth, honour, light and wisdom. Patriotism in this country seems to have fallen into the trap which interested parties laid for it in order to drag it by the nose to stupid retaliation. Haarlem stands on the side of what was formerly a lake. It has been drained, and 70,000 acres of good arable land have been acquired for cultivation. Large quantities of hyacinths, tulips and other "Dutch bulbs" are grown all around Haarlem, which are exported for seed to foreign countries. There was a mania in Europe for beautiful and rare kinds of tulips 250 years ago. At that time one little root is said to have been sold for more than Rs. 60,000.

In the evening, a few scientific gentlemen of Haarlem came to see the Bráhman from India. Among them was a Sanskrit scholar. The conversation turned upon Bráhmanical religion. I said that a true Bráhman belongs to no nation or no creed in particular: he belongs to all. He preaches universal charity. Long ago he found out that he was merely a part of the whole. But the world was not prepared for what he taught. So he succumbed under the weight of his premature growth. Endless compromises, extending over thousands of years, at length shaded the light so much as was best suited for the eyes of those that needed such a shade. But with the advance of knowledge an intelligent eclecticism is now sure to take place, which is likely to satisfy the religious aspirations of scientific minds all over the world for the time being. To the Sanskrit scholar I recommended a careful perusal of the Sánkhya system, the Yoga system, the Vaiseshika, the Uttara-mimánsá, but above all the Bhágvata-Gitá. I said that in my opinion two things have hitherto prevented European scholars from forming a clear judgment on ancient Indian matters. The first is their belief that the world has been created only six thousand years, and the second is their very natural predilection for countries mentioned in the Bible. They would rather say that we took Manu from Egypt, than Egypt got her Menes from us. They would have been quite ready to believe that we got Algebra from the Arabians, if the Arabs had not said expressly in their books that they got the science from us. Within the last fifty years, we helped European scholars to construct the science of comparative philology, but I do not see it suitably acknowledged. They would always admire more the Eddas and the Der Niebelungen Lied than the Puránas and the Sanskrit epics. My friends thought that it would be a good thing if we could send a mission to Europe to convert the people there to our religion. I said that we must put our own house right first. I further remarked:—" My country is now the scene of a great fight. A battle is going on there between Spirituality and Temporality, but not for the possession of a bit of ground as you are witnessing in Europe. Spirituality for long regulated all our temporal affairs, and compelled us to build our houses this way and not that way, to eat this food and not that food, to drink this beverage and not that beverage, to wear this cloth and not that cloth, to wear our hair this way and not that way, to take this medicine and not that medicine, to take a journey this day and not that day, to go to this country and not that country, to die here and not there, &c. Temporality wants to set us free from this iron bondage, but Spirituality has at her back all the prestige of the *status quo* and all the forces of divine authority, while Temporality has only the cowardly commonsense and the ever-hesitating ever-doubting science to aid her in her work. Yet, you may safely predict the result." My friend then asked me whether on my return home I intended to separate myself from those that believe in such things; for, he said, "you think like a European and not like an oriental." I replied—"Do not think lightly of an oriental. The sun rises in the East, not only in a material but also in its moral and spiritual sense. On the easternmost limit of the East, Confucius, on being asked by a disciple to include in a single word the sum of human duty, said—'Does not retribution do this? Thou shalt not do unto others that which thou wilt not that they should do unto you.' Five hundred and thirty years later, another great oriental said the very same thing on the westernmost limit of the East. In the middle, I mean in India, not only did our sages give expression to similar sentiments long before the birth of Confucius and Jesus Christ, but they also asked us to consider this golden maxim binding on us not only in our dealings with brother-men, but also in our dealings with all things that have life, that feel pain and the pangs of death, and that love to live. But to answer your question,—I do not think, I will separate myself from my people. Have you seen a centipede? It has many feet. Compare my country to a centipede, and me to one of its feet. If I separate myself from the body, I am dead and inert. Attached to the body, I help in its onward course. A number of such feet has got themselves loose from the cumbersome body, but they

1 P

are of no more value to move it onwards than the stray wheel of a locomotive engine to drag the train."

Next day Mr. Van Eeden took me to Amsterdam. We first went to Dr. Westermann, a gentleman of 80 years, one of the greatest naturalists in the world. The doctor received me very kindly, and asked me many questions about the progress of knowledge in British India. Dr. Westermann presides over the Zoological Gardens, which possess a fine collection of animals, among which I saw several lions and lionesses with cubs. We then went to Mr. K. N. Swierstra, Conservator, K. Z. G. Natura Artis Magistra. This gentleman has a splendid collection of butterflies and beetles from all parts of the world. I was very hospitably received by Mr. G. Janse, the officer in charge of the Aquarium. The Amsterdam Aquarium is one of the finest in Europe. They have both salt water and fresh water fishes here arranged in two rows. Four years ago, Mr. Janse obtained a supply of salt water from the sea. This water is conserved by maintaining an endless current, on one part of which it is filtered and pumped up. The most important sight in Amsterdam is the Ryk's Museum containing many pictures of great celebrity. Among these may be mentioned the celebrated Night-watch by Rembrandt, Le Confrère des Marchands de drap, Orphelines d' Amsterdam, the protrait pictures of the City Guard and Archer's Guild, &c. Amsterdam is the centre of an extensive canal system, by means of which the Dutch carry on an enormous trade with the rest of the world. The North

Holland Canal and the North Sea Canal connect Amsterdam with the German Ocean. The former is 130 feet and the latter 200 to 330 feet wide. The city itself is intersected by numerous canals, practically dividing it into 95 islands connected with each other by 300 bridges. As mentioned before, the soil is too soft to afford a secure foundation for buildings, so the Dutch drove piles through 50 or 60 feet of peat and sand and built their city upon them. The Palace at Amsterdam was built on about 14,000 piles. Secure as the foundation is, it is within the range of possibility for a building to sink under a heavy weight. The great Corn Magazine, with its 3,500 tons of grain, collapsed in 1822. Amsterdam is noted for its diamond-cutting industry, which gives employment to 10,000 workmen, mostly Jews. The most noted establishment is that of Kosters, where the wheel makes 2,000 turns a minute, *i. e.*, the wheel revolves more than 30 times by the time you can count "one."

In Holland many of the higher classes talk English, French and German. English is the commercial language, French the diplomatic language, and German the language of a powerful neighbour. "In French," once said a diplomat to me, "thoughts are expressed with the greatest precision." I asked him if that was not a disadvantage. He stared at me, evidently astonished at my simplicity. I put the question because the world entertains an opinion that precise language is the last thing a politician will care for. A plain "Yes" or "No," when the opposite is the fact, is an abhorrence; but an artistic rendering of the same sense excites admiration, at least is not practically condemned. Some are specially gifted with a natural talent in this direction, others acquire it. In Europe they are scientific: execution of criminals is an art, so is the murder of facts. In partisan-journalism alone facts are permitted to be murdered unscientifically. The blunter the weapon, thicker flow in the pennies. In savage life, the art I am speaking of is entirely absent; in a semi-barbarous society it is as a child, crude, open and delighting in trivialities; but in a civilised state it is in its highest perfection, grave, solemn and proud, yet charming. So much for the art and its worshippers. Its acquirement, however, is rather difficult for a European, for he labours under a disadvantage at the outset. The nursery atmosphere there is not congenial to its growth. When mothers every night make their little ones kneel at the bedside and pray, drop by drop the simple words cut in the soft minds an impression which it is not easy to efface in after life. This impression is dead against the art. Upheld by a strong sense of manliness and pride, the people as a body carry it through life in its fullest integrity. So it happens that the prince, patriot and the peasant among the two hundred and fifty millions in the remote continent of India have but one cry—"We will appeal to the British people!" That is the cry too of the highest intelligence in the country—The National Congress.

From Amsterdam I retraced my steps westwards. In due time I arrived at Paris. The prettiest fairy in the world seems to have made this beautiful city her bower. As light is the smile of the sun, beauty is the smile of such a fairy as this. Her smiles spread an unrivalled charm over this graceful city, over its well-laid parks, its wide scrupulously clean roads, and the symmetrical elegant palaces that line them on each side. Might I not fall on my knees, pour forth my heart to the presiding Spirit of Paris, and ask her for a charm to cast out the Malignant One we are possessed with, that would not permit us to make a little road connecting two railway stations even in the metropolis of India? Or would I rather first court the favour of her maids—the modest one, known by the name of Self-Abnegation; the one with sweet lips inviting all patriotic French to come and kiss her, called by the name of Unanimity; and the lovely little fairy who laughingly answers to the name of Good-Taste? Oh Paris! teach thou thy savage sister, Calcutta, how to make her toilet. Poor little savage! what can she do where in a far more touchy quarter loads of gold and silver usurp the place of decency?

On my arrival at Paris I first went to the Grand Hotel. In eastern countries royal magnificence belonged exclusively to royalty. Not so in the West. The poorest of the poor there can live like a king, if only for a day, by simply going to the Grand Hotel at Paris. Nothing can exceed the magnificence of the first class hotels in Europe, not even the palaces of kings. Here is the explanation why people prefer to live in hotels and boarding houses instead of having a place exclusively to themselves. Civilisation secures greater benefit from co-operative action than barbarism from individual effort. My countrymen often wonder why every English family does not possess a house all its own. They attribute it to poverty. No doubt it is through want of sufficient means, but it is a poverty which bears not the slightest relation to what is understood by that term in this country. For, a gentleman to have a house of his own to live in means a great deal more than the bare cost of erecting it. But the more palpable reason is that land is scarce in England, that the whole of it belongs only to a few individuals who jealously keep it, and that it is not the custom in that country to build, wherever one likes, a wretched hovel and live in it generation after generation. Besides, the idea of keeping a house in good order differs from what is entertained here. It costs them a great deal more time and trouble. Nor have they the custom of having a widowed sister or aunt to remain in charge when the family is absent from home. They do not send their roots deep down into the soil, but go from place to place, to London in summer, to Scotland, France or Germany in autumn, and to South Europe in winter. A house therefore becomes an encumbrance to a man with limited means; he finds it more convenient to hire one from a professional house-holder than to keep one himself, just as we buy a piece of cloth when we require it, and not keep a loom at home, as they do in Assam and Burma. In fact an individual with a palace in India and Rs. 2,000 a month all to himself will not command the same comfort as he will with Rs. 500 at the Grand

I had letters for M. Arnould and Professor Baillon, both scientific men of high repute. I was also introduced to M. Frémy, Membre de l' Institut, Directeur de Museum D'Historie Naturelle. Dr. Frémy is one of the greatest chemists in the world. He does not speak English. M. Maxime Cornu, Professeur Administrateur au Museum D' Historie Naturelle, and Membre de la Societè Nationale D' Agriculture, acted as my interpreter. Dr. Frémy received me very kindly. He takes special interest in fibres, particularly in Rhea *(Bœhmeria nivea,* H. and A.) I told him what we had been doing with it in India, and how we had signally failed to get a suitable machine for the extraction of the fibre from the stalk, notwithstanding repeated trials and the large reward offered by Government. He enquired if I was present at any of the trials. I replied that I saw two, and that in one I was not only present but was a judge appointed by the Government of India. Dr. Frémy then with great alacrity shewed me his sample collection, from the raw bark received from Algiers to the ultimate fibre ready for spinning. The clean fibre no doubt was what Rhea fibre ought to be, silky, glossy, unusually strong and exceptionally long, although in the process of manufacture it was subjected to a course of chemical treatment. Dr. Frémy has himself discovered the process. I could however elicit no satisfactory information about the cost of manufacture. At length I fairly told him that if his process was only intended to shew what Rhea could do and nothing more, he need not have taken so much trouble, for its capabilities were proved long ago. Dr. Frèmy smiled and remarked that not only is his process suitable for commercial purposes, but that it has triumphantly passed through the ordeal of practical application and that it is now used in the manufacture of the fibre so largely woven into fabrics at Lille. Dr. Frèmy further informed me that the supply from Algiers is not equal to the demand, and the market for dried bark is open for any one to come and step into it. He promised to test, and to obtain a valuation for any sample that may be sent to him from India. But he said the first consignment should not be less than six tons of the raw bark. I also told him about another species of the Urticaceæ, very similar to the Rhea, *viz.*, the *Maoutia Puya*, Wedd, which grows wild in the Sub-Himalayan regions of the Bengal Tarái and Assam. M. Jules Poisson, Aide Natureliste au Museum, and Professor Bureau then took me round the Chemical Laboratory, where a large number of students of both sexes were making experiments, and also round the Microscopic School where young men and women were engaged in making observations. I went to other scientific institutions in Paris, which it would be tedious to describe here.

In Paris I saw the Eden Theatre and the New Opera. Both very large places, and must have cost enormous sums of money. The New Opera is said to have cost upwards of two crores of rupees. I did not understand the plays, but I enjoyed the dance and liked the scenes. In the Eden Theatre a large number of girls danced together, as they do at the

Alhambra in London. These girls were bravely dressed, all glittering with gold and imitation stones, and when lights of different hues were thrown upon them as they danced, the whole scene formed a reality of fairy life, as far as it is possible for it to be real. Christmas pantomimes at Calcutta are good, but here they cannot afford to lay out so much money for dress and scenic decorations. Between the scenes I took a stroll over the building, and I met people who asked me for champagne. Let me thank my turban: I did not understand any European language whatever. As they tried one after the other, I mournfully shook my head, and replied in a language which I do not think was ever spoken by any nation in the world. But I did not quite enjoy the fun, for the remarks they made among themselves were equally Greek to me. I went to the Boulevards, but the trees at the time were mostly bare. Yet with their spacious foot-paths and brilliant rows of shops and cafès, they formed one of the most beautiful promenades in the world. I also went to the Champs Elysèes. What a gay multitude thronged there! All mirthful and neatly dressed, not however in rainbow colours or in thousand and one forms. I do not object to showy dress in a dark people, but the extensiveness of variety made available by imported materials has confused taste and destroyed its native congruity. The multitude there enjoy life, and know how to make the most of the least enjoyment. Notwithstanding all the philosophy the Indians are credited with, Europeans know better how to make cares take care of themselves. I saw many of the panoramas. One was a battle-field, depicted with such vivid reality, that even after such a long time I feel sick and sorrowful to call it to mind. O! the wounded man lying in the ravine all alone, bleeding, dying, perhaps very thirsty with no one to give him a drop of water to moisten his parched throat before he is past all thirst and pain! The sad face is yet in my mind. O mother! come and see how lies the boy whom thou so lovingly didst fondle in thy breast. O sister! the brother whom thou lovest so dear thinks of thee in this his supreme moment, thinks of the day when little child that thou wast, he plucked beautiful flowers from high above the tree to stop thy crying. O sweetheart! thou that nearly broke thy gentle heart at the name of parting, but yet hoped; what hope now? It was such a reality, that I yearned to run to the figure, take his head up to my bosom and to weep over him, to weep over the brutality of man!

I saw the Triomphe de l' etoile, a triumphal arch erected to commemorate the victories of Napoleon Bonaparte, and the Colonne Vendome, which the great Napoleon constructed by melting down 1,200 cannon taken in battle from the different nations he conquered. It was taken down from its pedestal by the communists in 1871, but has since been replaced. Napoleon's body now lies at the Hotel des Invalides, where disabled soldiers are quartered. Among the Museums I went to the Trocadero, where antique statues and ethnographical specimens are kept. But the most important place of this kind is the Louvre. The Museum of the Louvre is divided into different sections comprising antiquities; French sculpture; drawings; paintings of the Italian, Flemish and French schools; Spanish paintings; Greek, Roman and Egyptian antiquities, vases, statues, &c., and models of shipping. The original Venus of Milo is kept here. The most interesting part of the Louvre is the picture gallery, which contains one of the most splendid art collections in the world. The Immaculate Conception and the Beggar Boy may be named among the noted pictures in the Louvre. The Tuilleries Gardens are near the Louvre. Here stood the palace where so many incidents of French history took place. The communists burnt it in 1871. I visited the celebrated Notre Dame, a magnificent cathedral built in the twelfth century. It has three principal entrances, finely carved with subjects from the New Testament. There are two majestic towers which can be seen from a long distance. A large bell, called Le Bourdon, weighing 322 cwts., is only rung on state occasions. The choir inside contains beautiful paintings and carvings. The gallery is supported by 297 massive pillars. The glass windows are magnificent. The organ in the Cathedral has 5,000 pipes and is considered one of the finest in the world. The floor is of marble. Among other statues, I noticed that of Charlemagne on horseback with Roland and Oliver on foot. Near the Cathedral of Notre Dame is the Palais de Justice and La Sainte Chapelle, built by St. Louis for the reception of a portion of the true cross and the crown of thorns, purchased from the king of Jerusalem for 300,000 marks. The glass-windows are of beautiful colours, specially one rosette which is particularly good. Every visitor to Paris sees the Morgue, where dead bodies found in the Seine or in the streets are kept on view for identification until putrefaction sets in, after which their photographs are exhibited. I saw two bodies, found in the Seine, both of young men. The picture of a boy about five years old was also there. His body was found in the street a few days ago. Nobody claimed it. Such a thing is not possible in this country. I saw the Palais Royal with its courts, galleries and arcades, resplendent with jewellery shops. The Pantheon was formerly a Church, but is now used as a burial place for noted men, like the Westminster Abbey in London. Victor Hugo is buried here. My guide pointed out to me something as belonging to Voltaire, but I do not remember if he told me that Voltaire's remains have been removed to the Pantheon. I saw many other places in Paris, which it would be too numerous to describe.

I asked the guide, who conducted me to all these places, how he liked his present government. He threw a glance around to see if anybody was within hearing, and then said in a hushed voice—"Oh! it is an Opportunist Government, I don't like it at all." I do not know why he was afraid to say what he said, for it can hardly be that freedom of speech has anything to fear in the land of "Liberty, Equality and Fraternity." At all events we are better off under the British rule than the Continental Europeans under their own governments. This is a fact which I want to strongly impress upon my countrymen. Political offence is unknown in India, with its suspicions and cruel consequences. This is one of the happy anomalies under which we live. Indian mind, as represented by the bulk of the people, has scarcely emerged out of that darkness which prevailed in Europe in the Middle Ages. We have thus here the Middle Ages without their horrors. The Nineteenth Century gently taking the folds off the eyes of the Ninth Century. The morning twilight softly whispering to darkness the lesson to get bright. No violence, none of those throes and agonies under which parts of Europe still groan to give birth to that freedom which we British subjects claim as our birthright. None denies our right. I do not know what to admire most, the policy itself or the wisdom that dictated such a policy. Any other people but the British people would, I think, have *created* political offences, no doubt with suicidal results. Strong in its strength and confident in the righteousness of its cause, the great nation beyond the sea has laid down a policy the depth and breadth of which have to be fully grasped. Surely this nation has rightly deserved the love and loyalty of the two hundred and fifty millions of human beings. Thus we start with a general policy at the head the soundness of which no Indian can question. The controversy lies further down, in the working of its details. That kind of controversy always exists in every country, even under the best form of government which man has yet been able to devise or evolve. Care should therefore be taken to reduce it to its narrowest limits. A fearful responsibility rests upon the leaders of

Indian opinion as well as upon every member of the British people that have come to this country. A great change has overtaken one-sixth of the human race. It rests upon the leaders to wisely guide the nation through this transition, always remembering to whom we owe this change. Above all, we should not be hasty in judging men. Take an example. Nobody abused us (Bengalis) in more opprobrious terms than Macaulay did. But is there an educated Bengali now who would not like to make an image of that man and say?—"O, great spirit! inspire me with those noble sentiments that thou felt and expressed whilst thou animated this likeness." If I am not mistaken in the British people there can be but one answer to India's question—"Sister Britannia! will you look down upon me because I am dark?" On the other hand, every member of the British people in India must remember that he is not a private individual in this country. The millions around look upon him as a representative of the great nation that rules over them. The honor of his nation is thus in his hands, and though the eyes of his own people may not be upon him, the eyes of a vastly larger number of human beings are upon him, who are not like Africans or Australian aboriginals, but who from time immemorial have possessed a moral code not inferior to any moral code in the world. Therefore, the separate standard of civility and morality which Europeans evolve in non-European countries, as differing from that prevailing among themselves, for application to the people among whom they sojourn, is a mistake in India. Is there any man in the world so lost to self-respect as to like to be booked for a "low caste man" by his servants and inferiors? This is precisely what often happens, alas! not always without good reason.

It was snowing when I left Paris for Cologne. When I arrived at Cologne the whole country was covered with snow. Every thing outside was white, the fields were white, the trees were white, the houses were white and the crows were white. I went to the Hotel d' Hollande, just on the side of the Rhine. The river here is deep and as broad as the Hooghly at Serampur. The water was muddy. Numerous steamers went up and down the river, and the traffic seemed to be not inconsiderable. But nothing like what Cologne had in past days, when she was a free city, and when she compelled all vessels navigating her river to unlade their cargo here to be further conveyed by her own shipping. I saw on the river-bank small hand-carts, which the owner drags himself assisted by a dog that incessantly howls as it runs. The weather was so unpropitious that I did not care to see much of Cologne. I only went to see the Cathedral and the Church of St. Ursula. The Cathedral was founded in 1248 and completed only in 1880. It is needless to say that it is one of the most magnificent buildings of the kind in Europe. Like all such edifices it is built in the shape of a cross. The material used is red sandstone. This colossal structure is 496 feet long by 238 feet through the transept, and the height of the two west spires is 515 feet above the level of the floor from which they rise. Inside, there is a good model of Jesus

Christ, representing the scene immediately after the crucifixion. I was told that the figures are made of stone. They are very life-like indeed. The Cathedral contains the tomb of the three wise men who came from the East to see Jesus Christ just after he was born. I think some skulls were shewn to me as belonging to the Magi. A silver monument has been raised over this tomb, which is richly adorned with gold and precious stones. Among the last the attention of the visitor is always drawn to a big topaz. The stone thrown by the devil from the Seven Mountains has been carefully preserved here. The Church of St. Ursula commemorates the martyrdom of 11,000 virgins killed by the Huns in the eleventh century. Their relics are to be seen in the walls of the Church. Eau de Cologne is made at Cologne.

It was still snowing when I left Cologne for Berlin. I arrived at this place on Tuesday the 21st December 1886. It was very cold now, but I did not feel any discomfort on the way. The railway carriages in Germany are particularly good. They have a heating arrangement which maintains in them a genial temperature. Connected with the heating arrangement is a dial placed on the wall of each compartment, by turning the handle of which one way or the other the place can be made more hot or more cold. At Berlin, I went to the Central Hotel. It is a large hotel with more than five hundred bed-rooms. Like all first class hotels it is lighted with the electric light. The place is well decorated with frescoes and painted glass. In Europe they have a great fondness in decorations of this kind for symbolical scenes representing the four quarters of the globe. Attached to the hotel is a large hall roofed with glass, a sort of indoor garden, where people sit and sip their coffee. Amusements in the shape of theatres and concerts are also provided by the hotel in their theatre-room adjoining the garden. Lodgers go there free of any extra charge. One drawback of this hotel is that it is infested with guides who are more cruelly disposed towards their prey than others of their kind. It was now snowing night and day, but a constant temperature of 70 degrees Fahrenheit is maintained in the hotel by means of pipes. In ordinary houses they use stoves. In the Continent they have no open fire-place as in England, and I missed that very much.

Although I had quarters at the Central Hotel, during my stay at Berlin I was practically the guest of Professor Reauleux, Privy Councillor of the German Empire. Professor Reauleux is a Sanskrit scholar, and he takes great interest in all matters connected with India. He has lately discovered a close connection between chess and card as played in former times. While I was at Berlin, he was trying to find out the origin of a gold tablet lately dug up in Hungary. I think he is right in his supposition that it was an ornament which formerly adorned the head of an elephant. There is nothing against supposing that the Hun army possessed elephants. We had a close connection with this people, and whether Tibet was their original home or not, we still call our neighbours of the Himalayan tableland by the name of Hunias. Defeated by the Chinese on the east they moved towards the west and devastated Europe. The Magyars of Austro-Hungary are their descendants. I told Professor Reauleux how closely connected we have always been with the Huns, and how a similar ornament was used in ancient India to bedeck and protect the forehead of a state elephant. Professor Reauleux took me to see the various sights of Berlin. In one of the museums he shewed me some very nice pottery, the manufacture of which was extinct. It has lately been revived through an old man who saw the process of making it while he was quite a child. In Germany, they have also made in glass an excellent imitation of our metal-ware, glass-ware, lacquered-ware and pottery in their various shapes, designs and patterns. Professor Reauleux also showed me some pictures with carpets painted on them. From these pictures many old patterns of carpets have been revived. One evening the Professor took me to the Opera, and explained to me what was going on. As usual the scenes were very good.

I went to see the Ethnological Museum presided over by Dr. Bastian. Dr. Bastian came to Calcutta some years ago, and I think many of this city know him. He has been to all parts of the world making collections for his museum. I was introduced to this gentleman by Dr. Jagor. Dr. Bastian kindly took me round the place and pointed out to me everything that was of interest. He shewed me a carved piece of stone from ancient Mexico. It represents a human sacrifice. A dutiful scion of a noble family is offering the head of the victim to the manes of his ancestors, when lo! with outstretched hands another claimant appears for this dainty morsel. He is the king of the nether regions, whom the scent of the victim's blood has brought all the way up to the place of sacrifice. The brave young man however is not to be easily persuaded to give up to him, all the king of Death that he is, what he intended for the palates of his ancestors. A hot discussion therefore ensues, and the argumentative words of Death flow like a curl of smoke across the surface of the stone towards the ear of the obstinate sacrificer. How the dispute ended I do not know, for it is not shewn on the stone. It is a new museum, yet it is one of the best I ever saw. The new national life in Germany is visible everywhere.

The weather was so bad that it was impossible to go out much. All day and night it snowed. Heaps of snow lay on the roads, and sledges took the place of wheeled carriages in the ordinary street traffic. The railways were all blocked and I was practically snowed up in Berlin. I was fortunate however to see the late Emperor William I. My friends would have taken me to Prince Bismarck, but this great man was not at Berlin at the time. As it often happens with me wherever I go, I frequently lost my way in my wanderings through the streets and lanes of Berlin. One afternoon, I spent a long time in looking at the Christmas booths now set up on the banks of the Spree, and it was nearly dark before I thought of returning home. When I thought of coming back to my hotel, I could not find my way. For one whole hour I went through various streets in the hope of getting a sledge or a carriage, but I could see none. I asked several policemen and wayfarers to shew me the way, but they could not understand me. It was very dark now, and the matter looked serious. At length I met a little girl blind of one eye, returning from her day's work. To her I simply uttered the words "Central Hotel." She understood and made me a sign to follow her. As I subsequently learnt, the poor girl went about a couple of miles out of her way to see me home safe.

One evening, a friend invited me to his house. Among other gentlemen assembled there, I met a Philosopher. He told me many things about the German systems of philosophy and the progress which Europe had made of late in abstract sciences. He asked to know what we Indians thought of the subject. I said —" I am not fit to speak on such a grave matter, but so far I can judge my countrymen are not particularly edified by the conclusions you have drawn, however they may admire the subtlety of your reasonings. They hold that European mind, as constituted at present, is not able to grasp the higher truths inculcated by sages elsewhere thousands of years ago, and that Kant, Jacobi, Fichte, Schelling, Hegel, in short all European philosophers, seem to them to move more or less round and round the same groove. My countrymen are anxiously waiting for the time when in due course the European mind will be fitted to look beyond what you call the primordial force, which makes you see nature in a constant state of warfare, and leads you to take your lesson from what you understand not. So according to my countrymen, the following tribute to oriental wisdom is well rendered by an English poet :—

> 'Yours is the rain and sunshine, and the way
> Of an old wisdom by our world forgot.
>
> . . . .
>
> Well may we sons of Japhet in dismay
> Pause in our vain mad fight for life and breath
> Beholding you. I bow and reason not'."

I checked myself, as the thought suddenly came to my mind that I might be mistaken for one fit to hold a controversy with him on such a subject. I cannot be too careful on this point, for I am born under a particular evil star which constantly subjects me to be misunderstood by others. The least harmful of such misapprehension often takes the shape of my being credited with knowledge which I do not possess. Whom to contradict, how to contradict, and what good will come out of it? I might as well run after the wind to silence its whispering voice among the leaves! When the world once forms an impression, it is as difficult to erase it as the anti-resurrection belief in the mind of the Negro chief who, in answer to all Christian arguments, *would* say—"Can a dead man come out of his grave unless dug up?" For very shame, I had often to acquire a superficial knowledge of subjects I was credited with, perhaps with the result of making the first erroneous impression still deeper and still worse. But this cannot go on for ever, when the body in its frailty disobeys the mind, when the end of life becomes all but visible, and when adverse circumstances, cowardly as they are, at length close round their enfeebled foe! Then, if the world *will* so have it, let me go at the end to my funeral pyre nothing more than a pretender to science, politics and philosophy.

As soon as the snow was removed from the railway lines and the traffic resumed, I left Berlin for Vienna. I had a very pleasant journey up to Dresden. A military officer was in the same compartment with me, and he spoke English. He was in the Franco-Prussian war and his regiment took part in the siege of Paris. He related to me various incidents of the war with such a relish that I could not help thinking that he was anxiously looking forward to a renewal of that exciting sport. "Did not the horrors of war ever shock your mind?" I asked him. He said that the field after a battle somewhat tried his nerves. Then with a zest he entered into a long discourse on wars, battles, sieges, and the glories of the Fatherland. I said—"I take no cognisance of your petty jealousies, your neighbourly quarrels and your conception of glory. I see only the loss to the world from your vast armaments, which keep away millions of able-bodied men from the work of bettering the condition of humanity. A good many canals have yet to be dug, a good many marshes have yet to be drained, and a good many jungles have yet to be cleared. The earth wants roads and railways, the sea wants light-houses, the rivers want to be dredged and the mountains to be bored. Time was when war was necessary in the economy of the human race, but its functions have now ceased. The pressure of population can now be better relieved by emigration and occupation of spare lands in the remotest corners of the globe, the stamina of the race can be better maintained by scientific living, the integration of nations can be better accomplished by improved communication and free intercourse, and the extension of civilisation and the prevention of stagnation can be more easily effected by commerce and education. These warlike preparations in Europe make me think that the utmost development man has yet achieved is to get the head and the hand of a god, but he yet retains the heart of the ape." I laughingly made the last remark, and the gentleman with equal good humour replied:—" There is no use arguing this subject with you. I have read in books that you, Bráhmans, object even to kill animals. We are not so foolish. We slaughter beef and mutton for food, we kill game animals for sport, and sometimes we destroy animal-life with a humane motive too, as when we shoot lame and old horses at once to put an end to the pain and misery under which they would labour if their existence were prolonged." I said—" Excuse me, if I was under the impression that you killed lame and old horses to save yourself the expense of maintaining them. But if it is humanity, then the Hottentots are more humane, who practise this kind of charity nearer home, on their own kind, by exposing their aged and decrepit in the deserts to die of hunger and thirst." We conversed on other subjects, and we were soon fast friends. He got down at Dresden, and I continued my journey. After he left me, I found myself in a mood to moralize on the vanity of the world. With the eyes of a Bráhman, when I look down on the world below, what an evanescent mirage it appears! A fleeting panorama, with countless pigmies madly hustling out each other! So, our preceptors taught us to keep ourselves in the serene atmosphere above, where no clouds cast their shade, no winds howl, no storms rage, and to look down with a calm, careless, callous mind on the mad struggles beneath. But, Sir, there is hunger, there is pain, which though I can minimize, ignore or conquer in myself, I cannot do so in others! This painful sympathy for others and above all the vanity that is in me, throw me down from my dizzy height and recall to my mind that I too am a pigmy like the rest. Oh, let me be only worthy to untie the latchet of their shoes, who work to make these sorry pigmies good giants like themselves!

Shortly after, I arrived at a place called Tetschen, a town on the Austrian frontier. Here I asked the railway people whether it would be necessary for me to change my train in order to go to Vienna, for the tickets I had with me shewed—Berlin to Dresden; Dresden to Bodenbach; Bodenbach to Vienna. Either they did not understand me or I did not understand them, I concluded from what they said that I might proceed by the train. So I made myself comfortable and went to sleep, for it was night.

It was past midnight, the approaching dawn was the dawn of Christmas day, the train was running with all the speed of an international express, when the conductor came to my compartment and roused me from a deep sleep. He came to examine my tickets. Cold and drowsy as I was in no time I put them in his hand, in the hope to have done with him as quick as possible. But he was in no hurry to leave me to my sleep. He took a long time over his examination, and in my impatience I thought he must be spelling out every word and storing them all up in his memory. Not content with the knowledge which the dim light in my compartment enabled him to glean from my tickets, he went out, as I imagined, to seek better aid, a stronger light befitting the importance of the subject. By this time I was wide awake, and a doubt now flashed across my mind. Is an opportunity of satisfying the fondest ambition of a traveller going to be placed within my reach? Am I at length going to be the hero of a mighty adventure, with every prospect of coming through it safe and sound at the end? In short I wondered if they were going to mistake me for a blood-thirsty socialist or dynamiting nihilist. Just at this moment my eyes fell on the glass, where I saw my face reflected. This at once gave me a more exalted notion of my importance, and I consoled myself with the thought that in common decency they could not take me for a lesser personage than the Mehdi of Khartoum. So I straightened my beard, looked the very image of ferocity, and did all I could think of to prevent the world saying hereafter that the dignity of His Mehdiship suffered in my hands. Thus prepared I patiently waited for the return of my conductor. He came alone, *i.e.*, not with soldiers and guards as he ought to have done. But what was my disappointment when, instead of quailing before the awful dignity with which I environed myself, he in a simple matter-of-fact way began to explain, by words which I did not understand and by gesticulations which I did understand, that I was travelling by the wrong train and that I must pay down the excess fare, not a trifling sum either! I felt indignant and said—"Sir, I believe you are not the Caliph Harun-al-Rashid, that you are privileged to put wrong ideas into a man's head just roused from a deep slumber. Considering the way you looked at me and the care you took to examine my tickets, I have ample cause to think myself the Mehdi in disguise. If you wish to establish yourself in my good opinion, you better call your men and take me into custody. No doubt I am dangerous, as my looks must have told you; but you need have no fear, my Dervishes are not with me, and I promise you to make no attempt to throw away my valuable life in resistance to the superior force you are bound to bring for my arrest." I lumped the words together and brought them out as gutturally as I could, taking 'Altherthumswissenschaft' as my model, but yet the perverse conductor would not comprehend me. He would only shake his head and demand the money. At length I had to come down from my lofty pedestal, and explain how they at Tetschen told me not to change. But this did not do either; the conductor shook his head and demanded the money. I spoke again mighty words: I said, "Sir, if you have no conscience, I will have none for you. I decline to pay," and supported my words with signs. He then left me, and notwithstanding my disappointment, I congratulated myself that he left me for good. But in fact, as it subsequently transpired, he *did not* leave me for good. Although it was an express, he made the train stop at the next station, a mere shed among high mountains covered with snow from head to foot. Here he made me come down, threw my baggage after me, and gave his signal to the driver, and in the twinkle of an eye the train moved off, leaving me alone among the hills of Bohemia. The sky was cloudy and the night was dark, except what little light the dazzling snow reflected all around. I went up to the station, and seeing a man there caught hold of him in order to bring him to my luggage now lying on the rails. He was so taken aback by the sudden apparition which my person and dress presented before his eyes, that I feared he would run away taking me for something more than the Mehdi, expressly deputed from a hotter climate than Upper Egypt to join him and his friends in their Christmas carousals. He looked so scared that I could not help bursting out in a fit of laughter. He joined me, but a faint tinge of suspicion still lurked behind his merriment. I then partly led partly dragged him to where lay my luggage, which we removed to a place of safety. Next I repeated the word "Wien" many times, to let him know that I wanted to go to Vienna. I shewed him my tickets and put my finger on the name "Bodenbach" as the cause of all my trouble. A glimmer of intelligence gradually lighted his face; he understood it all, but instead of shewing any sympathy for my distress, at once demanded the excess fare due by me from Testchen to his station. I was a wiser man now, and would not demur to pay and would not aspire again to the Mehdiship of Khartoum. I laid all the marks I had with me on the table. He shook his head. Not enough? I added to it all the paper guilders I possessed. He shook his head. What! not enough yet? I put a gold coin alongside and asked for change. Got no change? Well, I can do no more; you now do your worst. So saying I sank down in a chair. He then called in a porter, held a brief consultation, wrote out a bit of paper and gave it to him.

The porter took up my luggage, bade me pick up my money and follow him. For a short time we walked across an even bit of ground, but the snow lay thick upon it several feet deep, except on the narrow pathway where it was trodden down to the consistency of glass, and as slippery. Of course I did not know where I was being led. A little while after, we began to climb a hill, our road winded along its side. On our right the mountain rose high; on the left, as far as could be judged in the darkness, was a precipitous descent clad in snow, looking at which I thought in my mind that if one of us were to fall his body would make a tunnel through the loose snow in getting to the bottom. My man went before me, I followed keeping a close watch upon his movements, as a precaution against any mischief he might take into his head to commit. Thus we trudged a long way on before we descended and came upon a large river. A wooden bridge was thrown over it which we crossed. Here the man took from me all the silver I had and went away probably to pay the toll. He came back shortly after and we again proceeded on our way as before, but now by a better road. We soon met a party of men, women, boys and girls probably returning home from some kind of Christmas amusement. At about three in the morning we arrived at a little town. It seemed half awake, for in going through the streets I frequently heard sounds of laughter, singing and other tokens of seasonable mirth. Coming before a large house, my man took the gold coin from me and went inside to change it, bidding me to wait for him on the road. I was tired and drowsy and my feet was numb, so I leant myself upon the half open door and shut my eyes. I did not stand long in this way before a man tumbled upon me, and both he and I fell to the ground. At first I suspected foul play, but the man lay all on a heap beside me and immediately began to snore. With some difficulty I picked myself up and tried to raise him lest he died of cold. After many vain attempts, I succeeded in making him sit and then dragged him to the wall on which I made him lean. He now partially regained his senses and assuming a threatening attitude talked violently. In the meantime the railway porter came, but I sent him back to tell the people inside that a man was at their door in a helpless condition who might go to sleep again. We then walked for a short distance until we came to a hotel. Here he shewed me the bit of paper the station master gave him, which was a receipt for the excess fare. He took the fare as also what was due to him, and made a sign to me that

I was to sleep there for the rest of the night. Then he wrote on a piece of paper "Aussig," and "9-18," from which I understood that the name of the town was Aussig, that the Bodenbach-Vienna line ran by this town and that my train would be there at 9-18. I guessed rightly. At 9-18, I got my train and left for Vienna.

From Aussig to Vienna was a long journey. The train rapidly swept across a country that looked like a vast expanse of snow diversified by high mountains, low hills, deep ravines, dense pine forests and picturesque towns and villages, on many of which the ruins of ancient castles looked sombrely down from overhanging cliffs. The snow will not be off the ground until weary earth, now asleep after her toil of several months, again rises refreshed when the beauteous spring whispers to her ear his joyful advent. On passing through this vast extent of country of dazzling white, I sadly felt the want of hedges, judiciously pruned, with branches aud branchlets running into all directions, interweaving and intermingling, on which my eyes grew accustomed to rest, and to unravel the intricacies of their compact mass was their constant delight, during journeys of a similar kind in Great Britain, Flanders or France. The holly with its prickly leaves, the hornbeam and the beach, the long-branched elder or the ornamental sweet-briar, the black-thorn and the white-thorn, the yew or the privet, formed by their solid body into an impenetrable fence on the boundary of fields, did not in this country afford to my eyes a pleasing variety against snow and rocks and houses and bare trees. My countrymen may smile at my raphsody on hedges, for looking at their unpruned and untrained *Euphorbias, Jatrophas* and *Zizyphus* they have little idea what science, care and taste can effect even in the commonest details of life. My companion in the carriage was an officer of the Austrian army, Lieutenant A. Bürger of Pettersgersse. All through the day, every half an hour, this gentleman would offer me a cigar, put his hand on his brow and bewail his fate that he did not know English so that he could converse with me. I have often doubts in my mind if the world on the whole is too selfish to be good. But may be those doubts arise from an ardent wish to see the world what it ought to be, forgetting that if there be a bright side it must have a dark side. At any rate men like my strange companion in the carriage make us wish to live in the world. In the afternoon we passed Prague, and it was dark when we crossed the Dwina and entered the precincts of the imperial city of Vienna. I went to the Hotel Metropole, where English and American tourists take their quarters, but in this city I was practically the guest of M. A. de Scala. As usual, this gentleman and his lady received me very kindly and put me in the way of seeing the sights of Vienna. Vienna resembles Paris in many respects, in its neat, clean roads, palatial residences, and public promenades thronged by cheerful faces with no thought but the enjoyment of the passing hour. I went to see the Danube, which is about two miles from the city. I also saw the Emperor's palace, which is an extensive museum by itself containing as it does a vast library, a large collection of pictures and engravings, objects pertaining to ethnography, minerology, natural history and antiquities, as also coins and a valuable assortment of precious stones.

What struck me most forcibly, both at Vienna and other places in the Continent, is the systematic and persistent encouragement the Governments of those countries give to manufacture of articles for foreign use. For instance, they have in Vienna a collection of the most important manufactured things used by different nations in all parts of the earth. The Austrian consuls, stationed all over the globe, keep the home authorities supplied with information about prices, demand, duties and all manner of facts likely to be useful to makers and dealers, which are published in a weekly circular by M. A. de Scala. Specimens of these articles are also freely lent to help the manufacturers in making imitations. The efforts made in this direction have not been in vain. German manufactures are not only ousting English goods from the markets of Europe and Asia, but they are successfully competing with English manufactures in England itself. Considering the primitive organisation of the Indian people, the method adopted in Germany will be of little practical good in this country; but even in England they do not possess a central bureau where the ends of all the strings of private enterprise can be gathered together to create for general benefit and guidance an intelligent momentum. In such matters we are just approaching the Tripotolemus Yellowley stage. At Vienna I was introduced to many scientific men, among whom may be mentioned Herr M. Fleischnar, Roezina, Finchs, Shindashner, Beck, Fraz Heger, Karl Anton, Ludwig, Von Lorenz, Liburnau and August Von Pelzein. With these gentlemen, as also with several merchants whom I saw, I had conversation about the introduction of Indian tea and other products and art-manufactures into Austria. They expressed their readiness to help us.

On Monday the 27th December I left Vienna. The greater part of the next day was taken up in crossing the Austrian Alps. The Alpine mountains resemble the Himalayas in appearance, but they are not so high or steep. Our train followed some of the watercourses that issued from these hills, the highest of which could not have been more than 4,000 feet in altitude. The rocky country here is however more under the dominion of man than are the Himalayas. The Alpine peasantry did not seem to be very well off, so far as I could judge from the small cottages they live in. These dwellings are like the little holes the Kanáits and Kolis burrow on the side of the Himalayan mountains. In the afternoon we arrived at Pontebba, an Italian town on the frontier. It took us sometime more to cross the Italian part of the Alps before we reached the plains. At 10-55 P.M., I arrived at Venice.

Before I reached my place of destination, the railway for sometime ran over a causeway which joins Venice with the Italian mainland, or as the Venitians called it the "*Terra Ferma.*" On each side lay the lagoon, far away towards the Adriatic. It is a sheet of shallow water, covering an area of about 200 square miles, which ages past the Adriatic set apart for the habitation of her future queen. A natural dyke or embankment, called the Littorale, separates the demesne of the now defunct royalty from the open sea. Several channels intersect the Littorale, through which vessels pass in during high tide and enter the artificial canals in the lagoon. Fifteen hundred years ago when the high tide filled the lagoon, many little islands peeped through the water, among which was a cluster of 60 or 70 naked islets. That was our Venezia in embryo, she who like our Goddess of Wealth rose like a vision from the sea, and held for many centuries her mighty sway not only over the Adriatic, but all over the eastern Mediterranean up to Tyre in Asia Minor. Early in the fifth century, the little islets in the midst of this marshy plain afforded refuge to numerous families from the mainland, who came flying there before the fierce barbarians under Alaric the Goth and Attila the Hun. Here for a long time they led a life too miserable to induce the destroyers of the Roman Empire to follow them, for they possessed "no wealth but their boats, no food but fish, and no merchandise but salt." Rome was not built in a day, nor was Venice. It took many centuries before the descendants of these emigrants founded a powerful republic, conquered large tracts of country in the mainland, planted their victorious banner in the islands of the Levant, fitted out crusading expeditions, absorbed all the trade between Europe and Asia, and arrived at that prosperous stage when the dying Doge (Tommaso Mocenigo, A.D. 1423) could declare on his death-bed:—"I leave the country in peace and prosperity; our merchants have a capital of ten millions of golden ducats in circulation, upon which they make an annual profit of four millions. We have forty-five galleys, and 300 ships of war; 3,000 merchant vessels, 52,000 sailors; a thousand nobles, with incomes varying from 700 to 4000 ducats each; eight naval officers fit to command a large fleet, 100 others fit to command smaller squadrons; many statesmen, jurisconsults, and other wise men." How slowly do powers rise in the western world! All the eastern powers we know of, except China, appeared and disappeared like the Napoleonic-flash. Worship of personality is too strong in the East to allow the development of commonalty, but without commonalty a persistent continuity of force cannot be maintained. The force generated by men like Cyrus, Muhammad or Tamerlane may go on acting for sometime after their death, but its continuity depends more upon the absence of external resistance than upon the healthy action of the machinery they set in motion. Yet notwithstanding the slow growth of Venice and the long time she took to arrive at maturity, her rise was due more to the absence in the neighbourhood of a resisting power of even mere ordinary compactness than to the virtue, valour and hardihood of the early emigrants. From the very beginning of her career, she displayed such a suspicious and fickle nature that the words of Napoleon —" the Venetian people were not made for liberty" —might have been rightly spoken even in the most glorious period of her history. People go into raptures about the expression "Semo a Venezia," as if it denoted anything more than the liberty to enjoy those vulgar amusements which the common herd delighted to enjoy. And what, pray, was the meaning of the old proverb current in Venice—"De Deo parum, de Principe nihil?" And, what, pray, was the use of the two little holes I saw on the wall of the Doge's palace? Were they not for the reception of anonymous letters on the strength of which any poor citizen could be secretly arrested, secretly thrown into a subterranean cell under the palace, secretly tried by the Council of Ten, and as secretly executed nobody knew when or why? Oh! how glad would have been the wretched man to be publicly tried and, if guilty, publicly executed at the *Ponte dei Sospiri* or the Bridge of Sighs. What mattered it if the people made their own Government, elected the Doges by acclamation, and got up the Great Council by a system of ballot the most complicated ever devised, as long as the Council of Ten with its *pozzi*,* on the background, pursued like a shadow every member of the republic in the *palazzo*,† in the *piazza*,‡ in the *Canalazzo*,§ in the *riva*,‖ in the *rio*, ¶ in *campo*,* and the *calle*,† wherever he went. The way they murdered and multilated their early doges would even horrify the most callous intriguer inside an eastern seraglio. Venice put chains upon chains on Liberty lest she ran away, until nothing could be seen of her but shackles on every side. Yet Venice succeeded, and not only succeeded, but her success

---

* State prison ; † palace ; ‡ square ; § the Grand Canal ; ‖ foot-way ; ¶ canal ; * small square ; † narrow lane.

lasted for centuries. It was because all was darkness in Europe at the time, and there was light in Venice, though in our point of view, it was a dim one. The moment Venice came in collision with a compact body, she signally failed to maintain her reputation. The sister republic of Genoa repeatedly defeated her on sea, the Turks expelled her from her distant possessions, and ultimately she was bought and sold between Austria and France. In the meantime the route to the East by the Cape of Good Hope was discovered, eastern trade had flown into other channels, and the new continent on the other side of the Atlantic created such a commercial activity in other states of Europe, that Venice if left to herself would have in the natural course of things declined to its present position. If Italy be wise, she would give up all ambition to be a great military power, and would devote all her energies to take full advantage of her close proximity to the Suez Canal.

These thoughts crowded upon my mind as I stood on the *Ponte de Rialto*, the famous bridge over the Grand Canal, consisting of a single spacious marble arch. This Canal is the main thoroughfare of Venice, with which are connected the 146 smaller canals that serve as streets and lanes in this singular town. Four thousand gondolas carry on the street traffic on this watery labyrinth. On my right was the famous Rialto, where the opulent merchants of Venice counted their enormous gains from trade in silk, cotton, spices and dyes which their argosies brought from the distant East. That little house over there, now occupied by a fishmonger, was shown to me as the one where

Shylock the Jew hoarded his money. From that lofty building on the other side of the road were thrown to the crowd below slips of paper containing the latest news, which were afterwards sold for a "gazetta" a piece, whence our gazette of the present day. In this manner my guide pointed out to me the various places of interest in the Rialto. But the most important place in Venice is the Piazza or the Square of St. Mark. Here stands the Church of St. Mark, on the front of which above the doorway are the four horses brought from Constantinople in 1205, and which were taken away to Paris by Napoleon, but afterwards restored. The inside of the Church is profusely adorned with carved work and glass mosaic, especially the sides and ceilings of the domes where biblical scenes are vividly represented. In the Creation scene, God is represented as an elderly gentleman with an oval face, eyes not very bright, and dark head surmounted by a crown. The next place I visited was the Doges' Palace with its council chambers and subterranean cells. I also saw the Arsenal, where among various other interesting objects the model of the boat, formerly used in the annual ceremony of "marrying the Adriatic," is kept. The original boat was broken to pieces by Napoleon for the gold used in its decoration. The Adriatic Sea was given in marriage to the Doges of Venice by the Pope himself. In the year 1177, in return for certain services, Pope Alexander gave to the doge Ziani a ring, saying—"Take this as a pledge of authority over the sea, and marry her every year, you and your successors forever, in order that all may know that she is under your jurisdiction, and that I have placed her under your dominion as a wife under the dominion of her husband." The glass and lace manufactures of Venice, of which I visited the principal ones, are of great commercial interest. At the Grand Hotel Victoria in S. Marco, I met an Indian gentleman from Sind.

From Venice I came to Florence, the Firenze of the Italians. After passing through one vast stretch of unvarying snow, I was delighted to behold the Etruscan Apennines, with their upper ridge naked and barren, rising three thousand feet above the plains, but sides clothed with chestnut and timber trees, and underclothed with a bright green covering that afforded abundant pasture to numerous herds of cattle and sheep. Large and small rivulets impetuously running down the Apennines, or as Dante would call them, "cool streams flowing down the verdant slopes of Casentino's hills" (Inferno, Canto 30), came to meet the Arno as she laboriously sought her way out from the mountain mazes to "the city of Flowers and the Flower of cities," across a lovely fertile valley, encircled by gentle eminences, and studded with metayer farms, flourishing vineyards, fruitful gardens and picturesque villas. She meets the fair town with fairer names, lays herself upon it like a silvery necklet, dividing it into two unequal parts. Four bridges cross the river within the precincts of the town, of which the *Ponte santa trinita*, with the central arch 90 feet in span, and adorned by marble statues, is the most beautiful. At Florence, visitors see the Duomo, commenced at the end of the 13th and completed in the 15th century. This Cathedral has a magnificent cupola which is said to have excited the admiration of Michael Angelo. Near the Duomo, at the Baptistery of San Giovanni, three bronze gates were shewn to me, which my guide told me took twenty years to complete. They are in bass-relievo, *i.e.*, the figures carved in them are only partially raised from the surface, and two of them have been immortalised by Michael Angelo with the name of "Gates of Paradise." But the most important place I visited in Florence was the Gli Uffizi, which contains the famous Florentine gallery of art. Never before did I see such a splendid collection of paintings, engravings, sculpture, bronzes, coins, gems and mosaics. I stood for more than half an hour before a Madonna by Raphael and knew not how to get away from her. Her face was so sweet and oh, so heavenly! I thought how happy human beings would be if they could only vividly realise in their mind the watchful care of such a sweet holy mother over them, to console them in their sorrows and to guide them safely through the ills of the world. The stern Father or the self-sacrificing Brother would not quite satisfy the want of the human mind in this direction; it wanted a mother full of love to sit with tearful eyes by the bedside, to teach her suffering child patience and resignation as he passed through the ailments and troubles of the world. Instead of glorying in my philosophy, I could almost weep that I knew so much and yet so little. I saw a lady taking a miniature copy of this picture. It was almost complete, and I asked her whether she would sell it to me, thinking that the price could not be more than twenty francs. She said it was for sale, and on my asking to know the price, she named 300 francs! Of course I could not have it. I also saw some of the principal Churches in Florence, notably that of San Lorenzo and Santa Croce. In the former, there are many altars adorned with the paintings of Florentine masters, and a sacristy in which are the celebrated monuments of Giuliano de Medici and of Lorenzo, Duke of Urbano, both by Michael Angelo. These two statues have been described as "marvels of deep and living expression and unsurpassable in their mute and eloquent beauty." The sepulchral Chapel of the Medici attached to this Church is gorgeously decorated with the rarest marbles and jasper, agate, lapis lazuli, chalcedony and other most valuable stones.

At the church of Santa Croce, I saw the monuments to Galileo, Dante, Macchiavelli, Michael Angelo, Alferi, &c., from which will be seen how many eminent men Florence produced in her day. It has always been a matter of wonder to me why Macchiavelli has got such a bad name in the world. After all, he had said in "Del Principe" what we see daily practised all over the civilised world. It speaks well of the world that it does not like to see its own true picture, but likes to set an ideal prototype before it. "In what manner ought a prince to keep faith?" He has answered the question in the 18th chapter of his book, but no matter how moralists or Macchiavellists may answer it, the practical reply to the question has always depended upon the strength of the prince. "The best fortification for a prince is to be liked by his own people," so said Macchiavelli.

Old and new books are replete with such sayings; but every man is wiser than his fellows, and the way his mind is bent is always the wisest in his point of view. Happy are they who are wise enough to be guided by wise men, specially the young who have sense enough to listen to the old. Knowing beforehand the mind of each, I would have very much liked to be present at the conferences between Macchiavelli and Cesare Borgia. Their hearts must have overflowed with admiration for each other. Macchiavelli highly extolled the political art of Borgia, but Cesare was no author to return the compliment. Yet with all his art, Macchiavelli did not succeed to keep out the Medici from Florence. He was no ordinary theorist, but a successful man of action in his early life, with a good eye to details. At any rate it is cruelty on the part of the world to set men of theory to practical work; they should only be asked to lay down maxims and to loaf about in their free and easy and eccentric ways. Macchiavelli was an infinitely inferior man both to Vishnu Sarmá as a writer on politics and to Chánakya as an active statesman. The fall of Florence is to be deplored. Whatever success she achieved she fully deserved it. She was only a little town, but the self-reliance, industry and good manners of her people raised her to a position of great eminence, in point of wealth and prosperity; I care very little for her military reputation. It is very strange that she could carry her democratic principles so far as to completely exclude all members of the noble families from public service, while Venice on the other hand was engaged in registering in her Golden Book the male adults among her aristocracy, who alone were permitted to hold office in the State. Signor Giglioli, *Professore di Zoologia del R. O. Instituto di Studi Superiori*, at whose invitation I came to Florence, Signor Carnel, another Professor in the same Institution, and Signor Paolo Mantegazza, *Senatore del Regno*, shewed me the utmost kindness during my stay in this city. I saw the scientific museums, and was very much struck with the most valuable collection of anatomical models kept in the Natural History Museum. They were prepared in the last century under the immediate supervision of a body of scientific men, and are guaranteed absolutely correct. From Florence I went to Rome.

On Friday, the 31st December 1886, I first saw the great city which ruled the political, moral and spiritual destiny of the western world for so many centuries. I went to the Continental Hotel, built on an elevated position in the Esquiline Hill, the *Mons Esquilinus* of the ancient Romans. This was the last and the seventh hill which Servius Tullius added to Rome, which thenceforth received the appellation of "The city of the seven hills." My countrymen should not understand by this that Rome is built on the sides of seven high hills separated from each other by deep ravines, as they see the hill stations of Northern India. Whatever it might have been in former days, the hills constituting modern Rome are only gentle eminences, the whole of which I would have called simply a broken ground, but for the respect due to them for their glorious past. I first went to see Signor Nicola

Miraglia, the Minister presiding over the Agricultural Department. My name was not entirely unknown to the Italian Government; for, a short time ago, with the permission of His Excellency the Viceroy, it presented me with a gold watch and chain manufactured in Rome. Signor Miraglia kindly requested his Secretary, Signor Tutino, to take me round the scientific institutions in Rome. After doing these, I spent what little time I had at my disposal in seeing the sights of Rome. I could pay a hurried visit to almost all the important places, but unfortunately I could not go inside the Vatican, it being closed at the time owing to the holidays, and I had no time to obtain a special permission on my behalf by private influence.

Of course, I saw the Colosseum or the Flavian Amphitheatre, the construction of which Vespasian began and Titus finished in 80 A.D., or ten years after the destruction of Jerusalem. Any one can write a book on Rome: it has so many things fit to be told about, and it sets one so much to think of past times. So I thought, standing on the second tier of the Colosseum and looking down on the great arena below, where gladiators engaged in mortal combat and wild beasts yelled and fought to the great delight of the emperors, the senators, the vestal virgins and the 87,000 of the Roman populace, who found accommodation in the open galleries formed by arches on columns of Doric, Ionic and Corinthian structure. I could call imagination to my aid, and see before me good Titus sitting in imperial splendour, in the *podium* below, under the temporary awning they called *velarium*, with the two patricians on his side who conspired against his life and whom he that very day pardoned simply saying—"Do not do it again; Providence alone distributes crowns." I could "see before me the gladiator lie" on the ground covered with wounds, with the foot of his victorious foe on his breast, anxiously looking askance for the public fiat that was to make him live or die. Alas, alas! the Emperor turns his thumb downwards, so do the senators, the patricians, the vestal virgins and the excited populace above, all thirsting for the blood of a fellow creature. The prostrate gladiator draws a long breath to bid adieu to the sweets and sorrows of this world, to the bright sunshine around and to the ultramarine sky above, but before he lets it out in a sigh of deep anguish, the victor puts an end of him by one fatal stroke of his *gladius*. Deafening applause greets him from all sides of the circle as he triumphantly salutes the Emperor and the public. These are brave men, they are gloriously brave men who murder helpless women and children; and those are despicable milksops, fit only to go under the table at the sight of a knife, who faithfully serve their friends in time of need and whose heart weeps that man is yet such a brute!

Here carefully note why I have so often praised the British nation. It is not that the British nation is perfection itself, but that all things are comparative in this world. Bull-fighting is a national sport in Spain: a similar thing will be a criminal offence in England. Duelling is allowed in the Continent: it will be homicide in England. Then, above all, I can overlook all the shortcomings of the British people for what they have done to abolish slavery and slave trade. It is England that by dint of unusual exertions persuaded other nations to give up this inhuman practice. France emancipated her Negro slaves in 1848, the Dutch in 1863, and so far as I know slavery still exists in the Spanish and Portuguese Colonies. If England were not in India to-day, if we found ourselves drifting into the clutches of some unknown power of Europe as all non-European nations seem to be doing now, if choice were given to us to elect that power, we would be awfully stupid if we did not select England to be our chief. Never had militarism such a thick veneer of mercy and justice as it is in the British people. Mercy and justice without militarism behind them will be like a vertebrate animal without its backbone. France to-day would have been the mistress of the greater part of Europe and Asia, if she had only known in her moment of triumph what it was that caused Sicilian Vespers which, though the incident itself occurred in Sicily, had its counterpart in a more or less aggravated form wherever she established her temporary supremacy. I assure my countrymen that the indigo or coolie oppression we hear of now and then is, when true, practised by men un-British in their character and who act in complete variance of the best traditions of their race. Alas! Have not these black sheep found blacker coadjutors in our own countrymen? The *Banians*, the *Gumáshtás* and the *Jáchandárs* of the old East India Company, who despoiled and flogged the helpless weavers of Dacca; the *Diwáns* of Indigo factories, who made never-to-be-liquidated advances to peasants; the *Zamindárs* and their officials in the Muffassal, who burnt down houses and confined their tenants for fourteen years at a stretch in rooms full of lime, are heroes of a long tale which nobody cares to tell. Nor do their successors of the present day receive an adequate attention in the hands of our knights-errant, who into other quarters heedlessly and recklessly fling too many venomous darts to be of any practical good for the great cause of redress of wrongs in this world. A knowledge of European history, coupled with a profound ignorance of the circumstances immediately surrounding us, has put many quixotic notions into our head. These must be eliminated, so that our countrymen of Bengal in the Panjáb, in the North-Western Provinces, in the Native States, in Behar, Orissa and Assam may not blame us for the persecution we might bring down upon their head, so that posterity may not curse us for obstacles we might raise in Bengal's path of progress. It seems we are less forward now to appreciate and assimilate the teachings of civilisation than the last generation, and it seems too that the people of Bengal are gradually coming down from the prominent position they hitherto occupied among the nationalities of India. The more we identify ourselves with the ruling power, at the same time preserving our nationality and retaining our national good points, the more we identify ourselves with civilization and progress.

When Titus opened the Colosseum, 5000 wild beasts fought and died in the arena during the festivities which lasted for about 100 days. The ancient Romans were very fond of such fights and wherever they went they built amphitheatres, while the Greeks, who were a more refined people than their conquerors, built theatres. The Colosseum though said to be in a better state of preservation than other existing amphitheatres is not however in a perfect state. One portion of it is entirely gone and the remainder is in a delapidated condition. The Colosseum is I think in the *Mons Palatinus, i.e.*, the Palatine Hill where Romulus founded his little city. Near the Colosseum are the remains of several ancient Baths, the most noted among them being those of Caracalla, Titus and Trajan. The ruins of another ancient structure also exists in the Palatine Hill, *viz.*, those of the sumptuous Septizonium, which the Emperor Septimius Severus erected as an ornament to the imperial palace. This edifice was in a good state of preservation until the time of Pope Sixtus V, who deprived it of its valuable marbles and carried them away to decorate the Vatican Basilica.

Until recently, it was the fashion among English historians and English writers to call Muhammad an impostor, and hold up the Muhammadans before the eyes of the world as the most ruthless "vandals" the world ever produced. I could not but smile as I recollected the early lessons I received from Christian teachers, when at Rome I beheld before me temples converted into Churches, ancient buildings despoiled of their decorative wealth for the sake of Christian edifices, and gods and goddesses mutilated and disfigured out of all recognition by the hands of Christian iconoclasts. The world always ignores the fact that man is man whether he be a Christian, Muhammadan or Hindu, and that his goodness or the reverse depends more upon the kind of man he is than upon the religion he professes. He esoterises a crude religion or exoterises a subtle religion in proportion to the capacity of his mind. Thus a Bradlaugh is a better Christian than many divines. Thus a crocodile remains a crocodile though immersed in the holy water of Mother Ganges. Thus a Hindu remains a Hindu though baptised in a Christian Church or a Theistical *Mandir*. Nay, in cases, it should be made an occasion of public congratulation, thanksgiving and rejoicing, if a precious convert to Christianity or Theism proves not worse than his benighted brethren, left behind groping in the darkness of the benighted religion. To punish notions of this kind, Religion sighs for fire, sword and the cross. Failing there, she out-castes men. Thus, I cannot be an orthodox Hindu, because I went to England; I cannot be a genuine Theist, because I have not renounced the sacred thread of a Bráhman; I cannot be recognised a Christian, because I asked no Missionary to put a little water on my head, nor bathed myself in the waters of the well which the Italian Jesuit, who assumed the name of Viraswámi, consecrated on the sly, in the small hours of the morning, long before the village maidens came to fill their pots, the villagemen to wash, and the village cattle to drink in the trough. Oh, let me only soar high, better to observe

1 v

the wild sports of men, amidst their struggles to emerge into better states!

Excavations are now going on in the Palatine Hill. My guide shewed me a house near the temple of Vesta among the excavations made in the Roman Forum, which he said belonged to Numa Pompilius. My guide also pointed out to me the sites on the Velia, Sub-velia and Via Nova where Tullus Hostilius, Ancus Martius and Tarquin Priscus are supposed to have lived. The last two kings, however, had also their palaces in the Esquiline.

Between the Palatine Hill and the Capitol was the Forum Romanorum. A forum was a large open space usually surrounded with public buildings. The fora of ancient Roman cities were of two kinds; *fora judiciala*, where courts of justice were held and political matters discussed, and *fora venalia* where citizens met to transact business of a commercial nature. The Forum Romanorum was of the former kind. During the Republic it was the central point of Roman political life. Its importance declined with the decline in the political vitality of the people, *i.e.*, after the time of Julius Cæsar and Augustus. It contained temples, statues, basilicæ, curiæ, rostra, triumphal columns and arches and the comitium where votes were taken on a public question. The rostra were the pulpits from which orators delivered their speeches to the people. It is said that before the rostra of the Forum Romanorum, Sulla caused the head of young Marius to be hung up. Among the ruins in this Forum were shewn to me three columns that belonged to the Temple of Jupiter

Stator, and the Arch of Septimius Severus. Besides the Forum Romanorum, there were many other foras in Rome; some bearing the names of the Emperors by whom they were constructed, while others taking their names from the use to which they were put. Among the latter may be mentioned the Forum Boarium or the cattle market, the Forum Suarium or the pig market, the Forum Piscatorium or the fish market and the Forum Olitorium or the vegetable market. Traces still exist of the last two foras. Among those called after the names of Emperors, I saw Trajan's Forum, in the midst of which stands the celebrated monumental column, known as Trajan's Column, of which I saw a plaster of Paris facsimile in South Kensington. It is made of white Carrara marble, is 132 feet in height, and was constructed by the architect Apollodorus of Damascus in A.D. 114, to commemorate the victories of the Emperor over the Dacians. The basreliefs on the pedestal and on the body of the column, giving the whole history of Trajan's achievements, have thrown much light on the subject of dress worn by the ancient Romans. A colossal statue of Trajan formerly crowned the summit of the column, which was taken down, exactly 300 years ago, by order of Pope Sixtus V, and one of St. Peter put in its place.

Crossing the Forum Romanorum, I came to the Capitoline Hill. It is said that this hill bore the name of Saturn before Rome was built, and was the site of a city founded by that god. Once upon a time long ago, Saturn got very unpopular among the gods, owing to his having mutilated his father Uranus with a hooked scythe and to his habit of devouring his own children as soon as they were born. He therefore came down from heaven and chose the Capitoline Hill for his temporary residence, until his misdeeds were forgotten by his friends and relations above. He found the people of Italy in a wretched state of savagery, and it required all his celestial eloquence and power of persuasion to induce them to come out of hollows in the trunks of trees and caves and caverns where they lived, in order to learn from him how to build houses, cultivate lands, to write, and all the arts of civilised life known to the gods of the Golden Age. In the opinion of my guide "a pagan divinity like him could not have been expected to turn out such a beneficent ruler." Mons Saturninus came to be known by the name Mons Tarpeius from the day the Sabines obtained possession of the stronghold through the treachery of the virgin Tarpeia, who was crushed to death under the shields of her tempters and hurled down from the top of the rock. Since that time state criminals were thrown down from this rock. A portion of the Tarpein rock can still be seen in the garden attached to the Palace of Caffareli, now the German Embassy. In order to increase the population of Rome, Romulus established on this hill the sanctuary which gave refuge to criminals from the neighbouring states. On the site of this sanctuary now stands the Piazza del Campidoglio. The Capitoline Hill received its Roman name of Mons Capitolinus owing to the head of a man, named Tolus, having been dug up in a fresh state, when Tarquin Priscus was laying the foundation of a temple for Jupiter. The present name of the place is Campidoglio. One of the summits of the Capitoline Hill is now occupied by a church called the Ara Coeli. In the other summit are three palaces of which two are used as a Museum for ancient sculpture, coins and other objects of interest found in the late excavations.

In modern times, Palazzo del Campidoglio was the scene of a pleasing episode, *viz.*, the award of the laurel crown to the poet Petrarch, which ceremony took place in 1341. This Francesco Petrarca was a remarkable man, and the story of his romantic love made quite a sensation all over Europe in his time. He was a Florentine by birth, but his family having been banished from its native city, he took up his residence at Avignon, where Pope Clement V then held his gay court. In 1327, as fate would have it, Petrarca met in a Church a beautiful young lady named Laura, for whom he felt a passion of the most violent type. But this lady happened to be the wife of another man. Nevertheless all through his life (he died in 1375) he was firmly constant in his love for the lady, which necessarily was of a pure platonic nature. He worshipped the goddess of his heart from a distance, and Laura and love were chiefly the theme of his Italian poetical pieces, which became famous for their charming sweetness, and which are said to be "enlivened by a variety, a rapidity and a glow which no Italian lyric has ever possessed in an equal degree. The power of preserving and at the same time of diversifying the rhythm belongs to him alone; his melody is perpetual, and yet never wearies the ear." So he got his laurel crown, while he sat clothed, as a mark of special honour, in the royal robes of Robert of Anjou, king of Naples, amidst the exclamations of an enthusiastic multitude crying "All Hail to the Capitol, All Hail to the poet." When Laura got old and all her beauty was gone, he still admired her with the same vehement constancy. His friends wondered at it, to whom he once answered by saying—*Plaga Per allentar l'arco non sana.* "The bow can no longer wound, but its mortal blow has been already inflicted. If I had loved her person only, I had changed long since." The answer which Majnun of the popular Persian story gave to his friends was of a different kind. Majnun was a handsome young swain who loved to madness Lailah, an ugly little girl. His friends expressed their astonishment at his choice, on which he quietly said—*Lailah rá bachashami Majnun badid.* "Ah, if you had only seen Lailah with the eyes of Majnun!"

My guide in Rome was a patriot. He was one of the besieged when the French invested the city in 1849 in the interests of the Pope, and had eventually to fly for his life out of the Papal Dominions. He fought under Garibaldi for the unity and independence of Italy. I do not mean to underestimate the services of my guide to his country, but I cannot but find fault with Patriotism for her one-sided views. She is always partial to fighting and bloodshed, and those of her worshippers who sacrifice themselves in their battle with ignorance, misery and widespread abuses scarcely receive a recognising nod from her. I am therefore glad that she has been called by a philosopher "the last refuge" of scoundrelism. But if truth is to be told she little deserves this withering aphorism. A scoundrel can never successfully play the role of a patriot, for he must be too well known or soon comes to be too well-known; and instead of being a paying business, to play the part of a patriot is a losing trade requiring a good many sacrifices. Were I a commentator of Johnson, I would explain that he meant to say—"Religion, philanthropy and patriotism are the last solace of unrestful disappointed." We often see men and women with an uncontrollable amount of energy born under adverse circumstances; we too often see men and women cast out of the world for some early mistake, for some hasty or heedless action of a more culpable nature, or through no fault of theirs but through the villainy of others. They find the outlets for their indefatigable energy closed on every side, and these are the individuals who find refuge in philanthropy and patriotism—not scoundrels. These individuals are down on the ground, and no wonder that everybody should kick them, philosophers included. As for the world, it is always ready to be led by the ears to kick the fallen.

I saw the Pantheon, which was built by Agrippa in 87 B. C., and was dedicated to all the gods. It has been converted into a Christian Church, called the Santa Maria Rotunda. On the summit of the Quirinal Hill I saw the famous pontifical palace and garden. This palace was used as a summer residence by the Roman Pontiffs, and the conclave for the election of a new Pope was also held here. It has now become the palace of the King of Italy. In the square before the palace, called the Piazza del Quirinale, is a majestic fountain with two colossal statues of Castor and Pollux with their horses. It is said that these figures were brought from Alexandria by Constantine the Great. They are magnificent specimens of the sculptor's art, and speaking of the horses a competent authority has said—"The two horses placed on the Piazza del Quirinale at Rome, and the four horses in bronze in the portico of St. Mark's at Venice are, in my opinion, the finest works that can be possibly conceived of their kind." But the most important sight in Rome is the St. Peter's. It is the largest Cathedral in the world, and is said to be erected over the grave of St. Peter and near the spot where he suffered martyrdom. Its construction was commenced in 1506 and finished in 1626 A.D. It has no fairy-like symmetry like the Tàj, but it is a heap of grandeur unsurpassed in the world. Everything is in a colossal scale here, but owing to the proportions maintained all round, the enormous sizes of objects within it become hardly perceptible to the eye. The walls are adorned with plates of the richest marble, and copies of celebrated pictures executed in mosaic. Before the mosaic at St. Peter's that of Tàj sinks into insignificance, so far as massiveness goes. The floor is paved with marble of different colours, beautifully arranged. But the finest part of the building is the dome which is supported by four arches. Under the dome is the high altar of St. Peter, and beneath the altar, the shrine where 112 lamps burn night and day. Near the vestibule, where a splendid mosaic of St. Peter walking on the sea is to be seen, is a bronze statue of the Apostle. Its right big toe is completely worn out by the continual kissing of pilgrims for centuries. In the square before St. Peter's there is a large Egyptian obelisk, which is said to have been brought from Heliopolis by Caligula. There are other Egyptian obelisks in Rome, the largest being the Lateran in the Circus Maximus. Cleopatra's Needle which is now in London is smaller than the Lateran. The Tiber divides Rome into two very unequal parts, and although so near the sea, it is a small river at Rome, barely 300 feet in width. I was informed that the depth varies from 12 to 18 feet.

In passing through the length of the Italian peninsula, I could not but remark the poor condition of the peasantry. The land is fruitful. There is silk, wine, olive oil and other valuable produce for export. But the soil does not seem to mellow under the plough for the benefit of those that delve and toil. In the north, in Lombardy, the silk grubs spin and spin their glossy thread, but yet those that rear for them upwards of 17 millions of mulberry trees live in miserable hovels and barely subsist on the commonest of food. Do they spin to produce £5,000,000 of revenue for cannons and ironclads? There is misery too in the middle country where, under the clear blue sky only freckled here and there by spots of fleecy clouds, and beside the sloping mountains the rich tints of which impart a warmth to the atmosphere, the elegant festoons of vine gaily swing from tree to tree, growing all the while, bearing thick bunches of luscious grapes and vainly striving to make the land a land of perpetual holiday, where Painting may sit at ease, watch and admire, Poetry may contemplate love, and sweet Melody may at leisure raise her strains to enliven or soothe. There is distress in the south where the mournful olive, stunted and hoary with age, makes its contribution in oil, where the plump peach turns its ruddy cheek to the sun, where the semi-tropical almond, fig and pistachio yield their produce to the orchardsmen and where the African date hangs from its neck huge clusters of green, gold and pink. There too occasionally a buffalo wallows in the slimy pool, the glowworm glows in the night, and the railway porter importunes you for *Bakhshish*, as, arriving at the railway station of Naples, you hurriedly take the train for Pompeii. Verily, you smell the rich spices of the gorgeous East!

Eighteen hundred and nine years ago, in A.D. 79, on the 24th of August, about one in the afternoon, the sister of the elder Pliny drew the attention of his brother to a pillar of cloud issuing from Mount Vesuvius. That cloud on the top of the Vesuvius portended a mighty catastrophe. Pliny put his vessels to sea, and went nearer to better observe the phenomenon and to help the citizens of the neighbouring towns in case they required his help. He landed at Stabiæ, where he found the daytime enveloped in a deeper darkness than it prevails in the most obscure night. The earth was rocking violently, and hot cinders and calcined stones fell in showers. He went out to the fields for safety with a pillow tied on his head. There he was suffocated to death. The earth, the hot cinders, the pumice-stones and black pieces of burning rock that Vesuvius incessantly rained soon engulfed the towns of Herculaneum and Pompeii. In a very short time Pompeii was entirely forgotten by the world, with all her hopes and aspirations and her petty quarrel with Nuceria only a few years ago, on which occasion Nero punished her by stopping all her theatrical amusements for ten years. She was as entirely forgotten as I and You and He will be, my friends, when other I and You and He take our place. Her very site was forgotten, and for 1600 years crops were sown and vines were trained on the spot under which all the while peacefully slept in the sleep of death the houses, the shops, the theatres, the basilicæ, the temples, the forum, the amphitheatre, the baths, the prison, the pantheon, the bakeries, the house of Sallust, the house of the Tragic Poet with *cave canem*, the villa of Diomed and the skeletons found in the soldiers barracks. These have now been brought out to daylight by excavations that have been going on since 1755. There is nothing particular to say about these sights. Herculaneum and Pompeii derive their interest from their singular fate, the state of preservation in which they have been found, and the light which they throw on Roman social life 1800 years ago. They have got a museum in Naples, where the most interesting objects found in these two places have been carefully collected, among which are some very fine frescoes, the colours of which are in excellent preservation. I went across the exhumed town of Pompeii from *Porta della Marina* to the *Gate of Herculaneum*. From Pompeii I came back to Naples.

The saying goes that "Shave your head in Prayág (Allahabad), and then, O sinner! go and die anywhere," and also "See Naples and die." I have done both and I may now die in peace. So far as Naples goes, I could, however, only literally fulfil the requirement of the ancient saying; for I had only a few hours at my disposal to see the various sights that were to be seen in this town. So besides the town itself and its beautiful scenery, I had only time to see the Museums, the Aquarium and Virgil's Tomb. *Palazzio Campodimonte*, near the Catacombs, is a fine museum containing paintings, porcelain, arms, &c., and the *Museo Nazionale* possesses a picture gallery and a fine collection of mummies, mosaics, gold and silver ornaments, coins, and various other objects found in Herculaneum and Pompeii. They have got a very fine Aquarium in Naples. A well-arranged catalogue in English is sold there, which makes it easy for ordinary visitors to study the habits of the fishes kept in their glasshouses. Near the Tomb of Virgil there is a large tunnel. On the Naples side of the tunnel I saw a little shrine, neatly covered with red cloth, on which a number of small and large brass images of gods were nicely arranged. The priest in charge of them ran to me and reminded me of my duty to make some offerings to the deities. So I went and respectfully made my obeisance to the gods and saints and while doing so laid some pieces of copper on the floor. The priest was satisfied with my humble gift; and when I saw that he would not ask for more, I was pleased that he was not like his kind elsewhere, and I gave him a lire. He was profuse in his thanks, and said many things which I did not understand. In the Vesuvius Hotel at Naples, I saw two countrymen of mine, both Parsis. I did not speak to them. From Naples I came direct to Brindisi. Here the mail steamer was lying ready to take me to Alexandria. At daybreak, on the 3rd of January 1887, I left Europe and travelled back to my native country by the usual mail route. My stay in Europe lasted for 8 months and 27 days.

INDEX.

A.

	PAGE.
Aberdeen	286
Aberfeldy	288
Aboriginal races	71
Accidents in railways	36
Accomplishments of a lady	41
of a gentleman	155
Ach-na-cloich	290
Aden	6
Adriatic, marriage of	374
Advertisements	34
African coast	21
Agitation in India	234
Agricultural experiments	239—44
Albert Hall	67
Albert Memorial Chapel	210—11
Alps	369
American beauty	92
American Missionary	16
Amsterdam	338—40
Andamanese	71
Anti-alcoholists	188
Artisans, Indian	99
Artistic instinct	223
Art-ware of India	90, 93, 222
Atlantic Ocean	25
Aussig in Bohemia	366
Australia, progress in	124—26
Austrian Alps	369
Autographist	31

B.

	PAGE.
Babel Mandeb	12
Ballater	282
Balmoral	282
Banker, an example	40
Bath	268—70
Bay of Biscay	26

	PAGE.
Beauty, womanly	90—92
love of	221
Bedford, Duke of	237
Bengalis, persecution of	156, 163
liberalism of	266—67
decline of	383
Benmore	289
Ben Nevis	290
Berlin	352—57
Big Ben	310
Birds, singing, in England	217
Birdwood, Sir G.	32, 205, 247
Birkenhead	262
Birthday Book	206
Blair Athole	279
"Blue Stocking"	42
Bohemia, adventure in	360—66
Bombay	1
Boxing matches	149
Boys in England	151
Bræmar	281
Brazil, aborigines in	307
Brig of Turk	295
Bright, John	192
Brindisi	397
Bristol	263—66
British Museum	321—23
British policy in India	349
Broughton S. Hunter	304—5
Buck, Sir E.	108, 194, 247

C.

	PAGE.
Cabs	37
Callander	294
Cambridge	247—49
Campbell, Sir G.	302
Capitol	387
Caste in England	154, 183, 197—200
Caste-food	5, 116
Caste-prejudice in India	27

INDEX.

	PAGE.
Change and progress	76
Channel Tunnel	119
Charity	120, 175, 182, 193
Chastity	52
Cheap food for England	172
Chelsea Election	139
Christian Vandalism	384
Christy, Mr. Thomas	84
Cleanliness	29, 30, 215
Clifton Down	265
Climate of England	191
Clyde	291
Coffee in Aden	9
Coffee-House	157
Coilantogle Ford	294
Cologne	351
Colonial & I. Exhibition	64—138
Colonies at the Exhibition	123
Colosseum	380, 381, 384
Comfort, love of	221
Commons, House of	311—12
Compulsory education	140, 286
Congress, National	140, 258, 286
Conservatives	139
Cost of living	45, 46
Country-scenery	215—16
Cows	113—115, 116, 253—57, 283
Crowd in England and India	38
Crows in England	216
Cruelty of Europeans	73, 122, 123, 148, 168, 170—71, 274, 307
Crystal Palace	320
Cuckoos	217
Curiosity, we excited	99—106

D.

Dairy, in England	113—16
Dalmally	290
Dalree	289
Decline of England	180
Dee, River	280—81
Diplomatic language	339
Diseases, in England	190
Distress in England	164, 173—75
"Diving" boys	7
Doune	293
Drawing Room	42

	PAGE.
Dress, cost of	160
importance attached to	161, 213
Drugs	85, 87
Drunkenness	187
Duff, Mr. Pierre	195
Dunsmore, R. Mr.	275, 276, 278
Dyes	82

E.

Early marriage	50
Eastern condition of mind	234
Economic products	81—90
Economical discussion	228—35
Edinburgh	271—75
Education in England	154, 155
Education, compulsory	140, 286
Election, fight	142
Election, General	139
Emancipation of women	51
English character	86, 117—23, 382
Eton College	213
Europeans & Indians	134, 297—302
Evening in England	42
Exhibition, Colonial & I.	64

F.

Family affection	121
Family concord	50
Family nest	177
Famine in India	230—31
Fashion	159—163
Feathers	333
Female dress	160—61
Fibres	88, 89
Fighting in England	142—48
Fire-side	42, 44
Fishes in England	287
Florence	375—79
Flying Fish	6
Food	4, 40, 45, 46
Food, cheapening of	172
Foot-paths in the Highlands	282
Forgiveness	274
Fort William	290
Forum	386

INDEX.

Freedom, in England	167, 171
in India	169
Free Trade policy	165, 166
Frogmore	211
Fruits	109
Furniture	45

G.

Garden Party	214
General Election	139
Gentlemanly accomplishments	155
qualifications	184
Germany, place of education	41
Ghosts	149—51
Gibraltar	22
Gladstone, Mr. W. E.	54, 60
Glasgow	290—93
Glencoe	290
Glen Tilt	279
Gods and their keepers	323
Grattan's sentiments	61
Grazing lands	282
Great Eastern Steamer	293
Great Tom of Westminster	311
Greenock	293
Guest in England	303
Guildhall Ball	223—25
Gums	81
Gypsies	284

H.

Haarlem	333—37
Haggling, absence of	117
Hedges,	366
Herculaneum,	395
Highlands	279—90
Highlanders	280—281
High-living in England	40, 221
Hobby	244
Holyrood	272—75
Home Charges	228—30
Home Rule for Ireland	53—61
Horses	37
Hotels	341
Hot-houses	109, 110
Houses	191, 342
Hunger, its work	136

I.

India, at the Exhibition	69
intellectuality of	39, 131
darkness in	126—38
partiality for	83, 89, 101
Indian Art	93, 222, 223
Indian Ocean	4—6
Indians, their position	324—28
International obligations	55
Ipswich	249
Irish Question	53—61
Italy, poverty in	393

J.

Jeffries, Mr.	250
John Bull	86
Journalism in India	284—85
Jungle Scene	69
Justice, sense of	55, 56, 57

K.

Kath, discussion about	9
Kelpie	294
Kew Gardens	329
Kilchurn	290
Killecrankie Pass	279
Killin	288, 289
Killing propensity	5, 72, 73

L.

Labour, competition in	165
application of,	232—35
Ladies, accomplishments of	41
occupation of	41, 158, 179
Lawes, Sir John Bennet	244
Leek in Staffordshire	308
Leith	271
Levée at Windsor Castle	206
Liberals	139
Liberty in Europe	348
Life-boat man, story of	43
Linn of Dee	280, 281

	PAGE.
Lion, Northumberland House	246
Litigation	185—87
Liverpool	261
Living, high standard of	221
Loch Achray	295
Loch Awe	290
Loch Etive	290
Loch Fyne	290, 293
Loch Katrine	295—96
Lochleven	277
Loch-Nell	290
Loch Tay	289
Loch Vennachar	294, 295
London, sanitation of,	29
immensity of,	39—40
morning in,	201—5
Long, Reverend Mr.	79
Long Walk	212
Longley, Miss	309
Lords, House of	311
Louvre	346
Love-making	46—49
Luxury	218—20

M.

	PAGE.
Macchiavelli	377
Macgregors	290, 296
Machines for begging, &c.	153
Madame Tassaud's	319
Madrigal	264
Mail-route	13
Malta	17
Mammon-worship	133
Man and his religion	385
Manchester	251, 252, 260—61
Manning, Miss E. A.	192
Mansion, English	216—21
Manufacture, encouragement of	368
Manures, experiments in	241
Marlborough House	213, 215
Mar Lodge	281
Mary, Queen of the Scots,	207—8, 273—75, 278
Max Müller, Professor	68, 94
Mediterranean	17
Mersey Tunnel	262
Military education	301—2
Milk in England	112—16

	PAGE.
Models of Indian races	71
Monier Williams, Sir	296, 297, 303
Monument of London	319
Morgue	348
Morning in London	201—5
Muir, Mr. John	293
Muir, Sir William	284

N.

	PAGE.
Naga tribe	72
Naples	396
Narsingarh, Rájá of	206, 247
National character in India	126—28, 253, 257—60
National Congress	140, 258, 286
Nationalisation of British Rule	59
"Native,"	132
Neighbourly love	176
Nicobarese	71
Nightingale, Miss Florence	194
Nihilists	62
Northbrook, Lord	193
Northumberland, Duke of	245
Notre Dame	347
Novelty, love of	99

O.

	PAGE.
Oban	290
Omnibuses	36
Orwell Works	249
Ostrich feathers	7
Oxford	94, 296, 297, 303
Oxford Street	32

P.

	PAGE.
Paisley	293
Pantheon at Rome	391
Parental duty	178
Paris	340—48
Parliament Houses	310—312
Party politics	60, 139
Passenger-ship	3
Past, reverence for	76, 77, 128
Patriotism, mistaken	76, 180, 334

INDEX.

	PAGE.
Patriotism in Italy,	390
Pedestrians, in London	38
Perfumery	88
Perim	12
Perjury	185—87
Perth	275, 278
Peter, St., in Rome,	392
Petrarch,	389
Philosophy in Germany	356
Piety	155
Pigmies of the world	360
Pine-apple fibre	333
Pitlochry	279
Plymouth.	26
Politics	60, 139, 140
Pompeii,	395
Poor life	44
Population, increase of	163
Port Said	16
Poverty in England	154, 174, 175
in India	227—32
Prices of food	157
Prince Consort	210—12
Prince of Wales	32, 64, 65, 196, 206, 213
Princess of Wales	196, 213, 214
Principle, fight for	62
Private quarrels	141
Progress in Europe	76, 180, 328

Q.

Quarrels, how settled	187
Queen-Empress	64, 201, 205, 206, 210, 212, 214

R.

Race animosity	172
Railways	33, 36, 216, 352
Rain in England	191
Rámáyana in Aden	10
Ram Mohan Roy's Tomb	265
Ransomes, Sims and Jeffries	249
Rationalism	167—68
Reauleux, Professor	353
Red Sea	12
Religion, decline of	283

	PAGE.
Religion for Europe	336
Religion of man	385
Religionism	39, 180, 245
Religious bigotry	21
Religious discussion	16, 19
Respectability	233
Rhea Fibre	343
Rialto	373
Rob Roy	296
Rome	379—93
Rosebery, Countess of	245
Rothamstead experiments	244
Rotterdam	332
Royal Agri. Society	239—44
Royal Procession	66

S.

Salisbury, Marquis of	245
Sanitation	29
Sanskrit Anthem	68
Savagery in England	146
Scala M. de	367, 368
Schools in England	154
Sciences, cultivation of	135
Scotch people	276, 278
Scotland, excursion to,	270
beauty of	288—89
Self-assertion and Self-abnegation	298—300
Selfishness	181
Self-sacrifice	119
Sentiment and duty	182
Seven Apostles	13
Shylock's house	373
Silk	95—99
Sion House	246
Smith, Mr. Bullen	195
Snake-skins	333
Sociability of the Indians	3, 176
Social intercourse with Europeans	183—84
Social unit	179
Somalis	7
South Kensington Museum	329
Spain	22, 170
Speaking, mode of	34
Spirituality and Temporality	336

INDEX.

	PAGE.
State Apartments at Windsor Castle	207
Steam-boat in London	37
Strangers, kindness to	117
Street Arabs	152
Struggle for existence in Europe	181
Suez	13
Suez Canal	14
Sun, time of rising	202
rays of, in England	237—38

T.

Tallow Chandler's Hall	226
Thames Tunnel	262
Theatres	226, 235—37
Tilt, River	279
Tooth-making	190
Tower of London	318
Trade competition	165, 166
Trade, foreign	82
Trade Unions	165
Traffic rules in London	38
Tramps	283
Treatment we received in England	100—9, 116
Tribute of India to England	228—30
Trosachs	293
Twilight in London	201
Twins in England	163
Tyndrum	290

U.

Underground Railways	33, 204

V.

	PAGE.
Valletta	17
Vegetables in England	110
Venice	369—75
Vesuvius, Mount	395
Vienna	367—69
Virgil's Tomb	396

W.

Wardle, Thomas	99, 308
War-preparation in Europe	358—59
Water in England	116
Water-scarcity in Aden	9
Wealth, pursuit of	133, 134, 135, 233
Western civilisation, our bondage to	130
Westminster Abbey	312—17
Westminster Bridge	32
Westminster, Duchess of	245
Whitehall Palace	32
Wife, price of	51, 74, 306
Windmills	332
Windsor Castle	205—13
Wine, use of	189—90
Wives, number of	100
Wives, responsibility of, in England	157
Woburn Agricultural experiments	237—44
Womanly beauty	90—92
Women in England	52, 53
their hard work	305, 306, 307
Women, persecution of	50, 74
Work, on board a vessel	11
in England and India	203

www.ingramcontent.com/pod-product-compliance
Lightning Source LLC
Chambersburg PA
CBHW081912170426
43200CB00014B/2710